Guide to
First-Year Writing

2012-2013 Edition

Dr. Lyneé Gaillet, Director
Dr. Angela Hall-Godsey, Associate Director
Diana Eidson, Assistant Director

Georgia State University

Lower Division Studies

GCB 840

FOUNTAINHEAD
PRESS

As a textbook publisher, we are faced with enormous environmental issues due the large amount of paper contained in our print products. Since our inception in 2002, we have worked diligently to be as eco-friendly as possible.

Our "green" initiatives include:

Electronic Products
We deliver products in non-paper form whenever possible. This includes pdf downloadables, flash drives, & CD's.

Electronic Samples
We use a new electronic sampling system, called Xample. Instructor samples are sent via a personalized web page that links to pdf downloads.

FSC Certified Printers
All of our Printers are certified by the Forest Service Council which promotes environmentally and socially responsible management of the world's forests. This program allows consumer groups, individual consumers and businesses to work together hand in hand to promote responsible use of the world's forests as a renewable and sustainable resource.

Recycled Paper
Almost all of our products are printed on a minimum of 10-30% post consumer waste recycled paper.

Support of Green Causes
When we do print, we donate a portion of our revenue to Green causes. Listed below are a few of the organizations that have received donations from Fountainhead Press. We welcome your feedback and suggestions for contributions, as we are always searching for worthy initiatives.

Rainforest 2 Reef
Environmental Working Group

Contents

Acknowledgments

Faculty, staff, and graduate teaching assistants in the Lower Division Studies program at Georgia State have created the *Georgia State University Guide to First Year Writing* in order to provide students and instructors with comprehensive information concerning the procedures and policies of the Lower Division Studies program. This handbook also offers a first glimpse into the world of writing in higher education. Among many other important topics, this book introduces the reader to writing instruction, various literacies, writing processes, research practices, and argumentative techniques.

This guide is the product of an exhaustive, collaborative effort, and it would not have been possible without the Editorial Staff, the Writing Contributors, the Student Essayists and their Instructors, the Essay Committee, and the Artwork Contributors. Special thanks go to Robert Manfredi, who helped greatly with writing the front and back matter and with editing the galley.

The Editorial Staff would like to thank Dr. Lynée Gaillet for her warm compassion, her tireless energy, and her pedagogical and rhetorical wisdom. This project would not have been possible without her superb leadership.

EDITORIAL STAFF

Lynée Gaillet, Ph.D., Professor of Rhetoric and Composition, Director of Lower Division Studies, and Director of the Writing Studio

Diana Eidson, Assistant Director of Lower Division Studies; Ph.D. Candidate, Rhetoric and Composition; and Advanced Teaching Fellow

Stephanie Horton, Ph.D. Student, Rhetoric and Composition and Teaching Fellow, Lower Division Studies

Brett Griffin, Ph.D. Student, Literary Studies; Teaching Fellow, Lower Division Studies; and Tutor, Writing Studio

Danielle Weber, Ph.D. Student, Literary Studies and Teaching Fellow, Lower Division Studies

Robert Manfredi, M.A. Candidate, Rhetoric and Composition; Teaching Fellow, Lower Division Studies; and Tutor, Writing Studio

WRITING CONTRIBUTORS

    I.   Introduction: Diana Eidson

   II.   Essential Information: Diana Eidson, Stephanie Horton, and Danielle Weber

   III.   The Writing Process: Stephanie Horton and Diana Eidson

   IV.   Analysis: Brett Griffin

   V.   Argument: Diana Eidson

   VI.   Research: Stephanie Horton

   VII.   Analyzing Images: Melanie McDougald

   VIII.   New Media Literacy: Peter Rorabaugh, Ph.D.

   IX.   ENGL 1101: Stephanie Horton

   X.   ENGL 1102: Brett Griffin and Danielle Weber

   XI.   ENGL 1103: Diana Eidson

   XII.   Wrapping Up: Robert Manfredi

STUDENT WRITING AND ART CONTRIBUTORS

Student Essay Finalists:

Michael Banks, Chelsea Johnson, Jocelyn Lopez, Mollie Mason, Lauren Taronji, and Chris Vaughn.

A very special thanks to Kerry McDonough and Taylor Pannell, who contributed essay drafts and peer review comments for the chapter on The Writing Process.

Essay Finalists' Instructors:

Dr. Jody Brooks, Matt Donald, Diana Eidson, Marta Hess, Juliette Kitchens, Alice Myatt, and Dr. Laurah Norton. A special thank you goes out to Sara Hughes, who supplemented our text with one of her assignments.

Essay Committee:

Lara Smith-Sutton, Jamie Korsmo, Jill Goad, Katherine Kincer, Lelania Ottoboni, Rahna Carusi, and Matt Donald

Coordinator of Student Essay Contest:

Danielle Weber

Cover Photo:

A GSU friendship and a unanimous vote for the cover by our editorial committee. Rachel Leigh Clark captures the spirit of her friend Olamide Olufemi at a familiar GSU location—a parking deck.

Artwork Finalists:

Nnerika Adibe, Alesa Barron, Mike Black, Rachel Leigh Clark, Ashley Dunham, Erin Fielding, Marissa Graziano, Michelle Ha, Kristen D. Johnson, Catherine Keo, Judith Kim, Hang Nguyen, Leslie Rivers, Graham Robson, Divya Sawhney, Joshua Sheridan, Timothy Short, Michael Stevens, Fenton Thompson, William Walsh, De-onta Wheeler, Kaitlyn Winey

Artwork Selection Committee:

Dr. Lynee Gaillet, Diana Eidson, Stephanie Horton, Brett Griffin, and Danielle Weber

Coordinator for Artwork Contest:

Stephanie Horton

"What are you?" by Hang Nguyen and Catherine Keo

Introduction to Lower Division Studies and First-Year Writing Classes

WHAT IS LOWER DIVISION STUDIES?

Welcome to the program of Lower Division Studies in the English Department at Georgia State University. Lower Division Studies comprises all first- and second-year literature and composition courses (1000-2000 level) in the English Department, along with Business Writing (ENGL 3130). We design curriculum, suggest textbooks, and support instructors who teach Lower Division courses. Our work is foundational not only to the English Department but to the university at large. Indeed, every student who begins a college career at GSU will take several of our courses. Over the three semesters of this past academic year, we offered approximately 256 First-Year writing class sections and 28 survey/introductory literature classes. Our courses offer many students the most intensive instruction they will receive during college in language theory, rhetoric and writing, and literature.

Beyond our normal responsibilities, i.e., providing services related to lower-division English courses, we also strive to foster a community for students and instructors. Our goal in Lower Division Studies is to offer the highest caliber of writing instruction and resources for students.

Lower Division Studies Administration

Dr. Lynee Gaillet, Director, Lower Division Studies

Designs curriculum and pedagogical strategies for Lower Division courses
Designs professional development for instructors
Approves transfer credits
Hires and schedules instructors
Approves LDS textbooks
Allocates travel money for TAs
Handles student/instructor issues

Dr. Angela Hall-Godsey, Associate Director, Lower Division Studies

Designs curriculum and pedagogical strategies for Lower Division courses
Designs professional development for instructors
Manages tuition waivers for GTAs
Approves transfer credits
Handles plagiarism issues
Solves LD course registration issues
Serves as Chair of Student Grade Appeal Committee

Diana Eidson, Assistant Director, Lower Division Studies

Designs curriculum and pedagogical strategies for Lower Division courses
Designs and maintains Lower Division Studies website
Maintains GTA database
Coordinates GTA professional development
Coordinates scoring of CLEP exams with faculty
Assists with credit transfer requests for LD courses
Serves on Student Grade Appeal Committee

Lower Division Studies Instructors

Our program is large, with over ninety faculty and graduate teaching assistants. Instructors research a variety of fields, including literary studies, creative writing, and rhetoric and composition. All of our teachers undergo extensive training in the art and science of teaching writing as well.

WEB RESOURCES

Our newly updated website, located at lds.gsu.edu, provides a wealth of information for students:

1. Information about courses we offer, course exemptions, CLEP exams, grade appeals, and credit transfers. Refer to the yellow box on our home page (also see "Essential Information" chapter of this book);

2. An online supplement with model essays, handouts, and additional information to help you succeed in writing courses;

3. Helpful strategies for improving writing, along with technological resources to help you with research, writing, and creating multimedia projects. Under "Resources," click on "Student Resources" for links.

http://lds.gsu.edu/

WHY DO I HAVE TO TAKE A WRITING CLASS?

You might be wondering what a required English class can offer you if you are not an English major. The simplest answer is that you do not write only in an English class—you write in every class and profession you might pursue. However, a deeper examination of the question would address the interconnectedness of all cognitive activity; thinking, reading, writing, and speaking all work together. Practicing one skill, such as writing, strengthens the others. Reading, speaking, and thinking improve your writing, too—that is why each is vital in a writing class. In 1101, 1102, and 1103 you have the opportunity to perform all of these tasks in a way that allows you to see how they work together to help you become a better critical thinker. Achieving a higher level of abstract thinking enables success in many areas of your life, including not only your academic and professional life, but also in your volunteer work, personal relationships, and leisure activities.

Not only does writing instruction improve your level of abstract, critical thinking, but it also enables you to tailor your writing to specific audiences for specific purposes. Understanding the rhetorical nature of academic and non-academic writing helps you to gain credibility with a wide array of audiences. In addition, writing fulfills our deep-seated desire to communicate. After making progress in your writing, you might discover that you actually enjoy crafting words into engaging texts that address an audience and purpose effectively. This accomplishment can be deeply satisfying. Your words can motivate, persuade, entertain, and educate your audiences.

WHAT HAPPENS IN A WRITING CLASS?

Writing classes at Georgia State provide unique opportunities to create communities of writers. In contrast to lecture classes of three hundred students where you may only listen and take notes, writing classes are small (capped at 25 students), and are centered on discussion and peer interaction. As a class, you form a discourse community, which means that you share a set of experiences and practices that set you apart from any other discourse community[1]. Your instructor and peers form a model audience to whom you address your writing. This unique opportunity to create a community of writers places responsibility on each member to contribute to the group. That responsibility entails attending class and participating in discussions and activities. Fulfilling your responsibilities is essential for the community to thrive.

In addition to creating a small community of writers who help each other to write more and write better, writing classes are skill-based, performance classes. You demonstrate success by crafting compositions that are clear, concise, and compelling. Writing classes offer a direct way for you to apply what you learn. Instead of having to memorize a body of content for a standardized test, you are creating texts that address a one-of-a-kind rhetorical situation—a particular combination of exigency, text, audience, and purpose. Finally, learning to write and writing to learn both enable you to engage in critical inquiry. Writing classes encourage inquiry, active reading, criticism, self-expression, analysis, research, and reflection. Achieving proficiency in these tasks will serve you well in every area of your life.

---

[1]You are a member of a number of discourse communities; for example, you are a GSU student, but you might also be a Latina, a fan of Arcade Fire, an RPG gamer, a diabetic, and an animal rights activist. All of these affiliations have related discourse communities. These groups of people, whether in organized groups or less formal arrangements, have different vocabularies, rituals or practices, and rules about who can speak and how.

"Lord of the Arts" by Joshua Sheridan

HOW DOES WRITING FIT INTO MY COLLEGE PROGRAM?

Types of College Writing

During your program of study at Georgia State, you will write for a number of different audiences and purposes. Most of the time, the audience will be your instructor and your peers. Occasionally, however, you will have (or will take) the opportunity to publish your writing to an audience beyond the classroom: on the Internet, on iTunesU, at the Pullen Library's Undergraduate Research Conference, or perhaps in publications such as the *GSU Guide to First-Year Writing* or an academic journal. Some of the assignments you will write for college courses are lengthy, but some may be only a page or so. Your instructor may assign you a topic, or you may have to come up with topics yourself. Most college writing entails five major tasks: summary, exposition, analysis, research, and argument. Sometimes, your professor may want to determine if you read the assigned material. In demonstrating your completion of a reading assignment, you may be asked to summarize or respond to the readings. You may write reports in which you provide information from your own experience and from research. On an essay exam, you may be analyzing a problem or a text, or you might be making an argument. You may be required to research primary and/or secondary sources and synthesize your findings for a research project. Other common types of writing for college include laboratory reports, proposals, research papers, multi-media projects, and oral presentations.

No matter the assignment, you are learning how to hone your critical thinking skills and demonstrating that you understand and are able to apply concepts and skills you learn in your courses. You are learning to craft particular genres for various purposes to an array of audiences. Your college writing tasks must be ethically researched and honestly documented, and they must be clear, concise, unified, and rhetorically sound. Correct grammar, usage, and mechanics will help you build credibility as a writer and researcher. The content and organization of your work must be substantial, accurate, and logical. Of vital importance is your ability to follow the professor's instructions for the writing task, so that you fully and ethically demonstrate your competence in the writing task. In order to make sure you follow instructions, complete the following steps:

1. Print out a hard copy of the assignment sheet and keep it in your notes;

2. Read the assignment sheet carefully and highlight action verbs in the prompt as well as assessment criteria;

3. If you do not understand something on the assignment sheet, don't depend on a classmate to help; ask specific questions of your professor in class, via email, or via phone;

4. Pace the steps of the assignment so that you will complete it on time. Mark dates in your phone or planner, and set up checkpoints for yourself to keep you on schedule; don't wait until the last moment to complete the assignment.

No matter what kind of writing you do for your college courses, ENGL 1101, ENGL 1102, and ENGL 1103 offer you the practice and guidance that will help you succeed in every course. Not every faculty member considers himself or herself a teacher of writing, but the instructors in Lower Division Studies are specially trained to guide you through the writing process and help you create effective texts for a variety of purposes and audiences.

English Major and English Minor

English studies is a great major for the private sector (corporate jobs), the public sector (government jobs), and the third sector (non-profit organizations). Why? Every employer wants someone who can read critically and write eloquently. A Bachelor of Arts in English offered through the English Department's Undergraduate Programs Office provides five areas of concentration: literary studies, creative writing, and rhetoric and composition, secondary English (for teachers), and British and American Cultures (a joint studies/exchange program with the University of Northumbria-Newcastle in the United Kingdom). For more information on the undergraduate programs in English, please visit http://www2.gsu.edu/~catalogs/2012-2013/undergraduate/ and http://english.gsu.edu/1559.html.

If you are interested in pursuing one of the challenging and useful English major or minor programs offered at GSU, please visit the Department Chair's Suite on the ninth floor of GCB to make an appointment to speak with an advisor.

Writing across the Curriculum:
Learning to Write and Writing to Learn

In your ENGL 1101, 1102, and 1103 classes, you learn to write, but you also write to learn. You learn to write by practicing various types of writing tasks, but you write to learn through writing about the things you are reading and about your writing process. Many instructors use "writing to learn" activities to help you think about the ways you learn, how your insights fit into larger academic conversations, and how you can use readings and class and online discussions to enhance both your writing and your critical thinking. Remember, reading, writing, speaking, and thinking all work together and support each other, so learning to perform one task better helps your performance in the others as well.

We have two programs at GSU that will help you with both learning to write and writing to learn as you go through your program. Writing across the Curriculum (WAC) offers "Writing Intensive" (WI) courses in virtually every discipline to engage students in a number of critical writing activities. WAC faculty members from various fields are highly trained to teach students how to write texts in their disciplines. When you begin to take classes in your major and minor, sign up for these WI classes.

Critical Thinking through Writing (CTW) classes are offered as part of a Quality Enhancement Program for accreditation through the Southern Association of Colleges and Schools (SACS). In these classes, a substantial portion of the grade is derived from critical thinking activities, many of which involve a writing component. Every department offers these classes , and, in order to graduate from GSU, all students are required to take two CTW classes in their major.

Both WAC and CTW classes are staffed with faculty and teaching assistants who specialize in teaching students how to read, write, and think critically. These courses offer opportunities for you to practice and hone your writing and critical thinking skills in fields beyond English studies. Research studies have shown that when students are given many low stakes, small scale, informal chances to write about the material they are learning, they improve critical thinking skills and content knowledge.

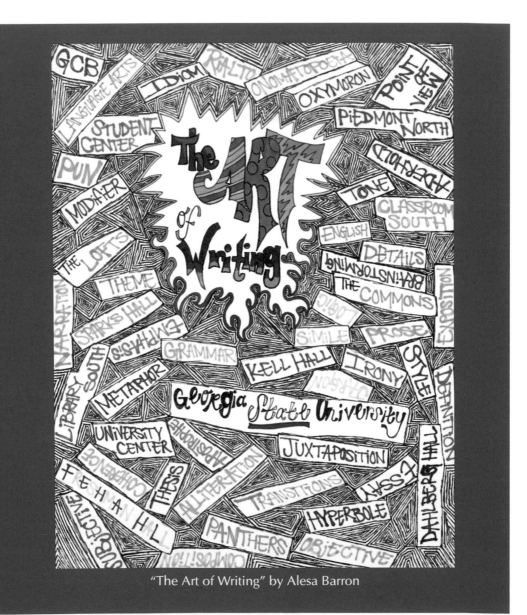

"The Art of Writing" by Alesa Barron

Writing in the Professions

"The other day, I went to get my car repaired at the mechanic. I told the service technician what the car was doing, and he typed detailed, clear directions so that the mechanic would know how to analyze the problem and repair my car. I was surprised and impressed with the amount and level of writing he does each day, and I told him that I thought he did a great job."

This (true) story illustrates the need to write effectively in nearly all professions. The College Board's National Commission on Writing put together a report of responses from 120 corporate leaders in the United States. In this report, "Writing: A Ticket to Work … Or a Ticket Out: A Survey of Business Leaders," the College Board found that writing is not only a "threshold skill for employment and promotion, particularly among salaried employees," but that two-thirds of all salaried employees in industry has some writing responsibility (3). The types of writing most often cited include technical reports, formal reports, and memos and correspondence (4). If you work in the private sector, writing will be a substantial part of your workload.[2] Furthermore, since most professional-level jobs in the public sector or the non-profit (third) sector have the same sort of administrative and interpersonal tasks as those of the corporate world, the jobs in these sectors also require a high caliber and high quantity of writing.

Business executives, public policy officials, educators, lawyers, nurses, doctors, scientists, engineers, analysts, and artists write for different purposes and audiences, but they all write extensively. Their on-the-job training typically does not include instruction in writing. Someone with a college degree is expected to know how to write correctly and skillfully. Taking advantage of multiple opportunities for writing practice and revision is, by far, the best method for improving your writing. The best way to prepare for your professional life is to practice the writing and speaking tasks you will perform in your chosen profession. In these pre-professional experiences, you can simulate writing tasks addressing colleagues or clients to inform, engage, and persuade them. If you want to know how much writing you will be expected to do in your chosen field, interview someone in that field and ask him or her. You might be surprised at the answer.

---

[2]National Commission on Writing. "Writing: A Ticket to Work … Or a Ticket Out: A Survey of Business Leaders." *National Commission on Writing*. The College Board, Sept. 2004. Web. 3 Apr. 2012. <http://www.collegeboard.com/prod_downloads/writingcom/ writing ticket to work.pdf>.

Lower Division Studies as a Student Resource

If you have any questions or concerns that this chapter did not address, please contact us. You may visit the Lower Division Studies suite in General Classroom Building 840, or you may call or email us.

Lyneé Gaillet, Director, lgaillet@gsu.edu, (404) 413-5842
Angela Hall-Godsey, Associate Director, ahallgodsey1@gsu.edu, (404) 413-5879
Diana Eidson, Assistant Director, dsullivan5@gsu.edu, (404) 413-5860

Essential Information

GSU AND LDS POLICIES AND PROCEDURES

Your Course Syllabus

The syllabus forms a contract between you and your instructor. This document defines teacher and student responsibilities, provides valuable information about the course, and offers advice for succeeding in First-Year writing. You should read the syllabus very carefully and ask questions about things that you do not understand.

According to the *GSU Faculty Handbook* (section 401.01), each syllabus at the university must contain the following elements:

1. complete course title and number; name of professor; term, year;
2. statement of faculty member's accessibility to students outside of class (e.g., office hours, telephone number);
3. prerequisites (if any) for the course;
4. course objectives that specify measurable and/or observable student learning outcomes. These learning outcomes should state course objectives in language that makes explicit the knowledge and skills students should have after completing the course. Consequently, these objectives may be quantitative or qualitative, as appropriate for the learning outcomes. The learning outcomes for general education courses are available at www.gsu.edu/~wwwfhb/goals.doc as approved by the GSU Senate 2/13/04;
5. course assignments (e.g., required readings and activities) and due dates;
6. specific course requirements (e.g., written and oral tests and reports, research papers; performances);
7. grading policy: how the final grade is to be determined with respect to the weights assigned to various course requirements;
8. attendance policy (there is a specific policy for courses in Lower Division Studies: see page 14 of this book and see current University General Catalog for University guidelines). Syllabi should state specific requirements for attendance, including requirements for the frequency and kind of participation by designated channels;

9. list of text(s) or other required course materials, optional materials, or supplementary readings;
10. make-up examination policy;
11. all syllabi should include the following statement: "The course syllabus provides a general plan for the course; deviations may be necessary";
12. all syllabi should refer to the Policy on Academic Honesty (Section 409 of Faculty Handbook);
13. all syllabi should include the following statement: "Your constructive assessment of this course plays an indispensable role in shaping education at Georgia State. Upon completing the course, please take time to fill out the online course evaluation";
14. all syllabi should include the following statement: "Students who wish to request accommodation for a disability may do so by registering with the Office of Disability Services. Students may only be accommodated upon issuance by the Office of Disability Services of a signed Accommodation Plan and are responsible for providing a copy of that plan to instructors of all classes in which accommodations are sought."

English department syllabi include a statement about Senior Portfolios as well:

The English department at GSU requires an exit portfolio of all students graduating with a degree in English. Ideally, students should work on this every semester, selecting 1-2 papers from each course and revising them, with direction from faculty members. The portfolio includes revised work and a reflective essay about what students have learned. Each concentration (literature, creative writing, rhetoric/composition, and secondary education) within the major may have specific items to place in the portfolio; information is available in the booklet located next to the door of the front office of the English Department. Senior Portfolio due dates are published in the booklets, or you may contact an advisor or Dr. Stephen Dobranski, Director of Undergraduate Studies. See the English office for additional information.

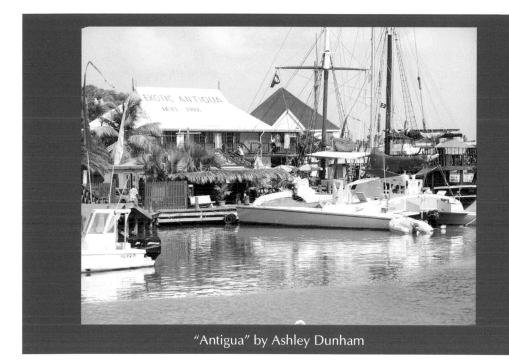
"Antigua" by Ashley Dunham

Disruptive Student Behavior Policy

(Section 401.08 of *GSU Faculty Handbook*):

"Disruptive student behavior is student behavior in a classroom or other learning environment (to include both on and off campus locations) that disrupts the educational process. Disruptive class behavior for this purpose is defined by the instructor. Such behavior includes, but is not limited to, verbal or physical threats, repeated obscenities, unreasonable interference with class discussion, making/receiving personal phone calls or [SMS texts] during class, leaving and entering class frequently in the absence of notice to instructor of illness or other extenuating circumstances, and persisting in disruptive personal conversations with other class members. For purposes of this policy, it may also be considered disruptive behavior for a student to exhibit threatening, intimidating, or other inappropriate behavior toward the instructor or classmates outside of class."

For additional information on expectations for student decorum, see the Student Code of Conduct adopted on January 19, 2012 at http://www2.gsu.edu/~wwwdos/wordFilesEtc/2011-2012_On_Campus_Handbook_Student_Code_of_Conduct_Revised_January_19_2012.pdf.

Lower Division Studies Attendance Policy

Attendance and participation are critically important in a writing course. The classes are small and focused on discussion, and most include some collaborative activities such as peer reviews and group projects. Instructors will take roll; your absence can affect your grade when you miss in-class assignments. You miss vital information when you are absent, your peers and your instructor notice, and the class is not the same without you. Put simply, class experiences cannot be replicated by getting the notes from a learning partner or by reading the required texts. Therefore, instructors expect all students to attend class regularly and to participate fully in class discussions and activities.

The following policies are in place for the 2012-2013 academic year:

- Instructors will take roll at every class meeting, record all absences, keep the records, and post them for student accessibility. Instructors are required to report absences weekly to University officials.
- If you miss the equivalent of more than two weeks of the class sessions, you will be in danger of failing the course.
- If you miss class, regardless of the reason, you may not make up any work that counts as a daily grade (homework, peer response, group work, short quizzes, short writing assignments, etc.). You will receive a zero on all of these activities. Participation cannot count more than ten percent of the final grade in the course, and that portion of the grade consists of measurable elements such as graded assignments or daily assignments with credit for completion. Put simply, there is NO make-up daily work in these courses.
- If you have an excused absence, you may make up or turn in late major assignments—tests, essays, or projects—upon presentation of a valid written excuse. It is your responsibility to contact your instructor immediately upon your return to arrange details for making up an assignment. Excused absences are only granted in the following cases: university-sponsored events; religious observations (with advance notice); legal (court) obligations; death or major illness in immediate family, illness of dependent family member; or a diagnosis of a severe or contagious illness of student.
- If possible, notify your instructor in advance of any scheduled absence. If you become ill, contact your instructor via email to make him or her aware of the situation. Most instructors are very reasonable about such matters, but only if you behave responsibly by keeping them informed of your situation.
- Instructors devise policies concerning tardies that are clearly stated in their syllabi (which is approved by LDS administration). Most instructors give quizzes and other graded assignments at the beginning of the class session, so it is important that you strive to be on time for class. Make sure that you

understand the policy and consequences for tardies. Your grade may be affected by excessive tardies.

Textbooks

English 1101, 1102, and 1103 focus on informational, analytical, and argumentative writing, as well as critical thinking and research strategies. The reading, writing, and critical thinking skills you acquire in First-Year writing courses prepare you for academic work in courses throughout the university curriculum.

Sometimes you might ask, "Why should I buy these textbooks?" The answer is simple: Learning to write is a skill, and reading attentively (and often) is the best way to hone that skill. This answer is true not just for English courses; across the board, the copious reader has a distinct academic advantage over those who read minimally.

While there are some variations in First-Year writing classes, each with different instructors designing their own syllabi, the following are texts you will most likely encounter:

1. A handbook such as *The Everyday Writer* by Andrea Lunsford, which addresses questions of grammar and usage. A handbook serves as a valuable reference for creating and revising your writing. Students often keep English handbooks throughout their college years and beyond.
2. A rhetoric, which is a collection of sample essays, writing exercises, and writing instruction. Rhetoric, to put it simply, is the art of persuasion; a rhetoric is a collection of writings and prompts designed to hone a writer's persuasive powers. The educational use of a rhetoric is part of a 2,400-year-long tradition of writers and speakers reaching back to classical Greece.
3. A reader, which supplements the books above and brings you the best of compelling and expert essays from around the world. Authors are often critically acclaimed writers and experts in the fields they write about.
4. Supplemental course readings, which enrich classroom experience, encourage critical thinking, and prompt writing topics and strategies. Your instructor will assign additional readings in your course.

In short, the more we read, the more literate we are—and the better we write and persuade.

"Amber Studies for a Test" by Judith Kim

Assessments

Typical Assignments and Their Assessment in ENGL 1101 and ENGL 1102

An English 1101 (English Composition I) course introduces you to a variety of writing genres. 1101 classes are designed to help you become a better writer and prepare you for the kinds of assignments you will encounter in courses throughout the university. Therefore, assignments are designed to help you develop an individual writing process and to improve your understanding of content, organization, style, grammar, and mechanics. Toward the end of the semester, instruction focuses on academic discourse. 1101 assignments may include informal writing exercises, such as freewriting, journals, reflections or responses, blog entries, and discussion forum postings; you will also be required to compose more formal pieces such as essays and multimedia and even multimodal projects[1]. Some in-

---

1 Multimedia refers to texts that have more than one technology component being used. PowerPoint and Prezi presentations are examples of multimedia texts because they could include photographs edited in Photoshop, texts created in Microsoft Word, and sounds created in Garage Band. A multimodal text uses various senses or modalities, such as visual, auditory, tactile, olfactory, gustatory. An art installation that engages with the audience by image, sound, aroma, and texture is multimodal. So, multimedia focuses on technology and multimodal focuses on rhetorical choices made by the author.

structors will ask you to create a portfolio of your work for the course, an assignment that will count as a formal, usually substantial grade in the course. Participation in the course is vital and will be measured through completion of class work and homework, responses in online forums, feedback to peers in activities related to review and other forms of groupwork, quizzes, and performances in and out of class. Daily work can constitute up to ten percent of your grade. For a detailed overview of English 1101 (learning outcomes, sample assignments, and sample student papers), read Chapter IX.

English 1102 (English Composition II) courses guide you into academic discourse, which means that you will be asked to engage in dialogue with authors on various topics by performing research; analyzing oral, visual, or written texts; and synthesizing source material to create research-based argumentative texts. You will research both physical and digital resources. You might create your own website or contribute to the course website. You may create multimedia, multimodal projects individually or in groups. In order to encourage you to engage with texts critically, instructors will create a variety of ways for you to read, analyze, and incorporate primary and secondary material into your own arguments. Many of the typical assignments parallel genres from 1101: journals, discussion forum responses, essays, and portfolios. 1102 courses build upon the knowledge and skills learned in 1101. Just as in 1101, participation counts for up to ten percent of your final grade, so it is a significant aspect of the course assessment. For a detailed overview of English 1102 (learning outcomes, sample assignments, and sample student papers) read Chapter X.

Keeping Records of Grades

To gauge your progress in the class and to effectively communicate with your instructor, keep track of all of your grades. You are responsible for keeping records of your own progress in the class. Keep all graded papers, and check on your grade periodically, either with your instructor or in the online format your instructor may adopt. You will find it useful to keep accurate records not only to improve your study habits and organizational skills, but also to make sure that you are successful in the class. Do not wait until after midterm to be concerned about your grade—it could be too late.

Grade Reporting (GSU PAWS)

At the end of the semester, letter grades A+, A, A-, B+, B, B-, C+, C, D, and F will be recorded by instructors for each student. However, only grades A through C are considered passing in 1101, 1102, and 1103. If you receive a grade of C- or below, you will be required to take the course over. A "C-" is equivalent to a 1.7 grade point, and you must have a 2.0 grade point from all Lower Division classes to proceed to the next level of courses. You will receive a grade of "W" if you withdraw before the midpoint of the term. You will usually receive a "WF" for withdrawing after the midpoint, which counts as an "F" in your GPA.

Grade Appeals

If you choose to appeal a grade that you can prove was assigned in an "arbitrary, capricious, or discriminatory" fashion, pick up and complete paperwork from Dr. Hall-Godsey in GCB 840. Try to address concerns with the instructor first, and only when this method fails should you turn in documentation to Dr. Hall-Godsey, who reviews the appeal before submitting it to the English Department Appeals Committee for review. More detailed instructions are available on the Lower Division Studies website at lds.gsu.edu.

Withdrawals

If you will not be able to complete the course, you must withdraw in PAWS prior to the mid-point of the term (posted in the GSU academic calendar). If you withdraw before the mid-point, you will receive a "W." Please note that if you withdraw after drop/add but before the mid-point, you will not receive a tuition refund. If you just stop coming to class, your instructor will assign the grade of "WF" at the end of the term, which is the same grade as "F" on your transcript and for calculation of your GPA.

If your name is dropped from the class roster for non-payment of tuition and fees or any other reason, you must go to the Registrar's Office to get re-instated. Instructors will not allow you to attend class until you get the issue resolved.

Incompletes

In order to receive an incomplete, a student must inform the instructor, either in person or in writing, of his/her inability (non-academic reasons) to complete the requirements of the course. Incompletes will be assigned at the instructor's discretion and the terms for removal of the "I" are dictated by the instructor. A grade of incomplete will only be considered for students who are a) passing the course with a C or better, b) present a legitimate, non-academic reason to the instructor, and c) have only one major assignment left to finish.

Evaluation of Instructor

At the end of each term, grades are posted in PAWS/GoSOLAR by the date listed on the GSU website. In order to view your grade, you will be asked to evaluate your instructor. Please take the time to complete an evaluation; your written feedback is particularly important not only to the instructor but also to the administrators in Lower Division Studies. We strive to improve the program by addressing your concerns.

Communicating with Writing Instructors and Tutors

Of course, becoming a better writer in your English courses will help you as you go through your program at Georgia State. In your First-Year writing classes, you and your instructor work as a team to improve your writing for a number of purposes and audiences. Your instructor's job is to provide clear directions; challenging, engaging assignments; and specific, helpful feedback and guidance. Your job as a student is to attend class, take notes, complete assignments, stay organized, ask questions, and seek assistance. In order to get the most out of your English classes, you must communicate your needs and questions to your instructor. That means that you need to ask questions in class or via email or phone, as well as take advantage of opportunities to meet in person with your instructor during office hours and during scheduled conference sessions. (Some instructors will set aside time during class or have you sign up for special sessions at various times during the semester.)

In addition, you may also meet with trained writing tutors in the GSU Writing Studio (see below for additional information about this important resource). There, you will engage in conversations about your writing at various stages, from the invention of topics and ideas to revising drafts in preparation for submission. Seek assistance from these experts early and frequently. When you meet with an instructor or a tutor, bring hard copies of drafts you are working on and prepare specific questions about your work. When you go to the Writing Studio, bring your assignment sheet from your instructor so that the tutor will be able to look at it alongside your draft. Finally, write down ideas and suggestions that you and your instructor or tutor discuss so that you can remember them as you continue to work on your text. These strategies will enhance the productivity of the conferences and tutoring sessions.

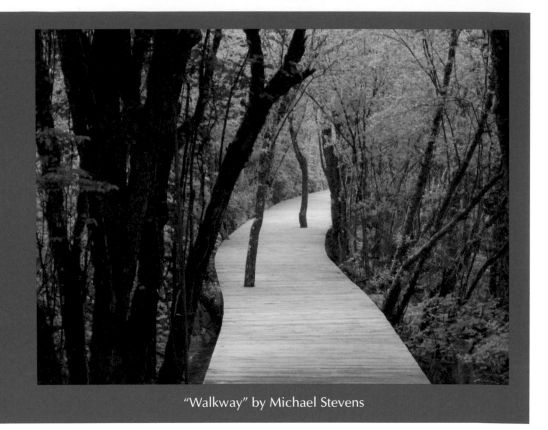

"Walkway" by Michael Stevens

RESOURCES AND OTHER PROGRAMS CONNECTED TO LDS

The GSU Writing Studio

976 General Classroom Building
writingstudio.gsu.edu
(404) 413-5840

Administration:

Lyneé Gaillet, Director
Owen Cantrell, Assistant Director

Sarah Dyne, Assistant Director
Kelly Elmore, Assistant Director

Office: 966 General Classroom Building
(404) 413-5829

About the Studio (from the studio faculty)

The purpose of the Writing Studio is to enhance the writing instruction that happens in academic classrooms, by providing students with an experienced reader who engages the student in conversation about writing assignments and ideas, and familiarizes the student with audience expectations and academic genre conventions. The Writing Studio focuses on the rhetorical aspects of texts and provides one-on-one, student-centered teaching that corresponds to each writer's composing process, especially invention and revising. Tutors in the Studio do not provide editing or proofreading services. Instead, they aim to create better writers, not "perfect papers," so we address "works-in-progress" in tutorials rather than finished texts.

Tutorial Services

The Studio offers face-to-face tutorials in 976 General Classroom Building, as well as Write/Chat, their online tutoring program. Visit our website at writingstudio.gsu.edu for more information. Remember to take a hard copy of your draft as well as your assignment sheet to your session so that the tutors may better help you.

Hours

The Studio is open year round. Hours will be posted on the website and the door the week before classes begin. The Studio offers online tutorials; the Write/Chat hours are posted on the Writing Studio website.

"Sculpture" by Mike Black

Non-Native Speakers of English
(from the Applied Linguistics faculty)

Reserved sections of English Composition 1101 and 1102 for undergraduate bilingual residents and non-native English speakers are available at Georgia State University.

- These courses have similar learning outcomes as the sections taught through the Department of English.
- Faculty have advanced degrees and training in the area of second language acquisition.
- The courses fulfill the university's English Composition requirements.
- Authorization is not required to register.
- Locate the courses by looking at the "Comments" column on GoSOLAR/ PAWS when you register. Look for "restricted to bilingual/non-native English speakers."
- To register, a student must be a non-native speaker of English—someone whose native/first language is not English, regardless of citizenship or visa status.

ENGL 1101: English Composition
for Non-native Speakers of English I

This course offers bilingual US residents and international students the opportunity to develop their academic writing skills while acknowledging and incorporating their unique language and cultural backgrounds. The course is designed to increase students' academic writing abilities, including organization and development of ideas, paraphrasing and summarizing of reading selections, use of academic language structures to create coherence, and basic research skills. Revision and editing skills are stressed, and grammar review is provided as necessary. This course fulfills the ENGL 1101 requirement and is taught by instructors trained to teach second language writing.

ENGL 1102: English Composition
for Non-native Speakers of English II

Prerequisite: Grade of C or higher in ENGL 1101. This course is designed to increase bilingual US residents and international students' academic writing abilities beyond the level of proficiency required by ENGL 1101. Paraphrasing and summarizing, revision and editing, and research skills are stressed. Grammar review is provided as necessary. This course fulfills the ENGL 1102 requirement and is taught by instructors trained to teach second language writing.

Support Services

ESL tutoring is available at the Learning Commons, Library North 2nd floor. For information and to schedule an appointment, visit https://sites.google.com/site/esltutoringatgsu/.

For more information, contact:

Sharon Cavusgil, ESL Director
Department of Applied Linguistics & ESL

Georgia State University
One Park Tower, 34 Peachtree Street, Suite 1200

404-413-5183, scavusgil@gsu.edu

FIRST-YEAR BOOK PROGRAM (FROM THE BOOK PROGRAM STAFF)

The First-Year Book Program at Georgia State University aims to provide all incoming freshmen with a common intellectual experience among First-Year students. The goals of the program are to promote academic discourse and critical thinking, provide an introduction to the expectations of higher education, integrate an academic and social experience into the campus community, raise awareness and tolerance of cultural likenesses and differences, and create a sense of community. All incoming students will receive a copy of the selection during Incept, and students are expected to read the book before the start of their first semester. The book will be integrated into the ENGL 1101 curriculum.

This year's First-Year book is *The Other Wes Moore* by Wes Moore. To find out more about this book, visit theotherwesmoore.com.

FRESHMEN LEARNING COMMUNITIES AND ATLANTA-BASED LEARNING (FROM THE OFFICE OF UNDERGRADUATE STUDIES)

What are Freshmen Learning Communities?

Navigate your First-Year courses with a cadre of 25 other freshmen. Take core courses themed to one of more than 70 areas of academic interest. Cultivate a higher college GPA and enjoy consistently higher retention (and faster graduation) rates than non-participants just by being a part of one program.

For nine years running, *U.S. News and World Report* has listed GSU's Freshmen Learning Communities as an "outstanding example of academic programs believed to lead to student success." Since its inception, the Freshmen Learning Communities have grown to include more than 1,600 First-Year participants. FLCs give students a broader, more hands-on introduction to the university and its resources by creating a small, friendly community; this eases not only the transition from high school but also further connects the student to the university, to other students, and to Atlanta communities. Rather than "going it alone," participants find an immediate sense of place at GSU, as well as peer mentors for additional support.

Each FLC offers clusters of courses geared toward a shared interest, and includes four courses that fulfill core degree requirements for all majors. You do not have to declare a major in order to register for an FLC. If at the end of the first semester you decide to select a major in a different area, your courses will still count as part of your general education requirements. A fifth course, GSU 1010 New Student Orientation, will help you gain study skills and familiarity with GSU resources. During your second semester at Georgia State, you may elect to remain with members of your FLC by taking one course together while choosing the rest of your courses independently. Most of the time, students stay together with their ENGL 1101 instructor and take ENGL 1102 as a continuing community through the first year.

A few of the 70-plus Freshmen Learning Community themes include:

- Emerging Leaders
- China and the World
- Global Business and Society
- Green Sustainability
- Why Math Matters
- Pre-Nursing
- Religion and Global Culture

- Media and Technology
- Your Life in Theatre
- People, Power and Politics
- Careers in Science
- Health and Society
- Atlanta-Based Learning: Culture and Community

Find the Freshmen Learning Communities informational booklet at http://www. gsu.edu/enrollment/images/Student_Success/FLC_2011_booklet_final.pdf.

For more in-depth questions on dual enrollment credit, math, and foreign language placement exams, e-mail FLC@gsu.edu, or contact Nia Haydel, Academic Professional for Freshmen Learning, at 404-413-2052, or Nikolas Huot at nhuot1@gsu.edu, or visit the Office of Undergraduate Studies in 224 Sparks Hall.

Atlanta-Based Learning

As part of the Freshmen learning Communities program, the Office of Undergraduate Studies offers a special option called "Atlanta-Based Learning." The information below comes from the "Student Success" website located at http://www.gsu.edu/success/ABL.html.

Atlanta-Based Learning promotes academic and civic engagement within the greater Atlanta community. As an urban research institution in Atlanta, Georgia State offers an opportunity for students to understand the context in which they are developing as learners. While engaged in "Campus Atlanta," students obtain the comparative advantage of attending an institution directly linked to its urban community. Engaging in Atlanta-Based Learning activities provides students with an opportunity to generate connections between the academic curriculum and the urban Atlanta environment.

The Atlanta-Based Learning program is open to all students and can be integrated into various academic courses. Program staff works closely with faculty and academic departments to include ABL activities into undergraduate curriculum. Students can participate individually or as part of a class in Atlanta-Based Learning along a continuum of engagement that includes four dimensions:

Learns About—Atlanta Settings

- Walking tour of Georgia State campus
- Walking tour of Atlanta to compare and contrast past and present buildings and landmarks

Learns From—Atlanta Systems

- Public health class tours Centers for Disease Control and Prevention (CDC) and learns about health issues in Atlanta
- Urban studies class meets with Central Atlanta Progress leaders regarding downtown urban development issues

Learns With—Atlanta Communities

- Pre-law class interviews a community member who attended elementary school during *Brown vs. Board of Education*
- Education class reads to children to improve literacy skills

Learns By—Atlanta Service-Learning

- Business class works closely with non-profit agency to design business plan
- Emerging Leaders class plants trees in the downtown Atlanta area

The Atlanta-Based Learning staff is available to assist you in developing and implementing engagement opportunities.

CONCLUSION

In this "Essential Information" chapter, we have presented vital information about GSU and Lower Division Studies programs and other resources available to you as a student. After reading the "GSU and LDS Policies and Procedures" section, you should be familiar with the elements of a GSU course syllabus, the behavioral expectations for all of your GSU classes, the new LDS attendance policy, the nature of textbooks in LDS classes, communicating with your instructors and tutors, the procedures for various assessments, as well as several grade-related procedures at GSU. The "Resources and Programs" section introduces you to several programs and resources connected to LDS classes: the GSU Writing Studio, programs and sections for non-native speakers of English, Freshman Learning Communities, and Atlanta-Based Learning. If you have additional questions, please ask your English instructor or contact the office of Lower Division Studies.

...nal writing process makes college easier, ...ove the impression one makes throughout ...ger role in academic and professional life than most students anticipate, regardless of major or career path.

PRE-WRITING

High school teachers emphasize prewriting strategies, including brainstorming, freewriting, outlines, and mapping exercises. Unfortunately, students tend to skip these prescribed pre-writing activities—viewing them as "extra work"—and dive headlong into writing a paper. This is a mistake. Years of studies in composition strongly suggest that prewriting strategies make writing easier; they also greatly improve its quality. Skip this step, and the finished product will suffer. Ten minutes of prewriting—even if few of these initial efforts make it into the final version—can do wonders. Prewriting generates good ideas, warding off the anxiety-ridden, "stuck" state of writer's block.

The following prewriting techniques provide suggestions for fruitful writing; they are not hard-and-fast rules. Consider two highly valuable tips, from years of college writing instruction experience: 1.) Read the assignment thoroughly. 2.) Begin these generative strategies the day a paper is assigned. Do not start the process the night before a draft is due.

Thinking about the Topic

The generative process of writing begins long before a writer sits down at a computer. Writers—and all students should think of themselves as writers—use free moments to think about what they are going to write, whether they are in the shower, the car, or walking to work. Professional writers report that many of their best ideas come to them during these "down" times; many dedicate a notebook, keeping it handy to record their ideas. This practice prevents the anxiety of sitting down to a blank screen.

Talking about the Topic

Brainstorm ideas with a bright friend, a pen and a notebook. Talking out ideas with another forces a writer to pull ideas into coherent form. A listener can tell a writer if an idea makes sense, or if additional ideas and perspectives should be considered. This strategy also helps a writer identify the *purpose* of the writing and to consider his or her *audience*—two of the most important elements of powerful, successful college writing (indeed, of all writing). In addition to a listening friend, the tutors at the Writing Studio can help writers generate ideas. Students are encouraged to make an appointment at any point in the writing process.

Free Association, or Brainstorming

A *heuristic* is a technique that prompts a writer's memory and ideas. Brainstorming—listing anything and everything that comes to mind about a topic—is familiar to most students. For more fruitful results, take brainstorming a step further—pick out specific words or phrases and do a secondary brainstorm on these narrowed ideas. This is called "looping."

These techniques generate ideas on any given topic; they also help narrow down what is most important about it, or give new directions to the writer. Not all ideas listed will be relevant, but brainstorming provides an excellent starting point. To stay focused, write the topic at the top of every page.

Ryan, a GSU student, brainstormed a list of ideas on why college football should be banned. Notice how brainstorming helps Ryan generate ideas and begin the narrowing process:

Brainstorm on Banning College Football (with Zack)

Football = not about academics, what a university's about

Costs too much money

Bad time for it

University funding going down

Tuition and fees going up

Athletes as celebrities—not educational

Bad-boy behavior

Track, swimming, other sports overshadowed

How do player GPA's compare—find the stats?

Georgia Dome lines out the wazoo—my argument a minority opinion

    She says think of the other side and respond—better be good

Head injuries

    Can be for a lifetime

Other injuries

School loyalty, image—a counterargument

Social aspect—a counterargument

Recruitment scandals

    No, stick with academics and player wellbeing

"Cheer" by Judith Kim

Freewriting

Putting pen to paper (or fingers to the keyboard), writers "freewrite" anything that comes to mind on a topic *for at least 10 minutes, without ever stopping the movement of the pen or keys and without worrying about grammar, spelling, or punctuation.* This technique does wonders to eliminate the stress of the first draft.

Write the topic at the top of the page, and write whatever drifts across the mind, no matter how extraneous it seems (for example: *"I'm not sure what she wants, I can't think of anything, this is dumb this is dumb ...."*). At some point, on-topic ideas will appear. Just as athletes must warm up before practice or competition, writers must "warm up" cognitive and emotional processes in order to write at peak performance. The following is Ryan's freewrite on banning college football:

> ### Ryan's In-Class Freewrite on Banning College Football
>
> *Okay, wht do I write, this is dumb I can't think of anything, thinking too much about tonite—how can I make this thing easier—she says cut it down—maybe I should limit to Georgia State, whether we should have ftball or not? High high higher student fees going to it, while people can't afford to stay in school. Talked to that basketball guy about practice schedules—he said brutal, it's really hard to keep the GPA—where to find a football guy and not use his name—ftball demands too much from these guys, and too much money from the school—saw somewhere that half of college football programs lose money evry year—find Georgia State financials? my audience is my 1101 class—going to be a tough sell—*

Cubing

This heuristic envisions a cube, which has six sides, to prompt thinking on multiple sides of a topic. The steps: 1) Describe the topic or argument. 2) Compare it to other topics or arguments. 3) Free associate. 4) Analyze the topic or argument: How is it significant? How does it work? 5) Argue *for* or *against* any part of the topic, or state your argument concisely. 6) What are the real-life ramifications of this topic or argument? Why should an audience care about this topic? Writing a little or a lot on each section, writers force themselves to see a topic from multiple angles.

Ryan's cubing notes made at home:

Side One: Okay. More people are starting to think it's a brutal sport can harm players for life, and it is not part of a university's mission. Has some socialization function, but in a time of financial need, money should go into building world-class academics.

Side Two: They say football brings people together, students, alumni, the community, etc., that it helps players more than it hurts (scholarships, etc.) and brings in revenue.

Side Three: What about some university up north (can't remember which one), a few years ago, some big alumnus gave 70 million to start a hockey team—what else could that money go for? Would have to find out what that university lacks. They certainly don't lack an athletic program.

Side Four: How it works . . . I don't know. Have to decide which part is most important, what to put 1st, 2nd, 3rd.. Split university mission? Some can't even stay, with all these tuition and fee increases. Help them?

Side Five: Argue against .....player brain injuries. Common sense says enough hits will damage soft brain tissue. Where will some guys end up? Andre Waters, Junior Seau.

Side Six: It's not the wholesome sport everyone says. That writer, writer I can't remember he wrote Outliers, compared football to dogfighting. How does this prepare the average GSU student's intellect for the world, for the fierce competition ahead? Can we dump the team we have? Alisha said Univ of Chicago did.

Questions and Answers

Writers often think of questions that they or others may pose about a topic, and then set out to answer those questions, with the writer (or a friend) recording the writer's answers. Again, this strategy is not concerned with grammar or spelling; rather, it helps to develop ideas and arguments. When writers answer questions, they practice explaining concepts—and building effective arguments—in their own words.

Ryan and Elise's Question and Answer session on "Banning College Football" over lunch:

Elise's question: *So, why do you want to ban college football? Isn't that a little extreme? Do you hate football?*

Ryan's answer: *"I actually like football, it's just that I don't think—that colleges should have teams, you know—I think football takes up too much focus. It has nothing to do with academic programs, which we should be focusing on if we want to compete in this tough global economy. I think football money could be better spent on academic programs that need it, and facilities—other things. The whole football thing is a social thing for students, but I don't think that warrants the cost."*

"Busy Day" by William Walsh

The Five W's and an H: Basic Questions of Journalism

Another specific technique some writers use is to list, and then to answer, the basic questions a reporter would ask: Who? What? Where? When? Why? How? These questions help writers find all the main points needed for expository or persuasive writing. They not only generate ideas but can help narrow the focus, aiding in the formulation of an argument. This technique applies to all types of writing, from creative stories to lab reports.

Ryan makes many general points, so he applies the journalistic questions to just one area—player head injuries. This takes him deeper into what he already knows, and provides new directions for research.

> **Ryan's Journalistic Questions, jotted down in the coffee shop:**
>
> ***Banning College Football: Reason II (Player Head Injuries)***
>
> *Who: Football players. Find out: how many? In other sports?*
>
> *What: CTE, permanent brain damage. Chronic Traumatic Encephal—look it up. These guys take dozens and dozens of hits a season. CTE=dementia, confusion, can't remember anything, may become suicidal. Every time a player takes a hit, it's like hitting a windshield at 30 mph??? find number. This enables them to tackle the world?*
>
> *Where: Throughout the sport.*
>
> *When: I think it's really bad when they're older, but a 21-year-old player, a big hitter, killed himself a while back. If use, must find the medical cause.*
>
> *Why: I don't know. I guess—everything costs something. Nobody likes to look at the cost of things that are fun and popular.*
>
> *How: Deon (friend, medic in Afghanistan) said repeated hits actually kill networks and shrink the brain, destroying the guy's ability to think and live normal. Guy actually laughed at "what about high-tech helmets?"*

Diving into General Research

Instructors sometimes assign a specific topic unfamiliar to a students, and even with a self-generated topic, a writer may not know the "lay of the land" of a topic, the geography of its issues and controversies (Tip: Ask a librarian about the site "Issues and Controversies," available through GSU's Pullen Library). Diving into general research may provide the background needed to formulate an argument. Rather than struggling to form a clearly thought-out thesis statement in the beginning, a writer can begin general research; an interesting argument may come during the process. See the chapter on "Research" in this book for ways to begin.

Here are Ryan's initial search results in the first week after the assignment, along with research questions that he generated (from searches of Google, Google Scholar, and the GSU Pullen Library databases):

Ryan's Research Questions:

What positive effects do football teams have upon the colleges and universities that have them?

What negative effects do football teams have on colleges and universities?

What is the graduation rate of GSU's student athletes?

How can colleges and universities create school spirit, focus on academics, gain prestige, and provide funding for students without resorting to having a football program?

Ryan's Initial Search Results:

Keywords and phrases: *"banning college football," "college football pros and cons," "effects of college football programs," "top colleges without football programs," "college football head injuries," and "graduation rates for GSU football players"*

a. *Chronicle of Higher Education, article called "The Education of Dasmine Cathey";*

b. *In Forbes.com, article by Chris Smith called "Would Banning College Football Actually Help Academics?";*

c. *Article on National Public Radio's Intelligence Squared debate on "Ban College Football";*

d. *Malcolm Gladwell, Intelligence Squared debater, author of The Tipping Point, Blink, and Outliers and New Yorker contributor, in article called "Head Games" in Slate.com;*

e. *Buzz Bissinger, Intelligence Squared debater and author of Friday Night Lights, in the Wall Street Journal on "Why College Football Should Be Banned";*

f. *Article in The Atlantic Monthly by civil rights historian Taylor Branch called "The Shame of College Sports" (EBSCOhost database);*

g. *Article on head injuries by Ben McGrath in The New Yorker called "Does Football Have a Future?" (EBSCOhost database);*

h. *Minutes of GSU University Senate Committee on Athletics, showing graduation rate of athletes;*

i. *Interactive image from National Geographic of 587 concussive hits from one UNC player's football season.*

Note that although Ryan has not found articles in scholarly journals on this issue, he is steering clear of any sources that are out of date or that are not in widely known, well-respected publications. No Wikipedia or personal blogs, for example.

DRAFTING: THE FIRST, THE SECOND, AND EVEN THE FIFTH DRAFT

The writer who 1) reads the assignment sheet thoroughly, 2) asks the instructor for clarifications, and 3) uses heuristic techniques to generate ideas will find drafting much, *much* easier than the student who does none of these. With ideas on paper, this writer can also think about the *purpose* and *audience* of the piece. The greater the command of these elements (of the *rhetorical situation*), the more powerful the writer.

Remember: Writing is a complex, recursive process, and early drafts will be messy. It does not matter what the first draft looks like—*as long as it is not the final draft you submit.*

Everyone's drafting process is different. This is true for children, for college writers, and for widely published and highly acclaimed authors. Some start with the introduction and write straight on through. Others begin with the body, saving the introduction for later. Some sketch the shape of the whole piece on screen or paper and start plugging in material, combing over and reworking the text repeatedly. In any case, writing research suggests a very important tip: *As you draft, try to ignore spelling and grammar. Just go with the flow of the ideas, and save revision for later.*

College writers can benefit from the following simple suggestions: 1) Shoot for *one thing per paragraph,* and clearly state it in a simple topic sentence. 2) Always provide transitions to the next paragraph, and certainly provide a lead-in for any quotation you use: *Gerald Graff has said that . . . / Miller asserts the following: . . . / As we have seen, writing centers help First-Year students (after a quote on writing centers.)*

REVISION: THE ART OF "RE-SEEING" WRITING

Revision takes a high priority in all writing courses. It takes time and effort, but it proves itself well worth it. Done well, it results in clearer, stronger, more effective writing, and a more interesting reading experience; consequently, it often results in better grades.

Studies suggest that First-Year college writers do not revise their writing. The writing of a student who *does* revise will likely stand out from the crowd. Revision gives students a distinct edge over almost two-thirds of their First-Year fellows.

Revision is not just editing, and it is not proofreading. Ideally, these come later in the writing process. Revision involves much, much more than running SpellCheck and adjusting a comma here and there. Rather, it involves a wholesale re-ordering and re-seeing of the very structure and style of the paper. The following three levels of revision may occur and recur during drafting; there is no set order to any writing process. Effective writers revise their papers with an eye to these three levels, circling back through earlier steps as needed.

The Organizational Level

Does the paper flow logically from beginning to end? Where might readers bog down, get lost, or lose interest? Does the thesis statement echo in every sentence of the paper, or can sentences or entire paragraphs be cut? (Students often resist this step until they see the results—a tighter, stronger, more effective paper). Does its tone provide consistent appeal, tailored to its audience? Does the paper contain transitions, guiding the reader smoothly between paragraphs and sections? Or does it jump around, jarring the reader?

"Alpharetta" by Judith Kim

The Content Level

Questions to consider: Does the paper make sense? Will it spark audience interest from the very first sentences? Is it informative? Does it say something unique, or does it feel like a rehash? Does its thesis—its main idea or argument—come through crystal-clear to its audience? Does strong evidence back up every point? Do any background or technical terms need brief explanation? Does the paper cite sources responsibly?

Calling on Creativity: New Directions in Revision

As we have seen, revision literally means re-visioning a paper through a new set of eyes; for best results, this process includes both the writer's and an editor's input, perhaps a peer response group's feedback as well. The following revision strategies are not employed all at once. "Stuck" writers, perhaps dissatisfied with a draft, can apply one or more of the following techniques within specific assignment guidelines:

1. Write a new introduction

2. Write a new conclusion

3. Switch the point of view (from first to third-person or from third to first-person)

4. Add dialogue to the description of an event

5. Re-write the conclusion as an introduction, and then write a new conclusion

6. Write a dialogue with a friend describing the paper, explaining why the topic matters, and specific points of importance

7. Write a stream-of-consciousness freewrite about what is going on beneath the surface of the action, arguments or explanations

8. Describe a place alluded to in the paper using all five senses

9. Open by starting in the middle of the action

10. Describe a person mentioned in the paper

11. Tell what happens after the paper ends

12. Describe what happened before the events of the paper

13. Describe a personal experience related to an argument in the paper

14. Argue from the opposite point of view

15. Create a dialogue representing two or more points of view

16. Write an argument as a narrative

17. Write an analysis as a letter to a friend

18. Write an argument as a stream-of-consciousness freewrite

19. Write to a different audience—GSU's president, a high-school student, a grandmother

20. Write a formal argument as a poem

21. Put the draft aside and write a quick outline of the points *you* want to make

22. Color coding: Write down the important points of the paper, assigning each a color. Then, color code each sentence in the paper, based on the point to which it refers. If the paper looks like a rainbow, or if randomly colored sentences appear in one paragraph (or sentences with *no* color), rework the structure of the paper.

EDITING: SENTENCES AND STYLE

Editing comes after revision, and for many good reasons. For one, efficient writers do not spend time fixing punctuation in a paragraph they might eliminate later. A proven editing technique for catching structural and sentence-level errors: Read the paper *out loud,* and slowly. Some writers editing their work read the paper backwards, last sentence first, focusing on one element at a time, like spelling or punctuation. If editing the entire paper proves overwhelming, read aloud one paragraph at a time. Editing does not have to occur all at once; some writers focus on one page, and then take a break. Will readers stumble over awkward phrasing, or be bored by redundancies or excessive repetition? Where can stronger, more descriptive words—and tighter sentences—enhance the reader's experience?

PROOFREADING: THE MICRO LEVEL

Proofreading is generally performed last, after several rounds of revision and editing have been done. Once you are satisfied that you have effective content, organization, and style at the level of paragraphs and sentences, you will proofread, or make sure that all elements of grammar, usage, mechanics, and manuscript form are taken care of. Proofreading entails performing tasks such as checking your spelling, capitalization, and punctuation; rereading the assignment sheet to make sure you have followed the correct heading and formatting guidelines; and making sure that all sources are properly documented in an appropriate documentation style (usually MLA).

A Revision, Editing, and Proofreading Checklist for Strong, Effective Writing

Purpose
- Did I follow the assignment guidelines?
- Did I make my purpose clear to the reader?
- Are audience, purpose, and content appropriate and effective?

"Telephone Remix 2" by Deonta Wheeler

Audience
- Does the paper effectively engage my audience?
- Does it appeal to my audience's logic and/or emotions?
- Does it establish my *ethos* as a writer (will the audience find my authorial persona reliable and trustworthy)?

Focus
- Is the thesis (main idea) clear, strong, and specific?
- Does every paragraph and idea relate to the thesis?

- Does the paper include irrelevant points? What can be cut to make the paper tighter and stronger?

Ideas
- Did I say what I wanted to say?
- Am I missing any important ideas?
- Did I include strong evidence to effectively state my point? Did I provide enough examples?
- Does the paper answer the "So What" question—"Why does this matter?"

Organization
- How can the introduction better engage the reader, establish the tone, and/or set up the main idea of the paper?
- Can I cut the phrase "In conclusion," and make the ending more sophisticated? Does the ending grab attention, giving readers something to carry away?

Structure
- Does the information unfold in the most effective order?
- Does the essay lead the reader through the essay in a clear and logical way?

Paragraphs and Transitions
- Does each paragraph focus on one main point, relevant to the thesis of the paper?
- Do I provide smooth transitions between paragraphs?
- Does each sentence connect to the one that came before it and the one that follows? Or does the writing feel disjointed?

Tone and Style
- Does the piece speak with a tone and writing style consistent and appropriate for subject, purpose, and audience?

Sentence Structure
- Does each sentence on its own make sense?
- Are sentences well-constructed, effective, and varied?
- Are there too many short, choppy sentences? Too many long, wordy sentences? Can these be juxtaposed to make reading more interesting?

Grammar and Spelling
- Did I consult my English handbook on use of commas and other points unclear to me?
- Did I not only run SpellCheck, but also look at *every single word* in the essay to ensure correct usage?

Citation of Sources

- Does the paper use the assigned style (most likely MLA)?
- Does the paper cite outside sources correctly within the text?
- Does the paper end with a properly formatted Works Cited page, including all outside sources? Do any sources appear on Works Cited that are *not* cited within paper?

SAMPLE STUDENT ESSAY FROM GSU ENGLISH 1101

In the next section, you will read about the writing process of GSU junior Kerry McDonough. Kerry is pursuing a Criminal Justice degree with a concentration in pre-law at Georgia State. She was enrolled in Diana Eidson's English 1101 FLC during the fall semester of 2010. Kerry continued with Ms. Eidson for 1102 in the spring semester.

The Assignment

On the following pages appears the assignment sheet from Kerry's instructor, Ms. Diana Eidson. For her ENGL 1101 class, Kerry was enrolled in a Freshmen Learning Community called "People, Power, and Politics." Her instructor used a theme of "Writing to Change the World," and encouraged the students not only to write about issues of concern to them but also to publish their works to a wider audience. Through publication in the *GSU Guide to First-Year Writing*, Kerry's story is now reaching a wider audience.

Diana Eidson wishes to thank Stephanie Horton, with whom she collaborated on designing the following assignment.

ENGL 1101/Essay 1
Diana Eidson, Office: GCB 952 Mon. and Wed. 1:30-2:30
Writing to Change the World
"I was (things were) never the same after that": a narrative essay*

THE ASSIGNMENT

OPTION 1. Write the story of an instance in which you encountered or experienced poverty, homelessness, hopelessness, joblessness, addiction, crime, unwanted pregnancy, a person/people facing huge obstacles, the abuse of the weak by the strong, the degradation of the environment, or hate/discrimination based on race, gender, sexual orientation, disability, etc., (whether as victim, perpetrator, or observer.) You may extend the list.

Example: Ms. Eidson's experience with the student who lived in the mill house

OPTION 2. Write a story about a book or article you have read, or a movie or documentary you have watched, that opened your eyes to a larger world and changed you in some way.

Example: Mary Pipher reading *The Diary of Anne Frank* in *Writing to Change the World*

Example: Ms. Eidson, *To Kill a Mockingbird*, and the inspiration to change the world in a positive way through fighting injustice

THE REQUIREMENTS

This must be the story of a GAME-CHANGING EXPERIENCE in your life.

It does NOT have to seem "big" or "important" to be significant. Small moments often bring life changes. If it has come to mind, chances are it will be good—if written with care.

The experience must have made you think, feel, change or grow.

In some capacity, it must have been a "turning point" in your life.

- **Did the experience make you more compassionate? What does that mean to you?**
- **Did it make you mad? Did it make you resolve to act?**
- Or conversely, did it make you go from idealism to cynicism?

- Did it change your worldview, or did it solidify your existing worldview?
- Did it prompt you to see yourself, another group of people, or the world, differently?

AT SOME POINT IN YOUR STORY, USE THESE WORDS

"I was (things were) never quite the same after that."

This essay will be drawn solely from your experience. This is not a research paper, but it must adhere to MLA page format and style (see *The Everyday Writer* and MLA handout).

Length: 6-8 pp. Bring 3 draft copies for peer edit workshop Wednesday, September 8.

Final due to Ms. Eidson Monday, September 13.

YOUR RHETORICAL SITUATION: AUDIENCE

Your instructor, members of the class, the undergraduate community of Georgia State University.

YOUR RHETORICAL SITUATION: PURPOSE FOR WRITING

To change the world, one millimeter at a time. To make a grade in 1101.

Narrative, Structure, and Organization:

A narrative has plot, a setting, and characters. It can analyze and persuade. However, it MUST say, "This happened. And then this, and then this. Here's what it all means."

Tell your story in the first person, using "I." "They (the American guards) asked if I was with Al Quaeda or the Taliban. When I insisted I was not, the abuse got worse. One guy used electroshocks on my feet, and joked that it would keep me warm. I was chained and hung by my wrists for a long time." Turkish student Murat Kurnaz, of his three-year detainment at Guantanamo Bay. In "In The Wrong Place for a Long Time," *The Washington Spectator*, 1 June 2009.

Tell your story chronologically, with introduction, body and conclusion. It's the most straightforward way. If it works better for you, you may begin *in medias res*—in the middle of the action—and tell the story through flashback. Or, 1. What I learned, then 2. How I learned it.

Use descriptive detail to enliven the story. "If you were to dig a hole 300 feet straight down from the charming French village of Crozet, you'd pop into a setting that calls to mind the subterranean lair of one of those James Bond villains. A garishly lit tunnel curves away into the distance, crammed with heavy steel structures, cables pipes, wires, magnets, tubes, shafts, catwalks and enigmatic gizmos." Achenbach, Joel. "The God Particle: The Large Hadron Collider." *National Geographic*, March 2008, pp. 95-105.

The Classic Narrative Arc:

There is no single "right" way to organize a narrative, but this one has withstood the test of time:

Exposition: Describes setting, or launches the story. Gives reader needed information.

Conflict, or Rising Action: Things ramp up.

Climax: Moment of highest intensity, usually toward the end. Think of when Captain Kirk and the bad guy fistfight on the catwalk.

Conclusion/Denouement: At the end of *Hamlet*, everybody dies. I'm sure this won't happen in your essay.

LEARNING OUTCOMES FOR THIS ASSIGNMENT
- You'll engage in writing as a process with various invention heuristics (like brainstorming); you'll consider audience and practice drafting, revising, editing, and proofreading.
- You'll engage in the collaborative, social aspects of writing.
- You'll use language to explore and analyze contemporary multicultural, local, global, and/or international questions, finding power in writing for social change and self-discovery.
- You'll express yourself through engaging, readable, colorful, coherent, meaningful prose.

OPENING LINES: WAYS TO BEGIN A STORY

By Establishing Point of View

"There was no exchange of body fluids on the first date, and that suited both of us just fine."

—T. Coraghessan Boyle

"Since Dr. Wayland was late, and there were no recent news magazines in the waiting room, I turned to the other patient and said, "As a concerned person, and as your brother, without meaning to offend, how did you get that scar on the side of your face?"

—James MacPherson, "The Story of a Scar"

With A Generalization

"It is a truth universally acknowledged, that a single man in possession of a good fortune must be in want of a wife."

—Jane Austen, *Pride and Prejudice*

With a Child Narrator

"When I was in the third grade I knew a boy who had to have fourteen shots in the stomach as the result of a squirrel bite."

—Ellen Gilchrist, "Victory Over Japan"

With a Description of a Person

"He was an inch, perhaps two, under six feet, powerfully built, and he advanced straight at you with a slight stoop of the shoulders, head forward, and a fixed-from-under stare which made you think of a charging bull."

—Joseph Conrad, *Lord Jim*

With a Description of Place

"The village of Holcomb stands on the high wheat plains of western Kansas, a lonesome area that other Kansans call "out there.""

—Truman Capote, *In Cold Blood*

"I am living at the Villa Borghese. There is not a crumb of dirt anywhere, nor a chair misplaced. We are alone here, and we are dead."

—Henry Miller, *Tropic of Cancer*

With Dialogue

"'Christmas wouldn't be Christmas without any presents,' grumbled Jo, lying on the rug."

—Louisa May Alcott, *Little Women*

Bernays, Ann, and Pamela Painter. *What If? Writing Exercises for Fiction Writers.* New York: Harper, 1990.

Mikos, Paul. *Opening Lines: First Sentences from Classic Plays, Poems and Books..* Appleseed Press, 2007.

ASSESSMENT

This paper is worth 10 percent of your final grade.

An A paper has:

- Ideas that are insightful, thought-provoking, and focused
- A clear thesis supported by specific, insightful details and examples that arouse audience interest
- A clear awareness of audience
- Coherent organization and relevant, logical use of evidence
- Appropriate transitions between ideas and paragraphs
- A confident and readable, style that incorporates varied sentence structure and precise word choice
- Grammar, spelling, and punctuation that are conventionally correct
- Correct MLA format and style
- In short, it *rocks.* An outstanding, model paper.

A B paper will contain:

- Ideas focused to a central thesis but not consistently insightful or thought-provoking
- Coherent organization
- Adequate but uneven details and examples that arouse audience interest. Evidence is relevant
- A general awareness of audience
- A style that is confident, readable, and rhetorically effective in tone, incorporating varied sentence structure and word choice
- Very few errors (less than five) in grammar and mechanics
- Correct MLA format and style
- "B" proud. Paper is above average in a college composition course

A C paper will contain:

- Ideas that support the topic and central idea with some focus
- Organization that is mostly coherent, but could be tighter and more effective
- May demonstrate weak transitions between ideas or paragraphs
- Development is adequate. Details and examples provide concrete, specific evidence
- An uneven awareness of audience
- Style that is readable and effective in tone, incorporating some varied sentence structure
- Few errors (five to seven) in grammar, spelling, and punctuation
- Generally correct format, with room for improvement
- "C" It's Complete and Competent

A D paper will contain:

- Clichéd, general ideas, but some support of a topic or central idea
- Organization that is generally coherent in support of the essay's purpose
- Abrupt or weak transitions
- Development that is general, providing adequate details and examples in some places.
- Evidence and reasons may lead to a few logical fallacies or unsupported claims
- Audience awareness is vague
- Inconsistent in tone, sometimes lacking sentence variety or effective word choice
- More than seven distracting, sometimes serious errors in grammar, spelling, and punctuation
- Format meets only some of the assignment's requirements

Obviously an "F" paper meets few, if any, of the assignment's requirements. I did not add the "F" category only because I hope I do not have any "F" papers.

Kerry on Pre-Writing

This assignment was to tell about an event that you were never the same after. I listed out a lot of topics that significantly impacted my life, but I did not know what the best topic or most appropriate one would be. The "I am from" poem I wrote helped me generate ideas by serving as a reference. That poem is essentially what I define myself as. In my prewriting stages, I oftentimes found myself referencing that poem and asking how this or that aspect of the event made me different from who I said I was in the poem. I was able to better explain how the event caused me to stray away from my identity with the poem.

Kerry's instructor asked her to write a poem called "I am from…" to help her generate ideas for this paper. This prewriting idea came from a book by Mary Pipher called *Writing to Change the World*.

I am from

by Kerry McDonough

I am from the whimsical Moira and the serious James

From two Yankee parents living in the South, talking with funny accents

From Irish blood that can drink like fish and love their corn beef and cabbage

From a Catholic family that occasionally attends Sunday mass

I am from a house that eats only New York style pizza, none of the "fake" stuff

From a long line of law enforcement that has inspired my majoring in Criminal Justice

I am from suburbia, with gas guzzling SUVs, gossiping soccer moms, and business suit dads

From girls in their summer sundresses and boys in their colorful polos

I am from a sports crazed father who got stuck with four girls

From a dad who taught me everything I know about basketball and tennis

I am from a school where I lettered in these sports, thanks to my dad

I am from a place that offered me every opportunity in the world

From a place that I am so grateful to have experienced

However, I am from a place that has inspired me to discover who I am in a place very different than where I am from possible topic?

- quitting basketball
  after 8 years
- DUI & getting
  arrested
- death of my
  grandfather

PROS/CONS OF DUI TOPIC

PRO:
- Easiest to write about
- I can put my full ~~feel~~ emotion into it
- every word is real than I feel

CONS:
- Very difficult subject
- just met teacher & don't want to make myself look bad
- good chance I will focus too much on ~~arrest~~ one also.
  at arrest

night before party

morning of arrest

process of booking

Most degrading feeling getting items handed to me

DUI

Release

calling parents/ bail $

Kerry on Drafting:

When writing my initial drafts, I take the topic I picked and the list of broad ideas I wrote about that topic and I begin to tell a story based off of these. For this assignment, I picked the topic of my arrest and then came up with the list of three main ideas which were the mistake (telling about the process of the arrest), the consequences of the arrest (injustice, friends, family, police) and then the lessons I learned. This made it easy for me to tell the story and create my drafts because in a sense, I'm just filling in the gaps of these main ideas with the inclusion of how I felt. The main strategies I use when writing my drafts are isolating myself, finding a quiet area, and making sure I designate a lot of time to work on the paper so I don't lose my train of thought by working short in short sessions. I do not save each draft I work on separately. I find it easiest if on my computer I save a rough draft, a peer review edit draft, and then a final draft of my paper. These strategies are very effective in helping me get my work done.

After Kerry wrote her rough draft, she asked her friend Taylor Pannell to review it. She asked him to give her feedback by responding to several questions. On the following pages appear Kerry's draft with Taylor's comments. The questions and answers appear at the end.

Kerry McDonough

September 13, 2010

English Composition 1101

Ms. Eidson

"I was Never the Same After That"

The morning of December 21st, 2009, my basic right of freedom was jacked when I was

Comment: Change to hijacked

arrested for a DUI. Driving to the jail, I remember feeling terrorized, shocked, and disappointed

at the fact that I was now a criminal. Having my rights confiscated for eight hours opened my

eyes to the meaning of consequence. The booking process and my spending time in the jail cell

Comment: Run-on sentence.

and all of the terrible consequences affected the aspects of my life that I valued most. Truly, lots

Comment: "Lots of stuff" is a colloquial expression. Consider appropriate diction throughout your paper. Keep in mind you are writing to an academic audience.

of stuff changed after my DUI. My opinion of the law, my family, my aspirations, and my way

of life were all turned upside down after this particular morning.

Comment: It is smoother to break this up using hyphens or parentheses rather than commas.

The night of December 20th, one of my closest friends, or so I thought, held her

eighteenth birthday party. There was laughing, dancing, and underage drinking. Nothing else

mattered. We were simply a bunch of teenagers with nothing else to worry about but having a

good time. We partied hard to make sure my friend's birthday was unforgettable and then

Comment: This is good, it expands a bit on your mindset at the time and will contrast with the reality of landing in jail later on.

crashed at about one thirty in the morning. My parents wanted me home early the next day, so I

woke up at seven thirty and headed home. I had not been in the car for more than a minute when

I suddenly saw the blue lights flashing behind me and heard the "whoop whoop" sound of the

police siren. I thought I was going to have a heart attack. Partly because I was groggy, and partly

Comment: Should change to a comma so that the next sentence isn't a fragment.

because I want to forget this morning all together. I vaguely remember my interaction with the

officer. My headlights were not on was the whole reason I got pulled over in the first place. The

whole reason I was pulled over was because my headlights were not on. The police asked me the

night before when I stopped drinking and where my license was. As I opened my wallet and

answered the officer, I remembered that my license was on my copy machine to be copied for a

school decal. Another officer showed up and said that because I lived close, he would go to my

house and tell my parents to pick up my car so it would not be towed. The officers talked with

each other for a while and then administered a series of diagnostic tests and a breathalyzer test.

After about thirty minutes, I was arrested on the charges of a DUI, under aged drinking, driving

without my headlights on, and driving without a license. Things were never quite the same after

that.

An officer asked me a series of questions about my health, many of which had me

thinking "people actually answer yes to these?" Then a female police woman led me to a room

where I was stripped completely of all my clothes and put in a jail suit that read Property of

Cobb County: Inmate. Stripping out of my own clothes unwillingly and being coerced to wear

these words on my back was the most degrading moment of my life. I was no longer considered

a person, but property of a government facility. This term property made me feel like I had

absolutely no value. After this, the booking process began. A smart ass officer laughed at the fear

in my eyes and asked "what is an innocent lookin' girl like you doin' here?" Ashamed, I

answered his question. He proceeded to take my fingerprints and my mug shot. At that moment a

face that once identified an innocent, high achieving, individual was now one amongst the

thousands of murderers, rapists, drug dealers and other criminals in the system.

Comment: Change in tense. Could correct by saying "wanted to forget that morning".

Comment: The second sentence is enough to make your point, no need to restate it.

Comment: Rewording is needed to clarify what the sentence is trying to say. "The police officer asked me for my license and when I had stopped drinking the night before" would suffice.

Comment: Not entirely required, but "diagnostic tests" and "breathalyzer test" could be consolidated.

Comment: Not needed since you are listing more than one charge.

Comment: A good way to add some length to a paper and make it sound less like "this is what happened" is to add in visual details. Describing the jail suit's color, form, or symbolism breaks up the monotony.

Comment: To keep tense correct, could change to "the".

Comment: Change to "that", proper tense usage, etc.

Comment: Great contrast to the earlier care-free Kerry!

The officer placed me in a holding cell where I called my parents to read them the information about my bail, which was two thousand five hundred dollars. My parents were already awaiting my phone call because of the officer's visit to my house informing my parents I was arrested and they would need to retrieve my car. I heard the fear in my dad's voice for his straight "A" student daughter who was now a Cobb County Inmate. I was then handcuffed to the hip of a sixty year old woman who was accused of making terroristic threats, and directed down a long concrete hallway to where the holding cells were. A butch woman threw me a feeble mattress, a blanket, and three rolls of toilet paper. These items suggested that I would sleep in jail for multiple days, which made me feel extremely anxious. I wanted to hand all these things back. A heavy concrete door slid open and I was shoved into a stone cold cell filled with about fifty other inmates.

Everything lay out in the open, including the toilets and the beds. It was unbearably cold and for the next eight hours goose bumps made the hair on my arms stick up. I stood the only white teenager amongst mostly black or Hispanic women that ranged from age twenty five to sixty five. This intimidated me because I was a little, white girl from the suburbs of East Cobb thrown into a cell filled with a diverse type of women with diverse convictions. In a chair I sat and put my head down when a large woman came up to me and said "That's my seat." I relocated to another seat avoiding any chance of trouble, put my head down again and cried for over an hour. When I looked up I realized many women were staring at me. An older woman asked me if I was okay and what I was in here for. I began to explain my situation to her and a bunch of other women. Strangely, talking to them alleviated some of my worry. Basically, we all talked down about petty and unnecessary arrests by many police officers. I distinctly remember talking to one young woman who had been in there for breaking her probation. She told me that

Comment: This section could be removed for a smoother read. If removed, add "the night before" to the end of "officer's visit to my house".

Comment: Could change to "of those" to keep tense correct.

Comment: It can be understood why, but expanding upon this could add more depth.

Comment: Wanted to make a note about this. I am unsure if this is the proper form of "lay" to use. It could be correct, but that word always confuses me.

Comment: Could change to "collection".

Comment: Could change to "various", unless you're going for repetition as a creative option here. In that case, it's fine.

Comment: Rearrange to "I had sat in a chair".

she could not wait to get out in nine days. I realized that Christmas was in four days and my

heart ached for the people who had to spend their holiday in this dark, depressing place. Then, I

heard my name accompanied with the words your going home. I jumped up and quickly walked

towards the officer for my release.

After picking up my belongings, I exited the doors of the Cobb County Jail. My eyes

painfully adjusted from the darkness of inside the jail to the intensity of the sun's rays. I walked

up a hill and heard my parents call my name. Both of them embraced me with a hug and a kiss

that never felt so comforting. However, stern looks and a silent car ride home followed this terse

moment of love. When we arrived back at my house, the yelling began. At the time, my father

was out of work and we were living off of my mom's miniscule teaching salary. Christmas was

only four days away, and money was extremely tight because my parents had been Christmas

shopping for a while. I had no money saved in the bank to pay for my own bail, DUI School, a

lawyer, or the many other expenses that getting arrested requires you to pay. My dad's intense

lecture still clearly replays in my head. He shouted that we were financially unstable because of

me and that I have had too many second chances. He concluded his tirade with the words "You

screwed up really bad this time Kerry. Sorry can't fix this one." These words cut through me

like a knife. I have two younger sisters who once looked up to me. My dad informed me that my

nine year old sister answered the door to the police officer that morning. Before this day, I served

as a role model for my sisters. When my dad told me that my youngest sister answered that

knock, I realized that I was a prime example of how not to act. I felt like there was nothing I

could do to earn back my family's respect. Having the police show up at their front door to tell

them that their daughter was in jail was the last thing my parents ever expected from their

seemingly innocent daughter. In addition to the guilt that ate me up inside, I had to live with the

> **Comment:** Change to "Those" to correct the tense.

> **Comment:** If you wanted, you could expand this into a little segment about your relationship with your dad and why his disappointment hit so hard.

> **Comment:** Change to "that", tense correction and whatnot.

frustration of not being able to fix this mess I created. Unpredictable, the court is extremely. All I thought about for days was how my present and future would be greatly affected by this whole situation. My court date continuously got pushed back. October of this year, the date is currently set. Not knowing what kind of punishment I am going to receive makes my stomach turn. In any scenario the judge assigns me, I know this arrest will affect my future forever. On all my applications, I am required to expose that I was arrested and charged with a crime. I constantly worry that when I am older I will find myself regretting this drunken night when I was eighteen because I will still be without a career. For a long time I wanted to work for the FBI. A tradition of law enforcement has inspired me to continue long line of New York law enforcement in my family has inspired me to continue the tradition. My heroes are my uncle, who was a New York detective, and my grandfather, who was the head of the New York DEA. By making it into the FBI, I wanted more than nothing to make them proud. However, with my lawyer, he told me this was no longer an option with a criminal record. This arrest complicates all the goals and dreams I strive to achieve.

> **Comment:** Reword this to "The court is extremely unpredictable".

> **Comment:** This needs to come before the previous sentence in order to keep the continuity in check.

> **Comment:** Reword to "The date is currently set to October of this year". Subject comes first in this instance.

> **Comment:** Change to "that" to correct tense.

> **Comment:** This sentence needs to be reworded/restructured in order to clarify what exactly you're trying to say.

> **Comment:** "Nothing more than" would be the correct phrase.

> **Comment:** This can be changed to "my lawyer".

Along with disappointing my family and interfering with my life goals, this mistake impacted my way of life tremendously. Christmas, New Years, and the rest of holiday break this past year were miserable. The anxiety from the legal troubles and the guilt I felt for putting my family through hardship induced me into a small depression. My room became the only place I desired to hang out. When school started back up, the constant questions of what happened made progressing forward with my life difficult. Everyone asked me what I got for Christmas, and it hurt me inside to reply "bailed out of jail." My senior year experience had been cut short. For obvious reasons, my parents grounded me. While all my friends shared stories about their crazy weekends, I sat and jealously listened. The girl whose house we drank at that night, supposedly

> **Comment:** Avoid clichés and overused expressions that don't really add meaning to your prose.

> **Comment:** Change to "listened jealously" to make better use of the adverb.

my best friend, asked me if her family would be in any trouble and then never spoke to me again. All the normality in my life had disappeared. Feeling alone and forgotten about, I stopped making an effort to enjoy what was left of High School. I knocked out my community service on the weekends, attended my DUI School, and continued to wallow in self pity.

> Comment: Here's another opportunity to expand. You could talk a little bit about how well you knew each other, to contrast with the abandonment.

My parents grew tired of my constant moping. My mom yelled at me to get on with my life. She preached that the past was the past and that I could not take back what I did, and that these words made sense when my mom said them out loud. I started to realize that constantly beating myself up was not resolving my issue in any way. The only thing I could do was learn from this massive mistake. For the next few weeks, I contributed significantly with housework. My parents used me as their babysitter, house keeper, and grocery shopper. Financially, my family was still struggling to pay for lawyers and DUI School. I had been job hunting and was thrilled when I landed a job at a frozen yogurt place called Yogli Mogli. By January, I was working three or four days a week and paying for some of the court fees. The one positive outcome that resulted from my arrest was being forced to grow up and take responsibility of my own life.

> Comment: This can be removed. You made your point with the beginning section of the sentence.

> Comment: Good ending, but try to hint at the next paragraph for a smooth transition.

I have a negative perception of the law as a result of my situation. My DUI School taught me that drinking and driving is one of the most irresponsible actions one can take and I strongly agree with this fact. However, I believe that my situation fails to be a true drunk driving incident. My reasoning for this is that I slept, sobered up, and passed the entire diagnostic test fine. The only evidence that says I was "drunk" was the number on the breathalyzer, which I am now aware I could have refused to blow in. This number I blew was over the legal limit for a minor. I find it ridiculous that this number overrides the physical diagnostic tests which proved I was capable of driving. A legal limit number that applies to everyone within that age group cannot possibly mean that every person is automatically drunk if they blow over that number. Everybody is different meaning that everyone has different tolerance levels. Despite the fact that there are many officers bravely protecting our streets, there are also quotas that these officers need to meet by the end of the month. Near the end of the month is when my DUI took place, and I question if the officer pulled me over because he had a quota to meet. His reasoning for pulling me over was such a minor reason, especially because the sun was shining. The officer claimed that there are certain times you had to drive with your headlights on, regardless of how bright the sky is. Feelings of anger run through me every time I think about my situation because a large part of me feels that bad luck had me driving in the wrong place at the wrong time; a perfect time for this officer to meet his quota.

> **Comment:** Could be removed for a more clarified read.

> **Comment:** Wordy, just say because.

> **Comment:** Change to a comma!

Today, I think about everything this experience has taught me ,and I am proud to say that I am a different, more mature person. My responsibility shows when I go to social events. Every time I go to a party, I keep the things in my life that I value most in the back of my head. Whenever I feel the need to drink, I question if the drink is worth jeopardizing the people or relationships that are important to me. Not only has being incarcerated prevented me from drinking and driving, but my situation has taught my friends to make good choices with their partying as well. My friends learning from my practices of making smart decisions proves I honestly have transformed my irresponsible ways. I now am aware of the dangers and repercussions of breaking the law.

Kerry's Peer Review Questions:

1. *Kerry: After reading my paper, does the sequence of events make sense? There were a lot of events I needed to explain, and my question is if I lost my reader in all the explanation of the events.*

   > Taylor: I did not have much to add to the paper in terms of clarification. Your sequence of events made perfect sense and I was not, at any time, confused as to when something occurred or how some details fit the overall story!

2. *Kerry: Are there any areas that need more explanation or any areas where I use too much detail?*

   > Taylor: I actually feel that you should use MORE detail. However, visual details could be used rather than just adding on to the story. I feel like you explained the events perfectly well, but going into a bit more detail on how things looked, how you felt, the smell of the prison, etc., can add so much more depth to a story without making the paper too long.

3. *Kerry: Do I answer the essay assignment, which is to write of an event that made you never the same. I feel that I may not focus enough on how my life has changed since the event because of all the explanation of the events.*

   > Taylor: I think you answered the question perfectly fine. Although not as much time is spent on showing how your life has changed since the event, your point is easily made. If you were to add more, I would recommend adding details in the relationships you had with your family/friends.

4. *Kerry: Is my diction in the paper okay? I want to sound educated, yet passionate. Also, I fear that I might have been too lax in some of language and it took away from my ethos.*

   > Taylor: It's good to keep in mind that passion doesn't ever have to be written less elegantly to exist. Passion is all about having the reader fully relate to what you are writing. Using more vivid details, expanding upon the relationships that were negatively affected… These changes will do wonders for adding ethos to your paper. Come to think about it, sounding more educated here would work better. The reader will be drawn in more to find out how such an intelligent person could find themselves in such a situation!

Kerry also submitted to Ms. Eidson a draft for an initial review. In Ms. Eidson's class, the students write a letter to her with questions about their draft, and she responds in a letter. The students and instructor keep up a semester-long correspondence about the students' writing progress. Kerry asked Ms. Eidson these questions:

- Are there a lot of verb tense errors?

- Does the paper flow smoothly with good transitioning?

- Do I focus too much detail in certain areas?

On the next few pages appear Kerry's first draft with comments from Ms. Eidson and answers to her questions.

Kerry McDonough

September 13, 2010

English Composition 1101

Ms. Eidson

"I was Never the Same After That"

The morning of December 21st, 2009, my basic right of freedom was jacked when I was arrested for a DUI. Driving to the jail, I remember feeling terrorized, shocked, and disappointed at the fact that I was now a criminal. Having my rights confiscated for eight hours opened my eyes to the meaning of consequence. The booking process and my spending time in the jail cell and all of the terrible consequences affected the aspects of my life that I valued most. Truly, lots of stuff changed after my DUI. My opinion of the law, my family, my aspirations, and my way of life were all turned upside down after this particular morning.

The night of December 20th, one of my closest friends, or so I thought, held her eighteenth birthday party. There was laughing, dancing, and underage drinking. Nothing else mattered. We were simply a bunch of teenagers with nothing else to worry about but having a good time. We partied hard to make sure my friend's birthday was unforgettable and then crashed at about one thirty in the morning. My parents wanted me home early the next day, so I woke up at seven thirty and headed home. I had not been in the car for more than a minute when I suddenly saw the blue lights flashing behind me and heard the "whoop whoop" sound of the police siren. I thought I was going to have a heart attack. Partly because I was groggy, and partly because I want to forget this morning all together I vaguely remember my interaction with the officer. My headlights were not on was the whole reason I got pulled over in the first place. The whole reason I was pulled over was because my headlights were not on. The police asked me the night before when I stopped drinking and where my license was. As I opened my wallet and answered the officer, I remembered that my license was on my copy machine to be copied for a school decal. Another officer showed up and said that because I lived close, he would go to my house and tell my parents to pick up my car so it would not be towed. The officers talked with each other for a while and then administered a series of diagnostic tests and a breathalyzer test. After about thirty minutes, I was arrested on the charges of a DUI, under aged drinking, driving without my headlights on, and driving without a license. Things were never quite the same after that.

> **Comment:** Omit one of these sentences.

> **Comment:** Explain what you did. If this is an important detail, elaborate a bit. This was for a parking permit at school?

> **Comment:** Thank you for remembering to add this sentence.

An officer asked me a series of questions about my health, many of which had me thinking "people actually answer yes to these?" Then a female police woman led me to a room where I was stripped completely of all my clothes and put in a jail suit that read Property of Cobb County: Inmate. Stripping out of my own clothes unwillingly and being coerced to wear these words on my back was the most degrading moment of my life. I was no longer considered a person, but property of a government facility. This term property made me feel like I had absolutely no value. After this, the booking process began. A smart ass officer laughed at the fear in my eyes and asked "what is an innocent lookin' girl like you doin' here?" Ashamed, I answered his question. He proceeded to take my fingerprints and my mug shot. At that moment a face that once identified an innocent, high achieving, individual was now one amongst the thousands of murders, rapists, drug dealers and other criminals in the system.

> **Comment:** Redundant—female officer is fine

> **Comment:** This seems to be something worth expounding on. Give more detail, with an emotional punch.

> **Comment:** Keep your audience in mind. Decorum gives you ethos.

The officer placed me in a holding cell where I called my parents to read them the information about my bail, which was two thousand five hundred dollars. My parents were already awaiting my phone call because of the officer's visit to my house informing my parents I was arrested and they would need to retrieve my car. I heard the fear in my dad's voice for his straight "A" student daughter who was now a Cobb County Inmate. I was then handcuffed to the hip of a sixty year old woman who was accused of making terroristic threats, and directed down a long concrete hallway to where the holding cells were. A butch woman threw me a feeble mattress, a blanket, and three rolls of toilet paper. These items suggested that I would sleep in jail for multiple days which made me feel extremely anxious. I wanted to hand all these things back. A heavy concrete door slid open and I was shoved into a stone cold cell filled with about fifty other inmates.

> **Comment:** Oh, my. Describe this scene a bit, if it is important enough. Kind of darkly comic, it would seem.

> **Comment:** Can you think of a more sensitive, less stereotypical term for her?

> **Comment:** Necessary?

Everything lay out in the open including the toilets and the beds. It was unbearably cold and for the next eight hours goose bumps made the hair on my arms stick up. I stood the only white teenager amongst mostly black or Hispanic women that ranged from age twenty five to sixty five. This intimidated me because I was a little, white girl from the suburbs of East Cobb thrown into a cell filled with a diverse type of women with diverse convictions. In a chair I sat and put my head down when a large woman came up to me and said "That's my seat." I relocated to another seat avoiding any chance of trouble, put my head down again and cried for over an hour. When I looked up I realized many women were staring at me. An older woman asked me if I was okay and what I was in here for. I began to explain my situation to her and a bunch of other women. Strangely, talking to them alleviated some of my worry. Basically, we all talked down about petty and unnecessary arrests by many police officers. I distinctly remember talking to one young woman who had been in there for breaking her probation. She told me that

> **Comment:** This part is not quite clear. I would suggest rewording or adding a bit of detail. How were you aware of their varying offenses? Did you talk to them?

> **Comment:** This scene could be one of importance, and it told with grace, could be really powerful.

> **Comment:** Do these injustices warrant elaboration?

she could not wait to get out in nine days. I realized that Christmas was in four days and my

heart ached for the people who had to spend their holiday in this dark, depressing place. Then, I

heard my name accompanied with the words your going home. I jumped up and quickly walked

towards the officer for my release.

> **Comment:** Direct quotation? If so, indicate it with quotation marks.

After picking up my belongings, I exited the doors of the Cobb County Jail. My eyes

painfully adjusted from the darkness of inside the jail to the intensity of the sun's rays. I walked

up a hill and heard my parents call my name. Both of them embraced me with a hug and a kiss

that never felt so comforting. However stern looks and a silent car ride home followed this terse

moment of love. When we arrived back at my house, the yelling began. At the time, my father

was out of work and we were living off of my mom's miniscule teaching salary. Christmas was

only four days away and money was extremely tight because my parents had been Christmas

shopping for awhile. I had no money saved in the bank to pay for my own bail, DUI School, a

> **Comment:** When? The previous day? Make the chronology clear.

lawyer, or the many other expenses that getting arrested requires you to pay. My dad's intense

lecture still clearly replays in my head. He shouted that we were financially unstable because of

me and that I have had too many second chances. He concluded his tirade with the words "You

screwed up really bad this time Kerry. Sorry can't fix this one." These words cut through me

like a knife. I have two younger sisters who once looked up to me. My dad informed me that my

> **Comment:** A clichéd simile. Can you think of a more compelling one?

nine year old sister answered the door to the police officer that morning. Before this day, I served

as a role model for sisters. When my dad told me that my youngest sister answered that knock, I

realized that I was a prime example of how not to act. I felt like there was nothing I could do to

earn back my family's respect. Having the police show up at their front door to tell them that

their daughter was in jail was the last thing my parents ever expected from their seemingly

innocent daughter. In addition to the guilt that ate me up inside, I had to live with the frustration of not being able to fix this mess I created. Unpredictable, the court is extremely. All I thought

> **Comment:** It seems you are trying to alter the word order for rhetorical effect. If deliberate, make sure it is effective. Here, it seems a forced, and therefore, jarring.

about for days was how my present and future would be greatly affected by this whole situation.

My court date continuously got pushed back. October of this year, the date is currently set. Not

> **Comment:** *Continually* means something that happens over a long period of time, but only intermittently. Continuous does not make sense here, because the court could not push it back 24/7/365 with no break. There were a few instances of pushing the date back over a long period of time, so use "continually."

knowing what kind of punishment I am going to receive makes my stomach turn. In any scenario

the judge assigns me, I know this arrest will affect my future forever. On all my applications, I

am required to expose that I was arrested and charged with a crime. I constantly worry that when

I am older I will find myself regretting this drunken night when I was eighteen because I will still

be without a career. For a long time I wanted to work for the FBI. A tradition of law

enforcement has inspired me to continue long line of New York law enforcement in my family

has inspired me to continue the tradition. My heroes are my uncle, who was a New York

> **Comment:** Revise this sentence to eliminate redundancy.

detective and my grandfather, who was the head of the New York DEA. By making it into the

FBI, I wanted more than nothing to make them proud. However, with my lawyer, he told me this

> **Comment:** More than anything? Take another look at this sentence and make sure it's clear. "By making it into the FBI, I would have been able to make them really proud of me." What do you think?

> **Comment:** Is something missing here? "However, when I met with my lawyer, I found out that this goal was no longer an option..."

was no longer an option with a criminal record. This arrest complicates all the goals and dreams I

strive to achieve.

> **Comment:** Be careful of verb tense. "I have striven to achieve" is correct, though a bit awkward. "I have tried to achieve"?

Along with disappointing my family and interfering with my life goals, this mistake

impacted my way of life tremendously. Christmas, New Years, and the rest of holiday break this

> **Comment:** "has impacted"... The use of "impact" as a verb is in dispute among grammarians, so you might want to say something like, "this mistake has changed, transformed, complicated"...find a synonym

past year were miserable. The anxiety from the legal troubles and the guilt I felt for putting my

family through hardship induced me into a small depression. My room became the only place I

> **Comment:** I'm not quite clear what you mean here. *Induced* is not the correct word, though, I think. "Reduced me to a depressive state" might be better, but doesn't seem quite right. Let's come up with something else.

desired to hang out. When school started back up, the constant questions of what happened made

progressing forward with my life difficult. Everyone asked me what I got for Christmas, and it

hurt me inside to reply "bailed out of jail." My senior year experience had been cut short. For

obvious reasons, my parents grounded me. While all my friends shared stories about their crazy

weekends, I sat and jealously listened. The girl whose house we drank at that night, supposedly my best friend, asked me if her family would be in any trouble and then never spoke to me again. All the normality in my life had disappeared. Feeling alone and forgotten about, I stopped making an effort to enjoy what was left of High School. I knocked out my community service on the weekends, attended my DUI School, and continued to wallow in self pity.

My parents grew tired of my constant moping. My mom yelled at me to get on with my life. She preached that the past was the past and that I could not take back what I did, and that these words made sense when my mom said them out loud. I started to realize that constantly beating myself up was not resolving my issue in any way. The only thing I could do was learn from this massive mistake. For the next few weeks, I contributed significantly with housework. My parents used me as their babysitter, house keeper, and grocery shopper. Financially, my family was still struggling to pay for lawyers and DUI School. I had been job hunting and was thrilled when I landed a job at a frozen yogurt place called Yogli Mogli. By January I was working three or four days a week and paying for some of the court fees. The one positive outcome that resulted from my arrest was being forced to grow up and take responsibility of my own life.

> **Comment:** This idea is highly important, so foreground it. Emphasize this lesson in the portion of your essay that deals with the present.

I have a negative perception of the law as a result of my situation. My DUI School taught me that drinking and driving is one of the most irresponsible actions one can take and I strongly agree with this fact. However, I believe that my situation fails to be a true drunk driving incident. My reasoning for this is that I slept, sobered up, and passed the entire diagnostic test fine. The only evidence that says I was "drunk" was the number on the breathalyzer, which I am now aware I could have refused to blow in. This number I blew was over the legal limit for a minor. I find it ridiculous that this number overrides the physical diagnostic tests which proved I was capable of driving. A legal limit number that applies to everyone within that age group cannot possibly mean that every person is automatically drunk if they blow over that number. Everybody is different meaning that everyone has different tolerance levels. Despite the fact that there are many officers bravely protecting our streets, there are also quotas that these officers need to meet by the end of the month. Near the end of the month is when my DUI took place, and I question if the officer pulled me over because he had a quota to meet. His reasoning for pulling me over was such a minor reason, especially because the sun was shining. The officer claimed that there are certain times you had to drive with your headlights on, regardless of how bright the sky is. Feelings of anger run through me every time I think about my situation because a large part of me feels that bad luck had me driving in the wrong place at the wrong time; a perfect time for this officer to meet his quota.

Today, I think about everything this experience has taught me and I am proud to say that I am a different, more mature person. My responsibility shows when I go to social events. Every time I go to a party, I keep the things in my life that I value most in the back of my head. Whenever I feel the need to drink, I question if the drink is worth jeopardizing the people or relationships that are important to me. Not only has being incarcerated prevented me from drinking and driving, but my situation has taught my friends to make good choices with their partying as well. My friends learning from my practices of making smart decisions proves I honestly have transformed my irresponsible ways. I now am aware of the dangers and repercussions of breaking the law.

> **Comment:** This section of the paper is highly important, and worth spending a bit of text on.

Kerry, here are my responses to the questions you asked about your draft:

1. *Are there a lot of verb tense errors?*

   I did not notice many errors. I commented within the text at a couple of points where I was confused as to the actual sequence of events. We will talk about how to organize the paper so that it is chronologically clear. Make sure that you lead the reader from the past to the present, or present to past in a smooth, clear way.

2. *Does the paper flow smoothly with good transitioning?*

   For the most part, yes. From the first paragraph to the second, I noticed a jump from present to past that was rather jarring. The organization of the paper started in the present, went back to the night of the party, the arrest, the jail, the aftermath with your parents, and then concluded with what you have learned. Except for the opening, this is generally effective. We will talk in our conference about navigating the times and places, as well as switching between the story and the reflections on the story, which can be difficult.

3. *Do I focus too much detail in certain areas?*

   Well, the paper certainly more than meets the page requirement for the paper. In some places, there is too much detail. The way to determine this is to ask yourself, "What are the most important things about this story that I want people to take away from it?" If a detail is not necessary for the story to move forward to emphasize these important points, then you could omit it. In some places, such as the jail uniform, the distribution of the items that you wanted to hand back, and the scene where you talked to the women, I wanted to find out more. These seemed like important parts of the experience and what you took away from it. You can give us a bit of the cake without giving us the whole slice. Give us a taste, and we can imagine the rest.

Kerry,

You have written a detailed essay that clearly conveys the importance of this experience in your life. Your organizational structure is effective and clear overall, but I think you can work on two things that we will discuss in more detail during our conference. First, the opening should engage the reader's attention much more strongly. Second, you might consider structuring your essay around the following frames that will help you tell the story. The first part is the mistake. It's about choices. The second part is about the consequences. It seems to be largely about irony and injustice. The third part is about the lessons learned. The theme here seems to be about responsibility and trust. Perhaps you can use these themes as you work through the chronology of the story. It might help. We will talk about it more during the conference.

I look forward to seeing where this essay takes you. It will prove to be a really powerful story, I'm sure.

CONFERENCE NOTES

Kerry and Ms. Eidson had a face-to-face conference regarding Kerry's initial draft. Here are the notes from that conference:

Ms. Eidson: Kerry, what questions do you have about my comments on the rough draft?

Kerry: 1) how to shift tenses when the story goes from the present to the past and vice versa; 2) how to smooth out the level of detail—too much in some places, not enough in others; 3) how to organize logically

Kerry and Ms. Eidson discussed the following strategies:

Refer to assignment sheet: we looked at assignment handout and discussed narrative structure/chronology, effective openings, descriptive details, learning outcomes, and assessment

Opening/hook: start *in media res* (middle of action) with the sirens and blue lights

Organization/transition: Shift clearly to the past, what led up to the police arrest; option—tell story, then reflect on it

Details: Select few scenes and expand instead of giving play by play —add vivid description for emotional impact; tighten writing/ redundancy/wordiness—will give Kerry more room to add vivid details

Learning Outcomes and Assessment: use assignment sheet as checklist for content, organization, language conventions, and MLA form

Frames/themes to help organization: mistake consequences lessons (injustice and irony responsibility and choices)

Goals for final draft:

- Create effective hook

- Navigating chronology: selecting and ordering events

- Level of detail: omit nonessential scenes and flesh out essential ones with vivid detail

- Frames: mistakes, lessons, consequences

Kerry on Revision:

Revising for me involves a lot of reading out loud. When I read my paper out loud, I can hear the grammatical errors or things that sound awkward. I usually cut things when I hear too much fluff or if there is too much detail explaining a minor idea. I add elements to my paper if there is something that is too vague. I usually move things around if I find I have made my paper sound too much like "This happened. Then, this happened. Then, that happened." I want to make sure I keep my audience interested with my style of writing. I find writing questions on my drafts to my teacher and to my peers who are revising my paper helpful. I ask questions that deal with mistakes I know I have a history of making in my papers. My questions usually ask if the reader thinks that I have answered the essay assignment, if they were interested throughout the paper, and areas where there needs to be more clarity or less detail. Asking a teacher or peers these questions on the draft they are editing helps not only with the assignment at hand, but it also helps you as a writer to not continuously make the same mistakes.

Kerry on Editing and Proofreading:

I address editing and proofreading concerns after I feel confident that I have addressed most of my structure/organization errors. Again, reading out loud is helpful because I can hear the grammatical errors. Sometimes I find it useful to find two friends to do a peer review focusing on style, organization and structural errors, and then have a separate third person edit my paper only identifying grammatical errors.

Kerry's final draft appears on the following pages with comments and a grade from her instructor.

Kerry McDonough

Ms. Diana Eidson

English 1101

8 September 2010

I Was Never the Same after That

I did a double take into my rear view mirror as blue and white flashing lights caught the corner of my eye. The howl of a siren quickly followed. I began to process what was happening and immediately pulled into the nearest neighborhood. As a young, handsome police officer walked toward my window, I gripped the steering wheel tightly, trying to remain calm during my first time being pulled over. The officer informed me I was being pulled over for not having my headlights on. He proceeded to ask for my license and registration. I cooperated with the officer and opened my wallet to grab my license that was nowhere to be found. As I began explaining to the officer why I was driving without a license, he interrupted me with the question "How much did you have to drink last night Ms. McDonough?" Little did I know that I would never be the same after this routine traffic stop on December 21, 2009.

> **Comment:** Kerry, this opening is much more effective, drawing the reader immediately into the moment.

Last year, my senior year of high school, I only cared about celebrating my last year with the friends I spent years making. The night of December 20th, one of my closest friends (or so I thought at the time) held her eighteenth birthday party. There was laughing, dancing, and underage drinking. Nothing else mattered. We were simply a bunch of teenagers with nothing to worry about except having a good time. I did not think there was any harm in our activities

> **Comment:** This transition effectively takes the reader back to the previous night, showing the way that the arrest originated.

because I knew I was sleeping where I was drinking. The night started out with a harmless beer or two. As the night progressed and the adults went to sleep, we let more friends into the basement where the alcohol was kept. One shot of tequila led to several more. We partied hard to make sure my friend's birthday was unforgettable and then crashed at about one thirty in the morning. My parents wanted me home early the next day, so I woke up at seven thirty and headed home.

I had not been in the car for more than a minute before I realized I was being pulled over. My heart sank when I realized I still reeked of alcohol. I vaguely remember my interaction with the officer, partly because I was groggy, and partly because I want to forget that this morning ever happened. As I opened my wallet and answered the officer, I remembered that I had left my license on the copy machine at my house the previous day. My high school required us to have a parking decal which was obtained by giving a copy of one's driver's license to a school administrator. I tried explaining this to the officer, but must not been convincing because he interrupted me with the question, "How much did you have to drink last night Ms. McDonough?" My response was unclear because I was so nervous, but the officer took this to be the slurring of my speech. I was told to step out of the vehicle and then I was directed through a series of diagnostic tests followed by a breathalyzer test. After about thirty minutes, I was arrested on the charges of DUI, under aged drinking, driving without my headlights on, and driving without a license. Things were never quite the same after that.

As soon as we entered the jail, an officer asked me a series of questions about my health, many of which had me thinking, "people actually answer yes to these?!" Then a female officer led me to a room where I was stripped completely of my clothes and made to put on a jail suit that read "Property of Cobb County: Inmate." Stripping out of my clothes unwillingly in front of a complete stranger robbed me of any sense of freedom I once felt I had. One of the most degrading parts of my life was when I stepped into the jumpsuit that classified me as property. I was no longer identified as the straight "A," athletic, high achieving Kerry McDonough that stood out from a crowd. In jail, the crime you committed comes to be what defines you. The only thing that made me different from the woman standing next to me was my inmate number. After this, the booking process began. An officer laughed at the terror I must have been displaying on my face as he sarcastically asked, "What is an innocent lookin' girl like you doin' here?" Ashamed, I answered his question. He proceeded to take my fingerprints and my mug shot. At that moment a face that once identified an innocent, high achieving, individual was now one amongst the thousands of faces of murders, rapists, drug dealers and other criminals in the "corrections" system.

> **Comment:** If the crime identifies the inmate, then what does the inmate number do? Are you saying that you are no longer a person, but merely a number and an offense instead? This part is not quite clear.

Next, the officer placed me in a holding cell where I called my parents to read them the information about my bail, which was two thousand five hundred dollars. My parents were already awaiting my phone call because of the officer's visit to my house informing them I had been arrested and that they would need to retrieve my car. I heard the fear in my dad's voice for his straight "A" student-daughter who was now a Cobb County Inmate. In the holding cell was one other woman, a sixty year old who was there for making terroristic threats. She saw my tears and tried to calm me down, but the fact that she had just told me she was in jail because of making terroristic threats scared me into maintaining a wide distance from her. My efforts to keep away from this woman were all in vain because before long, I was handcuffed to her sixty year old hip and led down a freezing hallway to where the population holding cells were located. A stern woman threw me a feeble mattress, a blanket, and three rolls of toilet paper. I wanted to hand all these things back and say, "My parents will be here very shortly, so I won't need these,"

> **Comment:** How might you transition more smoothly from the conversation with your dad back to the reality of the holding cell?

but I did as I was told and took the items gratefully. A heavy concrete door slid open and I was shoved into a stone-cold cell filled with about fifty other inmates.

Behind the metal door was an abhorrent scene. Everything lay out in the open, including the toilets and the beds. It was unbearably cold and for the next eight hours goose bumps made the hair on my arms stick up. I stood the only white teenager amongst mostly black or Hispanic women that ranged from age twenty five to sixty five. This situation intimidated me because I was a little white girl from the suburbs of East Cobb who was thrown into a cell with a diverse group of women. I sat in a chair and put my head down when a large woman came up to me and said, "That's my seat." Immediately, I relocated to another seat in order to avoid any chance of trouble, put my head down again, and cried for over an hour. When I looked up I realized many women were staring at me. An older woman asked me if I was okay and what I was in here for. I began to explain my situation to her and to some of the other women. Strangely, talking to them alleviated some of my worry. Several of the women had multiple DUI convictions. They shared with me their experiences, enabling me to gain an idea of what kind of punishment I should expect. I did not realize then how useful these conversations would be in the following weeks when my peers and family members who knew of my arrest tried to tell me what to expect or what my punishment would be, as though they had any clue. At least the conversations with the inmates were based off of firsthand experience and I could trust what they told me to expect from the criminal justice system. I distinctly remember talking to one young woman who had been in there for breaking her probation. She told me that she could not wait to get out in nine days. I realized that Christmas was in four days and my heart ached for the people who had to spend their holiday in this dark, depressing place. Then, I heard my name accompanied with the words "you're going home." I jumped up and quickly walked towards the officer for my release.

Comment: I'm not sure this sentence is necessary. You have already made it clear the discrepancy between yourself and the typical denizen of the county jail.

Comment: A nice touch of pathos through your connection with these women. They weren't as intimidating as they at first seemed.

After picking up my belongings, I exited the doors of the Cobb County Jail. My eyes painfully adjusted from the darkness of the jail's interior to the intensity of the sun's rays. I walked up a hill and heard my parents call my name. Both of them embraced me with a hug and a kiss—affection that had never felt so comforting. However stern looks and a silent car ride home followed this terse moment of love. When we arrived back at my house, the yelling began. At the time, my father was out of work and we were living off of my mom's miniscule teaching salary. Christmas was only four days away and money was extremely tight because my parents had been Christmas shopping for all four of their daughters over the three-week period prior to my arrest. I had no money saved in the bank to pay for my own bail, DUI School, a lawyer, or the many other expenses that getting arrested requires one to pay. My dad's intense lecture still clearly replays in my head. He shouted that we were financially unstable because of me and that I have had too many second chances. He concluded his tirade with the words, "You screwed up really bad this time Kerry. Sorry—can't fix this one." These words made me feel like throwing up. I have two younger sisters who once looked up to me. My dad informed me that my nine year old sister answered the door to the police officer that morning. Before this day, I served as a role model for my sisters. When my dad told me that my youngest sister answered that knock, I realized that I was a prime example of how not to act. I felt like there was nothing I could do to earn back my family's respect. Having the police show up at their front door to tell them that their daughter was in jail was the last thing my parents ever expected from their seemingly innocent daughter.

Comment: In this paragraph, you provided insight into your family dynamics, an insight that clarifies the depth of your parents' disappointment.

In addition to the guilt that ate me up inside, I had to live with the frustration of not being able to fix the mess I had created. The court system is extremely unpredictable. All I thought about for days was how my present and future would be greatly affected by this whole situation.

My court date was pushed back continually. The date is currently set for October of this year. Not knowing what kind of punishment I am going to receive makes my stomach turn. In any scenario the judge assigns me, I know this arrest will affect my future forever. On all my applications, I am required to expose that I was arrested and charged with a crime. I constantly worry that when I am older I will find myself regretting this drunken night when I was eighteen because I will still be without a career. For a long time I wanted to work for the FBI. A long line of New York law enforcement officers in my family has inspired me to continue the tradition. My heroes are my uncle, who was a New York detective and my grandfather, who was the head of the New York DEA. By making it into the FBI, I would have been able to make them really proud of me. However, when I met with my lawyer, I found out that this goal was no longer an option with my criminal record. This arrest complicates all the goals I have tried to achieve.

Along with disappointing my family and interfering with my life goals, this mistake has transformed my way of life tremendously. Christmas, New Years, and the rest of holiday break last year were absolute misery. The anxiety from the legal troubles and the guilt I felt for putting my family through hardship sent me spiraling into a depression. My room became the only place I desired to hang out. When school started back up, the constant questions of what happened made progressing with my life difficult. Everyone asked me what I got for Christmas, and it hurt me inside to reply "bailed out of jail." My senior year experience had been cut short. For obvious reasons, my parents grounded me. While all my friends shared stories about their crazy weekends, I sat and jealously listened. The girl whose house we drank at that night, supposedly my best friend, asked me if her family would be in any trouble and then never spoke to me again. All the normality in my life had disappeared. Feeling alone and forgotten about, I stopped

Comment: Nice transition from previous paragraph.

making an effort to enjoy what was left of high school. I knocked out my community service on the weekends, attended my DUI School, and continued to wallow in self pity.

Finally, my parents grew tired of my constant moping. My mom yelled at me to get on with my life. She preached that the past was the past and that I could not take back what I did. These words made sense when my mom said them out loud. I started to realize that constantly beating myself up was not resolving my issue in any way. The only thing I could do was learn from this massive mistake. For the next few weeks, I contributed significantly with housework. My parents used me as their babysitter, house keeper, and grocery shopper. Financially, my family was still struggling to pay for lawyers and DUI School. I had been job hunting and was thrilled when I landed a job at a frozen yogurt place called Yogli Mogli. By January I was working three or four days a week and paying for some of the court fees. The one positive outcome that resulted from my arrest was being forced to grow up and take responsibility for my own life. For the previous eighteen years, I had always gone straight to my mom and dad when I had a situation that was difficult and confusing. Considering that neither of my parents has ever been arrested, they could not help me more than I could help myself with this confusing situation. Realizing that my parents could not bail me out of everything, literally, was a major wake up call to the fact that I needed to be prepared to handle the consequences that all my actions would produce.

> **Comment:** At this point, the narrative shifts to a more mature, responsible Kerry.

> **Comment:** You do an effective job here describing the lessons learned and how you have changed as a result of this experience.

As a direct result of my DUI, I have a negative perception of the legal system. As I learned in DUI School, drinking and driving is one of the most irresponsible actions one can take and I strongly agree with this assessment. However, my situation does not fit the category of the typical drunk driving incident. I slept, sobered up, and passed the entire diagnostic test fine. The only evidence that says I was "drunk" was the number on the breathalyzer, which I am now aware I could have refused to submit to. This number I blew was over the legal limit for a minor. I find it absurd that this number overrides the physical diagnostic tests that proved I was capable of driving. A legal limit number that applies to everyone within my age group cannot possibly mean that every person is automatically drunk if he or she registers over that number. Everybody is different, with different tolerance levels for alcohol. Many officers bravely protect our communities, but they have quotas to meet by the end of each month. My DUI took place near the end of the month, and I wonder if the officer pulled me over because he had a quota to meet. His reasoning for pulling me over was such a minor reason, especially because the sun was shining. The officer claimed that there are certain times you had to drive with your headlights on, regardless of how bright the sky is. Every time I think about my situation, I feel angry because I am convinced that bad luck had me driving in the wrong place at the wrong time—a perfect time for this officer to meet his quota.

Comment: In this paragraph, I see the injustice theme repeated, but now in the form of a reflection.

Today, I think about everything this experience has taught me and I am proud to say that I am a changed person. This is not to say that I never do any of the things I did before my arrest. I am in college now, and I oftentimes find myself around the party scene. It is when I go to these festive events where my responsibility and maturity show the most. Before going to a party, I ask the location of it, the kind of people that will be there, and the number of people who will be there. My friends may find this "interrogation" irritating when they have simply invited me to a party, but I will not risk getting in trouble for one night of partying at a random place. Since my arrest, I have not driven under the influence, nor will I ever drink and drive again. I make this bold, passionate statement because I know now that drinking and driving has horrific consequences. Fortunately, no one was harmed by my intoxicated driving. I learned in DUI School, however, that there are thousands of individuals who have lost a loved one because of

Comment: Transition clearly here to the more positive theme of reflecting on responsibility and choices.

the selfish choice someone else made to drive when drunk. Several of my friends and family members have not experienced being arrested, or, in particular, a DUI, and always think they are fine to drive after having some drinks. I find myself watching over my peers at parties and making sure that they do not try to drive if they have been drinking, no matter how little it was. If I am offered a drink, I keep the things in my life that I value most in the back of my head. I now am aware of the dangers and repercussions of breaking the law.

I may be only a single individual. However, my DUI arrest taught me that my actions have the power to create significant change. For this reason, I need to think before my actions so that I am making positive change in the world around me. I said that I now have a negative view of the criminal justice system because of my experience with it and I also said that I do not believe my situation was true drinking and driving. I continue to stand by both of these, but I am fully aware that my poor decision to drink when I was not of age resulted in my arrest. My actions matter and their consequences go further than just impacting the one, single, and individual me. Therefore it is imperative that these actions reap positive consequences.

Comment: It is possible that this piece of writing could cause someone to think carefully before making choices. I hope so.

Comment: You conclude the narrative on a positive note, which I think is not only appropriate, but indicative of your moving into the future. It might be helpful to comment here that no matter what the outcome of court is, you must move forward with your goals. Not sure, though. Might be too didactic.

Kerry, In this draft, I see some of the improvements we discussed during our conference. You have revised the opening paragraph, added some details to crucial scenes, made more effective transitions, and organized your essay according to the themes of mistakes, consequences, and lessons. I still see same places where you might omit repeated ideas ("I am a little white girl from the suburbs" and "straight 'A' student" statements come to mind) and where you might tighten your writing so that it gets the ideas across effectively without overwhelming the audience with details. Using nouns and action verbs rather than a wealth of adjectives might help you accomplish this goal. However, this skill comes with enough practice. Remember: Instead of telling the story, try showing the readers the scenes and allowing them to draw inferences from the information that they are given. Holistically, you have created clear, vivid prose. In addition, you have followed language conventions and delivered virtually error-free writing. Based on the criteria for an outstanding paper, I would have to say that your essay fulfills the requirements to a moderate degree. You have included a clear thesis with specific, insightful details that arouse the audience's interest; you have a keen sense of your audience; your organization is clear and logical, and you certainly include plenty of evidence; there are appropriate transitions at most every point in the paper; you use a number of precise words to convey your ideas; your style is relatively confident and readable; and your grammar and language conventions are correct. Bravo!

GRADE: A- 92%

Kerry on Her Final Draft:

When I submitted my draft, I was most pleased with the fact that I was able to clearly organize a story that had several parts to it. Figuring out how to organize my paper can be very difficult, especially if the paper requires you to flip back and forth from present to past. I am proud that at the end of my writing process, and with the reviews from my peers and professor, that I was able to get my story out there clearly.

After looking at Ms. Eidson's comments on my final draft, my main question that remains concerns whether or not there is an easy technique to identify which details are unnecessary and which to expand on. It seems easy to know what detail is important because it is your story that you are telling, but I find it difficult to know what the reader is going to find important or insignificant. I believe that my final draft fulfilled the aims of the assignment successfully. In terms of saying how my life is different now, I think I could have expanded upon this idea more. Next time I write, I think I will really focus on identifying the crucial points and unnecessary detail. Good writing results from correcting your mistakes so you do not make the same ones in the future. Every piece of work can always be better.

FOR DISCUSSION

In whole class discussion or in small groups, respond to the following:

1. What do Kerry's pre-writing, first draft, peer and instructor comments, and final draft reveal about her writing process?

2. Compare the first, marked-up draft to the final draft as submitted to the instructor. What are some of the changes Kerry made to her draft? How effective are they? Why?

3. Did Kerry incorporate the changes suggested by her instructor? If so, how well did these changes improve the quality of the paper's argument and appeal to the audience?

4. What advice would you give to Kerry as she continues to improve her writing?

5. Did Kerry meet the specifications of the assignment as listed in Ms. Eidson's assignment sheet? Are there any components neglected? If so, what?

6. What is *your* writing process? When your instructor gives you an assignment, how do you approach it? Which prewriting, drafting, and revising strategies described in this chapter can you implement to make your writing stronger?

7. Why is the writing process so important? How does it improve the final "product"? What does it teach us about writing?

GETTING THE WORDS RIGHT

In an interview called "The Art of Fiction" with the *Paris Review* in 1956, Ernest Hemingway revealed his revision process:

> *Interviewer:* How much rewriting do you do?
> *Hemingway:* It depends. I rewrote the ending of *Farewell to Arms*, the last page of it, *39 times* before I was satisfied.
> *Interviewer:* Was there some technical problem there? What was it that had stumped you?
> *Hemingway:* Getting the words right.

If a writer like Hemingway feels he must revise one page 39 times, what then does a student writer need to do? You may not have the opportunity to revise your writing 39 times, but remember the importance of taking revision seriously, and taking advantage of every opportunity to improve your writing.

In the same *Paris Review* article, drama critic, poet, and short story writer Dorothy Parker responded to a question about her writing process: "It takes me six months to do a story. I think it out and write it sentence by sentence—no first draft. I can't write five words but that I can change seven." Clearly, professional writers have individual processes and have practiced strategies that work for them. Also, they understand that writing is an art, and that the process of excellent writing is painstakingly slow. However, they also know that the payoff is a deep sense of satisfaction and accomplishment.

Engaging, effective writing, like all other skills, takes time and practice. We hope that from reading this chapter, you will take away these essential pieces of advice regarding the writing process:

1. Start work early on writing assignments, and pace yourself so that you may complete each portion in a timely and exemplary manner.

2. Read the assignment materials carefully, and communicate your questions and concerns to your instructor in class and during one-on-one conferences.

3. Initial drafts are messy. Celebrate this by generating as much material as possible and then shaping it into something more polished. Think of someone making a pottery vase. He or she must have clay on the wheel in order to shape the vase. The first draft is the clay. When you write, you add "clay," remove clay and move clay around in order to make the vase. You must first have the clay. Enjoy both the "messy writer" phase and the "meticulous editor" phase.

4. Seek feedback on your work from peers and family members. Getting another set of eyes or ears to respond to your paper proves helpful in making sure that your ideas are clear and engaging.

5. Put forth effort into every phase of the process: prewriting, drafting, revising, editing, and proofreading.

6. Read your rhetoric text for help with content, organization, and style issues.

7. Refer to your grammar handbook for tips on correcting mistakes in grammar, usage, mechanics, documentation, and manuscript form. Make sure all sources are properly documented in the correct form (usually MLA).

8. Revise, revise, and revise some more. The great thing about writing is that it is never finished. You can always go back and make it better. Many instructors give the opportunity to revise work after it is graded. Take advantage of this opportunity to improve your writing.

Writing is a challenging and exciting journey. You see the results of our efforts immediately. Many people are available and willing to help you. Find strategies that work for you and use them. Enjoy the process!

Analysis

INTRODUCTION: THE DIFFICULTIES FACING FIRST-YEAR WRITERS PRACTICING SCHOLARLY ANALYSIS

The majority of writing assignments you have encountered in previous academic settings most likely asked you to do one of two things: 1) relate your personal feelings or experiences, or 2) repeat facts or an established informative narrative. Of course, many components of your college degree program will continue to privilege your ability to memorize and reproduce the basics of your field of study, but achieving a degree will also require a critical perspective that asks more of you. Central to this mode of critical engagement is *academic analysis*, which we define as the process by which one gathers information, assesses that information according to objective criteria, and articulates logical conclusions that expand our field of knowledge as scholars.

Generally, First-Year writers are equipped to *summarize*, or describe the "6 Ws" that are familiar as informative writing (who, what, when, where, why, and how). But, First-Year students often struggle to analyze that summarized material in the way that their instructors expect. Meeting these expectations is made doubly hard because an insightful analytical essay always requires some limited degree of summary as its foundation, and shifting from summary to analysis is a subtler move than most writers or readers realize.

Many qualitative differences exist between summary and analysis, but one particularly accessible way of describing analysis comes to us from the field of psychoanalysis and that field's practice of interpreting dreams. One remarkably common dream centers on the dreamer showing up to work or school or some other public place completely naked. It is safe to say that everyone reading this book has had the naked dream, or one very much like it. Summarizing this dream is easy: "I was running down the hall of Aderhold because I was late for an exam, and when I burst into the classroom everybody turned to me and started laughing. When I looked down, I realized that I wasn't wearing any clothes..."; where it goes from there is up to you. That summary encapsulates what analysts call the *manifest*

"Untitled" by Marissa Graziano

content of the dream; it is what "actually" happens in the dream, the plot of the little movie that you watch while you are asleep.

But, as we know intuitively, this dream is in fact about something else. When you have a dream about showing up naked to class, you are not truly worried that one day you are going to be in such a rush that you leave the dorm without putting on pants. This scenario is a classic example of an anxiety dream, where the embarrassing act of showing up to class naked is really your unconscious mind's attempt to process your worry about something else (like that exam). This constitutes the *latent meaning* of the dream. The manifest content or the surface of the dream is about showing up naked to class, but the latent meaning of the dream is easily recognized as anxiety about something else.

> Another set of terms may help us understand the difference between summary and analysis, or manifest and latent content. Borrowing from the fields of linguistics and literary studies, we may distinguish between *denotation* and *connotation*. Roughly, denotation is what a text explicitly states, while connotation is what a text implies. An easy way to observe this distinction in action is to look at nearly any advertisement, as the effect of an ad is built as much on the associations consumers bring to it as what is actually there. Using a print advertisement or a video advertisement from the Web, summarize it, or describe its manifest/denotative meaning. Then, think about what feelings the ad elicits in you, or what associations you make even though they may not be addressed specifically by the ad, which would constitute its latent or connotative meaning.

Analysis is not truly distinct from the "Who, What, When, Where, Why, and How" of a topic, yet pushing past simple summary and on to cogent analysis is one of the most difficult-to-achieve learning outcomes facing many First-Year writers. These students may find themselves in a bind because, even though they may be unfamiliar with the conventions of scholarly analysis, most assignments require it; indeed, First-Year writers are, in many cases, being graded on their ability to perform a scholarly task that they probably have not been taught yet!

Furthermore, instructors of First-Year English courses may have trouble articulating the nature of scholarly analysis because, as academic professionals, it is what we do every day and therefore second nature to us; or, having been trained for a decade or more in a specific field of study, we may focus on certain types of analysis to the detriment of others. This makes things exceedingly more complicated because analysis takes what appear to be many different forms across disciplines. To illustrate, here are two examples of academics performing analysis:

- A certain type of literary scholar might analyze an individual poem written, say, 250 years ago by first "close reading"; that is, by examining closely the constituent parts of the poem to arrive at a "meaning" that is greater than the poem's parts, or that is implicated by the poem rather than expressly stated by the author. After reading to get an initial impression, this scholar might investigate the etymologies of particular words to see if changes in the meaning of words over time could be helping to shape the effect of the poem. This scholar might also look at the number of stressed and unstressed syllables in individual lines and stanzas, and then compare the findings to other poems or whole genres of poetry. If this scholar is so inclined, he or she might move on to investigating the biography of the poet to see if events from the poet's life resonate with the poem under examination, or if the culture in which the poet lived might also be shaping in some way the content of the poem.

- A team of physicists searching our galaxy for planets that might bear the conditions for biological life as we know it might use one of the world's great radio telescopes to collect thousands of images of a single distant star. By comparing these images taken over time, the team might detect the signs of a planet passing between the star and our earth. Once identified, and under the right conditions, the light collected from one of these planetary bodies can be broken into a spectrum that details, incredibly, the temperature and chemical composition of the planet's atmosphere, and from that data the physicists may reasonably speculate on the possibility that the planet could harbor life.

These are only two examples, and they are from two very distinct disciplines—the Humanities v. the "Hard" Sciences. Seemingly, the methods, modes of inquiry, types of evidence, and nature of their conclusions are very different.

Similar examples are easy to generate. Try to think what these professionals must consider when given the following task:

- An international financier deciding whether or not to invest in a new company;
- A buyer for a retail clothing chain asked to increase sales of an old brand of jeans;
- A group of engineers hoping to build a more efficient electric car battery;
- A physical therapist working with a stroke victim to relearn how to walk.

The superficial differences in these scenarios are difficult to look past, but you may already notice similarities among these examples. Whatever the task, each of these professionals begins by conducting a careful analysis of the available information. This information will be evaluated according to *discourse community-specific criteria.* As stated in the Introduction, a discourse community is a group of people who share certain beliefs, methodologies, or interests, and who communicate using a specialized lexicon. Scholars of poetry and physicists constitute two discourse communities, as each has its own standards for evidence and argumentation, and each employs its own set of terms. Of course, there are innumerable non-academic discourse communities, like members of the military or skateboarders or yoga instructors. However, in all cases, employing discourse community-specific criteria allows one to address fellow members of the community according to agreed-upon standards, and to draw logical conclusions or argue in favor of a certain course of action in a convincing fashion.

Indeed, scholarly analysis is absolutely integral to our capacity to thoroughly understand a topic and to build an informed and persuasive argument. The remainder of this chapter will attempt to further define the basics of academic analysis and demonstrate how objective analysis is in turn the basis of all academic work, even among pursuits as diverse as the study of poetry or the search for extraterrestrial life.

Defining "Analysis"

Of course, scholarly analysis is not *totally* foreign to First-Year writers, and the types of analysis we conduct in the academy are not all *that* different from the analyses we complete every day outside of the classroom. In fact, complex analysis is frequently at play during even the most mundane moments in our lives.

Consider, for example, the decision to go see one movie over another. Whether you know it or not, the argument about which film to see that you and your friends have while standing in line for tickets is, in fact, predicated on a considered analysis. Think of the factors that go into deciding amongst yourselves what movie you will all pay to see that night: commercials on TV, the posters in the lobby of the movie theater, your personal preference for action movies over serious drama, the reviews your friend read online earlier that day, the time available until your dinner reservations later that night, etc.

Each bit of information is a factor in your group's decision, but each on its own is not enough to decide the point. Each bit of information must be weighed against the others, and in line at the movie theater we will do just that, often in the blink of an eye. What we don't realize is how much work goes into this split-second analysis, and how complicated this process is—perhaps because it

"Basketball Mascot" by Graham Robson

doesn't really matter all that much whether you go see *The Avengers* or *The Artist*. This analysis must take place so that you can then go on to argue why you all should see movie *X* rather than movie *Y*.

This type of trivial analysis is similar to academic analysis in that both are founded on *criteria,* which are the standards by which a thing is being judged, or the underlying assumptions that allow a writer to make an analytical claim.

Further, both the relatively inconsequential analysis described above and the scholarly analyses you will complete in the classroom are shaped by the surrounding *rhetorical situation,* which includes several elements: the exigency of the rhetorical act (what makes it desired or necessary), the purpose of the act, the audience for the act, the kind of text being created, the unique contribution of a particular author, and the constraints of the act (anything that limits or shapes the rhetorical act).

In both settings, your analytical approach will be determined by the nature of admissible criteria and the rhetorical situation, and both will undoubtedly shape the *claim* that you make.

At the movie theater, success will be a matter of getting your way and convincing your friends to see the movie that you want to see. In the academy the "success" of a claim is measured differently, and constructed instead around logical reasoning. Academic writing may, depending on the situation, also employ other types of appeals that are more personal and/or shared between you and your audience, but these are more likely to occur in certain argumentative models rather than in the analytical essay. Of course, each of these terms needs to be unpacked, so let's start by further detailing the nature of analytical criteria.

The most significant difference between choosing one movie over another and writing an analytical essay is that *all academic disciplines value judgments based on objective criteria over judgments based on subjective criteria.* Your decision regarding the movie is primarily subjective: that is, based on your personal preferences, impressions, or feelings that stem from your unique history and experiences. Think about the language you or your friends might use in arguing for one movie or another: "I think superhero movies are dumb." "I love that French actor, whatshisname." "Reading subtitles is boring." Each of these statements employs subjective criteria, which are being signaled in numerous ways, including the use of the first-person "I-voice" or emotionally charged verbs or modifiers like "dumb," "love," or "bored."

The precise reason *subjective criteria* are inadequate foundations for academic analysis or argumentation is that they vary from person to person. To contrast, *objective criteria* remain the same regardless of the person employing them. To return to one of our earlier examples, the reason physicists can reasonably speculate on the atmosphere of a planet thousands of light-years away is because chemical elements affect the wavelength of light the same way here on earth as they do on the other side of the galaxy; it doesn't matter if the telescope is in California or Peru, or if the scientist taking the measurements is a 24-year-old graduate student from Boston or a 76-year-old Nobel Prize winner from Mumbai.

Look again at these example scenarios of professional analysis from earlier in the chapter:

- An international financier deciding whether or not to invest in a new company;
- A buyer for a retail clothing chain asked to increase sales of an old brand of jeans;
- A group of engineers hoping to build a more efficient electric car battery;
- A physical therapist working with a stroke victim to relearn how to walk

Try to list the criteria that each individual or group might have in mind as they work. Are these subjective or objective criteria?

A set of objective criteria is the most important element of a successful analysis; without these criteria, the claim you go on to make may be dismissed as biased, under-considered, or (perhaps worst of all) pointless. Therefore, thinking about what criteria you should employ when approaching a given topic is a reliable way to begin an academic analysis. You might also begin your analysis by examining some other aspect of the *Rhetorical Situation*, which encompasses the entire constellation of circumstances that surrounds a writing project. Your analysis will be directly shaped by the rhetorical situation, as it implicates not only the thing being studied, but also the one doing the studying (that is, you—the writer), the analytical methods that your field of study privileges, and the audience that will ultimately read your writing. Furthermore, the rhetorical situation can be informed by things as narrow as the constraints of particular research/writing projects and as broad as the historical context of the object or phenomenon being analyzed.

One handy way of thinking about the rhetorical situation posits that each piece of writing comprises its own triangle of relationships, with each corner roughly mapping onto the roles of writer, reader, and text. In practice, this formulation is always an over-simplification, as the role of "writer" is not exactly the same as the flesh-and-blood person who actually composes a text, and the role of "reader" can include abstract elements, like emotions or cultural values, that the text communicates. Similarly, "text" includes more than the words visible on a page or screen. It includes the line of thinking that leads the writer to make the claims he or she does and that leads the reader to react to these claims in his or her own way.

Just as academic analysis is founded primarily on objective criteria, most rhetorical situations in the academy will privilege a certain type of thinking—*Logical Reasoning*. Like objective criteria, the value of logical reasoning is not determined by the individual doing the reasoning; everyone who reasons logically from the same set of data should (at least in theory) arrive at the same logically derived conclusion. As stated earlier, the types of analytical claims that we can make vary greatly depending on the field of study within which we are working. In all fields of study, these claims should be built on a foundation of logical reasoning.

The two major forms of logical reasoning have been defined for millennia as *Deductive* and *Inductive*. When we employ deductive reasoning, we examine a set of premises or conditions, and on the basis of these general terms we draw a specific conclusion. Perhaps the most famous example of deductive reasoning is this syllogism:

> Premise #1: Socrates is human.
>
> Premise #2: All humans are mortal.
>
> Conclusion: Socrates is mortal.

Premise #1 is built on a simple observation: Socrates (that really ugly guy with the beard) is a man. Premise #2 is also built on a simple, cheery observation: all men and women eventually die. The Conclusion is arrived at by logical consideration of the known Premises: since Socrates is human, eventually he will die. We knew that already, didn't we?

Inductive reasoning operates along similar lines, but in reverse. Where deductive reasoning draws a specific conclusion from general premises, inductive reasoning takes a multitude of specific examples to draw a general conclusion. For instance, if you did reasonably well in your ENGL 1101 course and earned a "B-," but were committed to earning an "A" in your ENGL 1102 course, you might want to analyze the practices of students you know to have earned "A's." Say you pick three and interview them to find out about the following: their study habits, their tendencies to seek additional help or tutoring, and their majors. Let's say that you discover that Student A studies three hours a night, goes to the Writing Center twice a week, and majors in Nursing; Student B never studies, goes to the Writing Center every time he has a long writing assignment, and majors in Early Childhood Education; and Student C studies only on weekends, visits the Writing

Center once a week, and majors in Spanish. Inductive reasoning may not tell you how much you should be studying in order to improve your grade or what major you should pick if you want to get an "A" in ENGL 1102, but you can logically reason that visiting the Writing Center will beneficially impact your grade. (As an aside, in addition to being a concise example of a conclusion arrived at via inductive reasoning, the preceding claim about visiting the Writing Center has the great virtue of being true.)

"Freedumbs300" by Fenton Thompson

Analyzing an Analysis: The Sample Student Essay

By now, we have a fairly comprehensive outline of academic analysis, so let's take a close look at one successful model. Using selections from Jocelyn Lopez's essay "My Frappuccino: A Rhetorical Analysis of a Caffeinated Commercial" as a guide, we can articulate the things that a successful analysis should do, and those things it should be careful to avoid, in order to retain its persuasive power.

Criteria

Because this is an ad analysis, the writer's analytical criteria are, to a certain extent, already established and may not need to be addressed specifically in the body of her essay. Of course, all advertisers have the goal of drawing consumers' attention to the product in order to increase sales. Jocelyn's goal, then, is to see if the composition of the commercial generates the intended effect; in other words, does this ad make the viewer more likely to buy a Starbucks Frappuccino®? There are other ways of analyzing texts like advertisements that may require further an elucidation of criteria. For instance, a reading that is specifically attentive to gender, race, or other cultural dynamics would need to spell out its criteria explicitly at the outset.

Context and Summary

Here is the first paragraph of Jocelyn's essay:

> "In the summer of 2011, television viewers around the nation tuned in to witness America's most popular coffee shop franchise, Starbucks, release its 'however-you-want-it' Frappuccino blended beverage commercial. The purpose of the TV commercial is to sell Starbucks' unique product: a blended iced beverage that one can customize with various kinds of milk, toppings, and flavors. The ad was aired in May of 2011, a time when the weather is warm in many parts of the United States, therefore making an iced beverage a refreshing choice for potential customers....Starbucks' 2011 Summer commercial successfully utilizes its layout, highlighted elements and symbolism to advertise the 'however-you-want-it' Frappuccino blended beverage and attract customers to the company and to its products."

Note that Jocelyn begins the analysis by contextualizing the ad under scrutiny; we read up front who produced the spot, what it advertised, and when it aired. Furthermore, she articulates an analytical thesis statement that proposes who the intended audience is, what effect the advertisers hoped to achieve, and how the ad attempts to generate this effect. Note, too, that these things are only broadly sketched at first. Jocelyn spends the remainder of the essay (six full pages) detailing each of these assertions. Especially in the draft stage, writers often act on a tendency to try and pack their entire argument into the first page or paragraph; this is, of course, impossible (otherwise we wouldn't need the rest of the essay!). So, only outline the parameters of your analysis at first, and allow it to expand as needed in the body paragraphs.

Jocelyn's essay will only succeed if the reader has a clear picture of the advertisement being analyzed, so she goes on to provide over the next few pages concrete detail regarding the composition of the advertisement:

> *"Apart from the commercial's layout, Starbucks has incorporated many visual elements used to emphasize the advertised beverage. These elements are clearly displayed from the beginning of the commercial. When the commercial begins, a large plastic Starbucks cup is suddenly set heavily onto the table, making a loud crashing sound and grabbing the viewer's attention. Starbucks' newest green logo on the cup stands out against the white background, introducing the advertised brand. Other elements highlighted throughout the commercial are the ingredients used to make the beverage: coffee beans, coconuts, caramel, strawberries, chocolate, ice, milk, etc. These ingredients are largely emphasized and are shown whirring in a blender since the beverage is in fact a 'blended' drink. The coffee beans are shown swirling in a clockwise direction, as though they are being blended. The clockwise direction could symbolize the progression the Starbuck's company has made over the years as well as the company's success with their new drinks. Strawberries are also shown being squeezed in an actor's hand over a sea of strawberries, showing how the strawberries are made into pieces when blending. Also, a block of ice is smashed with a hammer, showing the crushed ice used for iced beverages. These elements are purposely enhanced to make the ingredients stand out in a unique way compared to other commercials that simply show the finished product. Ultimately, these shots of the individual ingredients make the product seem even more appetizing for potential customers."*

Throughout this analysis, Jocelyn provides a clear account of what is actually on screen during this commercial. In each case, the descriptive paragraph concludes with her describing how the images and sounds generate a certain effect in the viewer. Here is another effective paragraph:

> *"Furthermore, the use of symbolism in the Starbucks commercial reveals embedded meanings behind some of the images shown. For one, a small trophy is held up in the air towards the middle of the commercial, symbolizing*

the success of the Starbucks brand and its products and attracting those who would like good-quality beverages served to them. There are also objects seen in the commercial, such as a toy dog and a piñata that symbolize youth and innocence. These objects tie in with the feeling one might get when one tries this beverage, the feeling of being young again and having the kid in you shine through, despite drinking a grown up beverage such as coffee. Other parts of the commercial prove this childlike theme, such as when the pie gets thrown at the young man s face, when the female actor jumps up in joy on what might be a trampoline, and when the young man squirts a can of whipped cream into his mouth. Another form of symbolism can be seen in the actors themselves. The actors are all young men and women, ranging from teenagers to those in their early 20s, which clearly demonstrates the intended audience for this commercial...."

Reading through this paragraph, we can see how Jocelyn looks at both the latent and manifest, or denotative as well as connotative, content of the commercial to determine its meaning.

Claim

Ultimately, these assertions culminate in an analytical claim:

"Overall, Starbucks successfully advertised its Frappuccino blended beverage during the summer of 2011. Its layout—a fast-paced, thirty-second commercial packed with much detail—keeps its audience's attention and interest. The use of visual and aural components also highlights particular images used. Furthermore, words and color equally play important roles in the commercial, emphasizing the ingredients and other images used in making the beverage. Finally, symbolism brings out the deeper meaning in the images used in order to attract the viewers to Starbucks and its products. When the components of the commercial are looked upon as a whole, Starbucks' thirty-second Frappuccino commercial not only makes viewers aware of the brand and the beverage, but also creates an advertisement that is both convincing and enjoyable to watch."

Jocelyn's conclusion answers the questions that motivate most advertising analyses: namely, what feeling or response is it that the advertisers hoped to achieve, and, did they achieve it? In her opinion, they did so successfully, and her claim is supported by the many details about the commercial she has so meticulously provided.

Support

This writer was asked to complete an individual, close-reading of the ad that did not require support from secondary sources or critiques by other writers. However, most substantive analyses, particularly those you complete during course work for your major, will ask that you also integrate the analyses of other scholars. Sections to follow in this Guide will help you to evaluate and employ this academic support.

To inventory, these are the things that an academic analysis must do to be considered successful:

1. Adequately *summarize* the thing being analyzed. The level of detail will vary depending on whether or not you know that the readers of your essay are familiar with the thing being analyzed, the constraints of the assignment, or the standards for your field of study. Remember: the thing must be introduced to your reader before you can go on to analyze it.
2. Provide clearly stated and objective *criteria* for the analysis.
3. Make a *claim* based on logical reasoning from the evidence presented.
4. *Support* this claim with pertinent details or backing from reputable sources (research).

The preceding list can be very helpful during the draft stage of your composition process, or when revising in order to determine if your analytical essay is doing the work that you (and your instructor) want it to do. Ideally, set your draft aside for a day or two and come back to it with "fresh" eyes. Read through carefully, but don't make any changes at all—not even to correct typos or spelling errors; treat it as if it belongs to someone else. Then, compose responses to the checklist above in a separate document and review. Is your analysis doing everything that a successful analysis should?

ANALYSIS ASSIGNMENTS IN FIRST-YEAR COMPOSITION

Many assignments that you encounter in the First-Year composition classroom are going to ask you to conduct a *rhetorical analysis* of a text, like the sample student essay examined in the previous section. While the specifics of the assignment will vary, the essay that you compose will almost certainly ask you to provide the following:

1. Introduction: a brief summary of the text and detail about the context it appears in, as well as a thesis describing its rhetorical effect.

2. Body: a series of paragraphs that discuss the specific rhetorical features that create this effect, using textual evidence/direct quotes to support your claims.

3. Conclusion: statements that make clear why your account is important for readers to understand.

Depending on your instructor or the focus of your particular composition course, the "text" you examine could be any number of things:

- A piece of imaginative writing (poem or short story);
- A non-fiction article or news broadcast;
- A political speech;
- A movie or documentary;
- A public or private place;
- An event where people come together for a common purpose;
- An advertisement;
- A static image, like a photograph or painting;
- persuasive essays that employ specific argumentative models, like the Journalistic, Classical, Toulmin, or Rogerian models;
- A process, or the steps one takes to complete a certain task or make a certain impression in others;
- A phenomenon and its causes;
- A group of people (ethnography).

Whatever type of text you are analyzing, the following checklist can help you determine what elements of it you should focus on in order to understand how the text creates a particular rhetorical effect:

- Layout, or the elements placed in the foreground, background, top, bottom, left, right, or center of an image/film/screen/document;
- Those elements highlighted by the author for particular notice;
- Those elements that are deemphasized or noticeably omitted by the author;
- Intensified, exaggerated, or repeated elements;
- The use of color;
- Music (including its tone, recognizability, or other rhetorical effects);
- Particular words, specifically (of course) their meaning or (in a film or picture) their relationship to the image(s);
- Symbolism;
- Allusions (explicit or implicit references to other texts);
- Genre-specific formal qualities (like meter and rhyme for poems, or guitar tone for pop music, etc.);

In some cases, particularly for longer or major assignments, your instructor will also ask that your rhetorical analysis takes into account:

- The medium of the text;
- The author of the text;
- The time period in which the text was created;
- The exigence, or what possibly caused the author to create the text;
- The purpose (entertain, inform, educate, sell) of the text.

As you can see, there is a lot to consider when conducting a rhetorical analysis, and it can often be difficult to decide where to start. However, the task is simpler than it seems. Simply stated, academic analyses ask you to determine the overall meaning of a text by breaking it into its constituent parts.

Here are the two major questions to ask yourself: *What effect is it that the author(s) hope to achieve?* And, *what strategies are used to try to achieve that effect?* Frequently, the best analytical theses are generated by a third question: *Did the author(s) achieve the intended effect, or was some other effect generated?*

Your instructor will provide additional materials to guide your analysis or help you to read specific types of texts. The three questions above and your responses to them will form the backbone of any successful analysis you compose.

Argument

WHAT IS ARGUMENT?

Argument does not have to mean raised voices and angry facial expressions. The art of argument helps us to appeal to others in order to get what we want. In addition to the everyday argument, *academic argument* has a longstanding tradition of reasoned debate among thinkers in and across fields of study. When you make an academic argument, you make a *claim* with *reasons* for which you provide an array of *evidence*, and you lead the *audience* from point to point in a *logical* fashion. You are asking your audience to consider your argument, and, as a result, to think differently, to take action, or to contribute ideas to a conversation. In your First-Year writing classes, you will write arguments using your own ideas and synthesizing or integrating your ideas with material from other sources; also, you will learn how to ethically document source material. These First-Year writing assignments enable you to hone your research and argumentative skills in order to use them in other classes, as well as in life outside the university.

WHAT IS RHETORIC?

In your ENGL 1101, 1102, and 1103 courses, your instructor will often use the word "rhetoric." Like "argument," *rhetoric* often has a negative connotation. We frequently hear this word used in political campaigns as a synonym for empty or deceptive uses of language. In this usage of the word, rhetoric sounds like a synonym for *propaganda*. However, when used effectively and ethically, rhetoric provides a treasure trove of strategies and techniques for you to use in your writing and speaking. The following definitions of rhetoric come from thinkers and practitioners of this ancient art.

Plato defined rhetoric as "the art of winning the soul by discourse." Aristotle, another famous ancient Greek philosopher, saw rhetoric as the "faculty of discovering in any particular case all of the available means of persuasion." The great Roman orator Cicero perceived in rhetoric "speech designed to persuade," and Quintilian, who taught rhetoric to young men in Rome, called rhetoric "the art of speaking well."

Composition scholar Andrea Lunsford sees rhetoric as "the art, practice, and study of human communication," and philosopher and rhetorician Kenneth Burke defined this term as "the use of language as a symbolic means of inducing cooperation in beings that by nature respond to symbols." As a field of study, rhetoric is profoundly and powerfully useful; it is the art of persuading an audience.

FOR DISCUSSION:

In small groups or as a whole class, discuss the following topics:

1. What are some common key concepts among all (or most) of the definitions of rhetoric listed above?

2. Compose your own definition of rhetoric, choosing essential qualities from the definitions given above or from your own knowledge of the term. For more on rhetoric, see *Sylvia Rhetoricae* ("The Forest of Rhetoric") at rhetoric.byu.edu.

3. Think of examples of rhetoric from everyday life. Where have you seen or heard rhetoric used effectively? Who are some effective rhetors?

4. Visit Americanrhetoric.com for a database of audio and video files of famous pieces of rhetoric from movies and political speeches, as well as definitions and examples of common rhetorical strategies. How many of the "Top 100 Speeches" have you heard before? What are your favorites? Visit the movie clips for scenes of rhetoric being used in film.

WHY STUDY RHETORIC?

Anytime you need to make an argument—for a writing class, another academic class, or in your personal or professional life—knowing the concepts and strategies of rhetoric will help you make a more convincing case. From previous English classes, you already know the basic parts of an argument—the introduction (including thesis), the supporting evidence, the refuting of counterarguments, and the conclusion. This model of argument originated in ancient Greece, where citizens in Athenian democracy needed to know how to speak in public forums to hold on to or gain property, citizenship, or other needs. Rhetoric formed an integral part of education for elite youth in Greek, and later Roman, societies.[1]

As mentioned above, the term "rhetoric" (as a 2,400 year old field of study) has a vastly different meaning than what is typically used in popular culture or political debates. At Georgia State, you will use rhetoric to make more effective arguments in English and other classes—and throughout your lifetime. You will learn how to address specific audiences, create particular genres of texts, and fulfill purposes through practicing the craft of rhetoric.

These are valid reasons for studying rhetoric. Remember Aristotle's definition of rhetoric? He said rhetoric means "the faculty of discovering, in a given instance, the available means of persuasion." Each part of this definition contributes to the idea of rhetoric's *power*. To the Greeks and Romans, the person who could use rhetoric effectively wielded great power because he could persuade his audience to action. The orator could shape the future by winning court cases, influencing legislation, and sending a nation to war or negotiating for peace. The same is true today.

"But," you say, "I don't need to do any of those things. I am not going into law or politics." Skill with rhetoric wields power in all spheres of influence. Educated people today use the craft of rhetoric not only to speak in public but also to craft written texts such as books, articles, letters, proposals, or reports; they also create visual forms of communication, such as advertisements, photographs, drawings, films, and websites. In our highly visual society, images and texts convey especially powerful messages that persuade audiences (readers and viewers) to act by donating, buying, sharing, working, or voting.

The principles of rhetoric will help you think critically. By knowing these principles, you can analyze intelligently and make conscious choices, not irrational ones based on persuasive techniques you do not understand. On a typical day, you might encounter the following forms of rhetoric:

1. An ad wrapping around a MARTA bus, advertising a new soft drink or a brand of jeans;

2. A recycling bin on the GSU campus located right next to the trashcan;

3. A political ad on TV that rips apart the spending record of the candidate's opponent and suggests that he is having an extramarital affair;

---

[1] The Classical Model of Argument will be covered in a later section of this chapter.

4. A tweet about a rally on human rights, including a link to a website about the organization;

5. A t-shirt emblazoned with the message, "At least the war on the middle class is going well."

You are constantly bombarded with various forms of rhetoric, some of them so subtle that you do not realize someone is trying to persuade you. Being fully literate requires that you think critically about the images and texts designed to grab your attention and get you to act.[2]

"Okay," you say. "I get that. But why do I need to learn the art of argument? I will only use it in English class." Not so fast. Consider the variety of arguments that you might need to make now, in your everyday life inside and outside GSU.

1. The Gwinnett County Sheriff's Department gives me a speeding ticket, but I was not speeding. I need to convince the judge to throw out the ticket;

2. My statistics professor wants us to research data and make an infographic that argues a case about what caused the recession of 2008;

3. I am late on the rent again. My landlord swore that the next time I was late he would throw me out. I have to convince him that I deserve another chance;

4. Someone on facebook is posting negative things about homosexuals, saying that they are unnatural and sinful. I must dispel that hatred before it becomes contagious;

5. It looks as though Congress is about to raise the interest rate on student loans. I've got to convince my legislators that they cannot let this happen to current and future students.

Argument, in some way, constitutes much of our everyday conversation and activity. Every day, we find the need to devise arguments for some audience to achieve some purpose.

---

[2]In the chapters on analyzing images and new media literacy in this *Guide to First-Year Writing,* you will find out more about ways to analyze and create visual and digital texts.

ACTIVITY: RHETORIC JOURNAL

Is rhetoric really all around you? Test the theory and find out. For one day, write down all the arguments you see or hear. List the author, the text, the intended audience, the purpose, and the effect on you. For example, "My dog goes to the door. His body language says I need to take him out; that's his 'argument.' I do take him out as soon as I get dressed."

ACTIVITY: MY ARGUMENT PORTFOLIO

If you were interviewing for an entry-level job after graduation, how would you talk about your writing and public speaking experiences? Write an informal, narrative résumé listing and describing several arguments you have made orally, visually, or in writing. Conclude each item by recounting the results:

Invited Speaker: My high school English teacher asked me to visit her class to talk about my experiences in English classes at Georgia State. I presented a talk about the importance of staying on top of assignments, attending classes, working well with peers, communicating with the instructor, reading assigned texts, revising my writing, and practicing academic honesty. The students asked me a number of questions about what kind of papers I wrote and about how hard the classes were, among other topics. I could tell they were surprised by how much writing we do in college and how much the professors expect of us in terms of workload, work ethic, grammar knowledge, and writing skill. Perhaps they will be better prepared for college, having heard these things from me as a college student instead of from Mrs. Hathaway, my former teacher.

"Greenway" by Judith Kim

THE RHETORICAL SITUATION

When you read or write an argument, keep the *rhetorical situation* in mind. The Rhetorical Triangle models this concept, consisting of three elements: author, audience, and text. The triangle in Figure 1 illustrates the relationship among the three concepts; notice also that a circle labeled "Context" encloses the triangle. Writers and speakers create rhetorical texts in particular contexts: time, place, circumstances. These elements affect each of the three aspects of the triangle.

The deeper you consider each side of the triangle (author, audience and text), the more convincing your argument will become. To charge your persuasive power, ask the following questions when you analyze or write arguments:

FIGURE 1

Writer or Speaker (Author):

- Who is the author? What gives him or her credibility with the audience?
- What impression does the author want to make upon the audience?
- What does the author do to establish credibility (ethos)?
- In what ways does the author create common ground or consensus with the audience?

Reader or Viewer (Audience):

- Who is the intended or target audience?
- What kind of text (genre) might appeal to audience members? What does the audience expect regarding the form and content of the text? Does the author use the most effective genre for the intended audience?
- What background knowledge does the audience already have? What bias or prejudice might influence their reception of the message?
- How might an ethical appeal (ethos) influence the intended audience? An emotional appeal (pathos)? A rational appeal (logos)?[3]
- What does the audience expect from the author?

Text (Purpose and Subject):

- What kind of text has the author created? Oral? Written? Visual? Which specific genre (i.e., letter, speech, blog, ad, etc.) constitutes this text?

---

[3]These three concepts—ethos, logos, and pathos—will be dealt with in more detail In a later portion of this chapter.

- What is the purpose of the text? How does the author convey his or her purpose?
- If the purpose is to persuade, what is the audience being persuaded to think or do?
- What is the thesis of the text?
- How is the evidence organized? Is the organization logical?
- How is the "so what?" question addressed? Why should I pay attention to this text?
- What effect does this text have on me?

These three concepts are powerful tools for analysis, as well as for building a convincing argument. You will use them to gain deeper understanding of other authors' works. In addition, these concepts become essential tools for analyzing and strengthening your own argumentative texts.

ACTIVITY:
APPLYING THE RHETORICAL TRIANGLE

Select two of the assigned readings in your composition class. Identify the author, the audience, and the purpose. Then analyze how each element affects the content and the effect of the reading upon the audience.

Context and Kairos

As pointed out above, all of the elements in the Rhetorical Triangle exist in a particular time, place, and set of circumstances, or *context*. This context shapes the author, audience, and text by providing limits upon what can be said or done. Social conventions, time constraints, page limits, audience attention spans, the quality of the sound system in the auditorium—all of these provide *constraints* or limits upon the rhetorical situation. A skilled *rhetor*, or practitioner of rhetoric, knows how to maximize his or her effect using these circumstances as tools.

The Greeks had a word for skillfully taking advantage of an opportunity. They called this agility *kairos*. No exact word exists in English for this concept, but loosely translated, kairos means the right or opportune moment to do something. When you hear someone say, "I saw my opening, and I took it," or "I really made that message stick," that person is referring to kairos. Kairos both restrains and enables what a rhetor can do or say in a rhetorical situation. Effective rhetors use every opportunity to make their message stick by using kairos.

USING KAIROS TO MAKE YOUR ARGUMENT

Take advantage of the kairotic moment when you make your own arguments. Here's how.

- *Timeliness.* What is the latest information on your chosen issue, and how can you emphasize it in your argument? Make sure your research is current/up-to-date. Use case studies from recent news stories.

- *Know your audience.* What are the characteristics of your audience? Make allusions they will understand and use examples of interest to them. Use humor if appropriate. Be conscious of offending people's sensibilities by being crass or by being insensitive to identities such as race, religion, class, gender, and sexual orientation. Act with decorum, which also increases your ethos with the audience.

- *Aim for the middle.* Just like political candidates aim for swing voters, aim your message toward those who might not yet agree with you but are not hostile to your message. You have the greatest chance of success hitting the "target" when you pitch to the middle.

- *Find a place to stand.* Location makes its own argument. President Obama made his famous "A More Perfect Union" speech (also known as the "race" speech) at Constitution Hall in Philadelphia. This location provided a symbolic backdrop for his speech on the principles of equality, unity, and tolerance found in the U.S. Constitution. Find a way to symbolically "stand" in a particular location by making reference to a historical moment or figure. Dr. Martin Luther King, Jr. used the words of President Lincoln as he stood in Lincoln's shadow at the Memorial in Washington, D.C., where he delivered his "I Have a Dream" speech. Careful use of words, phrases, and quotations will evoke images in the reader's mind, even if you cannot physically stand in the desired symbolic place. If you are constructing a multimedia argument, videotape at or use photographs or illustrations of an evocative locale.

"Excellence, Energy, and Entertainment" by Judith Kim

THE ARISTOTELIAN APPEALS:
ETHOS, LOGOS AND PATHOS

Aristotle, in his treatise *On Rhetoric*, discusses three appeals, or "proofs," to use in making arguments. The three appeals are *ethos*, or ethical appeals, which argue from the credibility of the author: *logos*, or logical appeals, which argue from logic or reason, and *pathos*, or emotional appeals, which target the audience's imagination or emotions. Sometimes, this triumvirate is known as the "Aristotelian Triangle." Some theorists even use these three to discuss the Rhetorical Triangle (or Rhetorical Situation), so we will make that connection below as well. "Figure 2" below illustrates the Aristotelian Triangle.

Ethos

Ethos connects to the *author* point of the Rhetorical Triangle. The *ethos* appeal consists of an argument through the author's *character*. In order to make an effective argument, the author must make the audience believe, respect and trust him or her. The author's character thus forms part of the persuasive appeal. The author's personality, reputation, and ability to appear trustworthy are key elements in this appeal.[4] According to Aristotle, ethos consists of four elements: 1) the vir-

[4]Jay Heinrichs's *Thank You for Arguing* devotes several chapters to this notion, and his readable, engaging style definitely pulls in the reader. He uses many references to familiar things such as popular culture and everyday family situations to teach about rhetorical strategies.

tue or moral character of the author; 2) the good-will created by the author toward the audience; 3) practical wisdom, or common sense displayed by the author; and 4) disinterestedness, that is the extent to which the author conveys that he or she does not have an ulterior motive in making the argument.

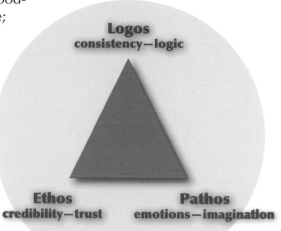

FIGURE 2

In order to enhance your ethos, you must act with *decorum*. That means that you must act as the audience expects you to act; you must demonstrate yourself as authentic, informed, honest, mature, formal, compassionate, and engaging. Doing extensive, ethical research certainly contributes to your ethos. Paying attention to details such as grammar, mechanics, and manuscript form in your writing enhances your ethos. So does using a tone that conveys passion without being overbearing or strident. Sometimes, when we feel strongly about something, we use emotionally charged language and a judgmental tone that could offend some audience members. Instead of saying, "Climate-change deniers are just plain ignorant. Why can't they see the facts?," a better approach might be something like this statement: "Before being so quick to dismiss the scientific evidence of climate change, the deniers should ask themselves why all of the world's top scientists and international policymakers are convinced of humankind's destructive effects on the environment." In what ways does the second sentence convey more ethos to the audience?

Appeals based on ethos are not confined to any one statement or element of an argument. If you make an ethical argument, each element contributes to the overall effect—that you come across as knowledgeable and forthright. Ethos, then, infuses every element of the powerful argument.

Pathos

Pathos connects to the *audience* point of the Rhetorical Triangle because the audience must engage with the author and the text largely through imagination and emotion. The word *pathos* has cousins in the words "sympathy," "empathy," "pathetic," and "pathology." People act on their emotions. You might change their minds through reason, but you get them to act based on your ability to tap into their compassion, anger, empathy, idealism, and joy. When you tell a story that evokes memories and tears, when you paint a picture with words that evokes visions of a better world, you are using the pathos appeal. In order to accomplish the goal of persuasion, you must know what your audience will respond to, what will captivate them and spur them into action. What does your audience desire? Fear? Doubt? Believe? Hope?

Using narratives, metaphors, humor, images, and carefully chosen words and phrases enables you to make effective appeals based on pathos. For example, using words associated with deep-seated feelings and affiliations will cause the audience to believe you and become inspired by your words. Think of words like "liberty," "equality," "justice," "family," "patriotism," "reform," and "prosperity." These words evoke images dear to many hearts in the United States. Consider the difference between these two phrases: "global warming" and "climate change." Which one do you think environmentalists use? Which one do people use if they are arguing against environmental science that says the Earth is getting warmer? How does framing an issue in a certain way (that is, choosing an evocative name or theme) change how people feel about it?

In order to use pathos appeals optimally, you must sympathize or empathize with your audience. Mirror your audience's emotions. When you encounter a friend who is sad, do you look sad, too, or do you say, "Cheer up!" Your friend would rather you commiserate with him or her, correct? Talking down to people does not work. Commiserating with them is much more effective. This reaction of sympathy (or empathy, if you actually *do* feel their pain) serves as a foundation from which you move the audience toward feeling the way you want them to feel. You serve as an emotional barometer for them, modeling the reaction you want. You start with sympathy/empathy and move toward identification and action.

Logos

Logos concerns most of what we would call the proof or evidence in an argument. In Greek, the word has gained a number of meanings, including "word," "plea," "opinion," "speech," or "reasoned discourse." Because most of the argument uses the logos appeal and because logos refers to the purposive argument itself, logos aligns with the *text* point on the Rhetorical Triangle. Aristotle argued that logos formed the most important consideration for an orator. Aristotle wrote, among many other things, on legal rhetoric, very common in ancient Greece; he discusses deductive reasoning strategies such as using expert opinion (testimony), as well as a set of memory joggers called "commonplaces," which you will read about in a later section of this chapter. Here is an example of a "syllogism," an argument an attorney might make:

> To qualify as a "citizen" of a state for purposes of diversity jurisdiction, a party must (1) currently reside in that state and (2) intend to remain there indefinitely. (*Major premise; states a rule of law.*) Here, the plaintiff does not currently reside in North Carolina. (*Minor premise; makes a statement of fact.*) Therefore, the plaintiff cannot be a "citizen" of North Carolina for jurisdictional purposes. (*Conclusion; correctly applies the law to the facts.*)[5]

In order to make a proper logos appeal, you do not have to devise sophisticated syllogisms like the one above. You just need to provide facts, statistics, examples, and statements from experts, documented carefully; furthermore, you must put pieces of evidence together in such a way that your conclusion arises inevitably from your evidence.

To use an appeal based on logos for an audience means that the text contains a clear claim or thesis that is substantiated with reasons and evidence, and that all of the material is presented in an internally consistent, well-organized manner. Typically, a rhetor will proceed from the weakest point to the strongest, from the strongest to the weakest, or will compare different solutions to argue for the best, or will show cause and effect through a chronological examination of events. Since audiences best remember what they hear first and last, most rhetoric texts suggest placing the strongest support for your argument near the beginning and end of your piece. Together, the content and the organization (logical form) contribute to the logos of the argument. Each of the three appeals—ethos, pathos, and logos—works together to create a cumulative effect.

To sum up: Think deeply about both 1.) the rhetorical situation and 2.) the rhetorical appeals when you analyze and create arguments. Think of the role of each appeal in fulfilling the ultimate purpose of your argument: to compel your audience and to persuade them to think or act differently. Some arguments use more of one appeal than the others, depending on the audience, purpose, and context.

---

[5]You can read more about this example of a syllogism in "Logic and Legal Reasoning: A Guide for Law Students," online at http://www.unc.edu/~ramckinn/Documents/NealRameeGuide.pdf

ASSIGNMENT: WRITING ABOUT ETHOS, PATHOS, AND LOGOS

Choose a text you are reading this term in your English class (example, in ENGL 1101, use First-Year book *The Other Wes Moore*) and write an essay that identifies the ethos, pathos, and logos appeals of the text. You could organize your paper in this way:

First, explain how the author makes character, reason, and emotion appeals, and to what extent each one is employed.

Next, analyze how the author uses the three appeals together to produce the overall argument. What is the general effect?

Finally, evaluate how well the author has used each of the three appeals. Use the information on appeals and fallacies in this text to evaluate your chosen text. To what extent are you convinced of the author's claim(s) and evidence?

Conclude your essay by providing an overall assessment of the effectiveness of the appeals based on both intended audience and purpose of the text.

RHETORICAL FALLACIES

The Rhetorical Appeals of ethos, pathos, and logos, when used ethically and accurately, contribute to effective, forthright arguments. Using one of the appeals incorrectly or unethically, whether deliberately or accidentally, constitutes a *fallacy*. In rhetoric, a fallacy means a misleading or unsound argument. Because there are three types of appeals, there are also three types of fallacies. We will take a brief look at some of the most common ones.[6] Keep in mind that the rhetorical fallacies, like the appeals themselves, often overlap. For example, a fallacy might simultaneously use faulty logic and unreasonably advance the writer's character, so it might be both a logical fallacy and an ethical fallacy.

---

[6]For more examples of fallacies, visit the Lower Division Studies website at lds.gsu.edu.

Ethical Fallacies

Ethical fallacies unfairly or unreasonably advance the character or credibility of the author.

False Authority. The "False Authority" fallacy asks audiences to agree with the author's claims based on testimony by the author or by someone who does not have the authority to advance the claim, i.e., someone who does not have expert qualification in advising on the matter. *Example*: "Michael Jordan drinks Gatorade, so electrolytes must be good for you."

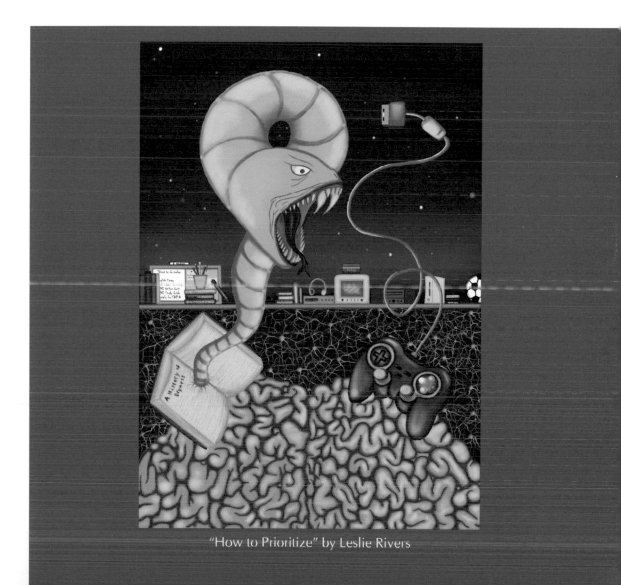

"How to Prioritize" by Leslie Rivers

Using Authority Instead of Evidence. In this fallacy, the writer insists that the audience believe him or her without any proof. First-person narratives, when produced as though they are irrefutable, fall prey to the essentialist claim that no one can argue with personal experience, no matter how prejudiced or limited the perspective. *Example*: "Believe me; no one could have won in an election against such an opponent."

Guilt by Association. The writer calls into question an opponent's character by pointing out that person's friends or associates. *Example*: "John must be a snob. He's on the debating team, which is full of snobs."[7]

Dogmatism. Dogmatism shuts down debate by insisting that the author's views are the only acceptable ones. *Example*: "Well, I believe nuclear energy is clean, and that's that."

Moral Equivalence. The "moral equivalence" fallacy equates a minor issue to a major moral crisis. *Example*: "'An anti-smoking moralist barks: 'Smoking cigarettes is nothing short of suicide—the smoker is willingly killing himself.' National anti-smoking campaigns often avoid the moral argument because the public understands that smoking is a personal choice that probably will not impact one's morality."[8]

Ad Hominem. In Latin, *ad hominem* means "to the man." In order to avoid dealing with the issue, writers will often attack an opponent personally. Many of these abuses involve the use of labels or loaded words that have negative connotations in the minds of the target audience. This fallacy often appears in mudslinging attack ads during political campaigns. *Example*: "The lifestyle of a political candidate is addressed in the press, rather than the candidate's ideas and platform issues."[9]

The "You, too!" Fallacy. This abuse of ethos sets up a new moral standard, generating an example of someone else's breaking of the original rule. In other words, "Somebody else did it, so it is okay for me to do it, too." The arguer's words either contradict an earlier position on the issue, or the arguer's words and actions do not match. *Example*: "Peter: 'Based on the arguments I have presented, it is evident that it is morally wrong to use animals for food or clothing.' Bill: 'But you are

---

[7]From http://online.santarosa.edu/presentation/page/?36896

[8]From http://ksuweb.kennesaw.edu/~shagin/logfal-analysis-moralequiv.htm

[9]From http://www.uta.edu/english/SH/Fallacies.htm

wearing a leather jacket and you have a roast beef sandwich in your hand! How can you say that using animals for food and clothing is wrong!'"[10]

The "Who Says So?" Fallacy. This abuse of ethics also provides a variety of the Ad Hominem attack. The ethical problem relates to *who* says something more than *what* the person says. In other words, the very source of the argument is given by the opponent as a reason not to believe it. *Example*: "Look who's talking. You say I shouldn't become an alcoholic because it will hurt me and my family, yet you yourself are an alcoholic, so your argument can't be worth listening to."[11]

Straw Man. This fallacy sets up a "straw man," or false opponent, which misrepresents the opponent's claims. In this way, the writer appears to defeat the second party/opponent, while in reality only defeating a weaker, inaccurate version of the opponent's argument. *Example*: "*Opponent*: 'Because of the killing and suffering of Indians that followed Columbus's discovery of America, the City of Atlanta should declare that Columbus Day will no longer be observed in our city.' *Speaker*: 'This is ridiculous, fellow members of the city council. It's not true that everybody who ever came to America from another country somehow oppressed the Indians. I say we should continue to observe Columbus Day, and vote down this resolution that will make the City of Atlanta the laughing stock of the nation.'"[12]

Emotional Fallacies

Emotional fallacies unfairly appeal to the audience's emotions, generally by using emotions to distort or ignore logic. These fallacies often appear in political propaganda and in advertising.

Sentimental Appeals. This fallacy uses emotions to draw the audience away from facts. *Example*: "Millions of cats and dogs undergo cruel, invasive surgery each year to reduce their population. This horrific treatment of spaying and neutering should not be practiced."

Red Herring. A "red herring" is designed to distract the audience from the real argument. The name comes from fox hunting, where servants would drag dried, smoked herring (a fish that has a red color when dried) across the trail of a fox to hide the scent from the hounds. *Example*: "*Student*: 'The opinions of the students

---

[10]From http://www.nizkor.org/features/fallacies/ad-hominem-tu-quoque.html

[11]From http://www.iep.utm.edu/fallacy/#TuQuoque

[12]From http://www.iep.utm.edu/fallacy/#StrawMan

are completely ignored in the process of determining both curricular changes and social programs. The students should have a much greater voice in campus governance, because we have a very great stake in this institution, and we think that we have a positive contribution to make.' *Professor*: 'The faculty are the ones who need a greater voice. Professors can be fired without explanation, and they have no control over who is promoted or given tenure. Their opinions about budgetary allotments are completely ignored. Why aren't you concerned about the injustice the faculty is experiencing?'[13]

Scare Tactics. The writer tries to convince the audience that his or her plan is not adopted, something dire will happen. Example: "*David*: 'My father owns the department store that gives your newspaper fifteen percent of all its advertising revenue, so I'm sure you won't want to publish any story of my arrest for spray painting the college.' *Newspaper editor*: 'Yes, David, I see your point. The story really isn't newsworthy.'"[14]

Slippery Slope. Similar to the Scare Tactic, the Slippery Slope argues that one thing will lead to another, with calamitous results. *Example*: "*Mom*: 'Those look like bags under your eyes. Are you getting enough sleep?' *Jeff*: 'I had a test and stayed up late studying.' *Mom*: 'You didn't take any drugs, did you?' *Jeff*: 'Just caffeine in my coffee, like I always do.' *Mom*: 'Jeff! You know what happens when people take drugs! Pretty soon the caffeine won't be strong enough. Then you will take something stronger, maybe someone's diet pill or an energy drink. Then, you will try something even stronger. Eventually, you will be doing methamphetamines. Then you will be a cocaine addict! So, don't drink that coffee.'"[15]

Bandwagon Appeals. This fallacy plays upon the audience's need for belonging and affiliation. "Jumping on the bandwagon" means going along with what other people are doing. *Example*: "Everyone who's anyone has tattoos. If you don't have a tattoo, how will you fit in with the cool people?"

Either/Or Choices (False Dilemma). This fallacy reduces a complex issue to only two possible choices, when in actuality there are likely several other choices. All complex issues have a number of varying perspectives. *Example*: In his book *Hostages to Fortune*, David Newnham describes a woman using an either/or (false dilemma) fallacy: "Gerda Reith is convinced that superstition can be a positive force. 'It gives you a sense of control by making you think you can work

---

[13]From http://www.txstate.edu/philosophy/resources/fallacy-definitions/Red-Herring.html

[14]From http://www.iep.utm.edu/fallacy/#ScareTactic

[15]From http://www.iep.utm.edu/fallacy/#SlipperySlope

out what's going to happen next,' she says. 'And it also makes you feel lucky. And to take a risk or to enter into a chancy situation, you really have to believe in your own luck. In that sense, it's a very useful way of thinking, because the alternative is fatalism, which is to say, "Oh, there's nothing I can do." At least superstition makes people do things.'"[16]

False Need. This fallacy plays upon desires by creating a need and then promising to fill it. *Example*: "You must have the latest in smart phones. You deserve the best; people will think of you as someone who is tech savvy."

Logical Fallacies

Logical fallacies depend upon faulty informal and formal logic.

Hasty Generalization. The author draws a conclusion from insufficient evidence. This fallacy uses faulty inductive reasoning, establishing a conclusion from too few examples. *Example*: "I will never shop at that store again. The customer service is terrible. Once, one of the clerks rolled her eyes at me when I asked a question."

Post Hoc Ergo Propter Hoc **(After This, Therefore Because of This).** Just because something happens after something else does not mean that the first event causes the second. The Romans called this slip-up *"Post hoc, ergo propter hoc,"* or "After this, therefore because of this." *Example*: "Two years ago, the school system cut its funding by 30 percent. Last year, teacher attrition doubled and student dropout rates increased by 20 percent. Clearly, funding cuts have a dire effect on retention of teachers and students."

Cum Hoc Ergo Propter Hoc **(With This, Therefore Because of This).** This fallacy assumes causation where none may in fact exist. Just because two things coincide does not mean one causes the other. *Example*: "He sometimes behaves violently when I am around him. I don't know what it is that I am doing to make him become so violent."[17]

Non Sequitur. Latin for "it does not follow," the *Non Sequitur* Fallacy makes a statement that does not logically relate to what came before it. The author may have left out an important link in the chain of logic. That is, the conclusion the ar-

---

[16]Quoted in http://www.fallacyfiles.org/eitheror.html

[17]From http://www.outofthefog.net/Treatment/CumHocErgoPropterHoc.html

guer makes can only be supported by weak or irrelevant reasons. *Example*: "Nuclear disarmament is a risk, but everything in life involves a risk. Every time you drive in a car you are taking a risk. If you're willing to drive in a car, you should be willing to have disarmament."[18]

Equivocation. This fallacy obscures the whole truth by revealing only a partial truth. In court, the oath "tell the truth, the whole truth, and nothing but the truth" is designed to subvert the possibility of witnesses committing this fallacy. The author committing this fallacy uses a word that proves ambiguous; that is, the word could be interpreted as meaning two different things. In other words, the word shifts meaning within the statement. *Example*: "Brad is a nobody, but since nobody is perfect, Brad must be perfect, too."[19]

Begging the Question. The writer restates his or her claim in a different way, appearing to make an argument. Have you ever looked up a word in the dictionary or online, and the definition has the word in it? If so, you have encountered a similar phenomenon, the circular definition or "tautology." *Example* of "begging the question": "'Women have rights,' said the Bullfighters Association president. 'But women shouldn't fight bulls because a bullfighter is and should be a man.'"[20] (That is to say, women shouldn't fight bulls because women shouldn't fight bulls.)

False Analogy. In this fallacy, the author draws an analogy between two things that are not comparable. We sometimes call this "comparing apples to oranges." *Example*: "Clogged arteries require surgery to clear them; our clogged highways require equally drastic measures."[21]

Stacked Evidence. This fallacy entails framing a debate in such a way that all discourse not friendly to the arguer's position is precluded. In other words, the writer of the Stacked Evidence Fallacy sets up the argument in such a way that his or her points are the only ones discussed and he or she fails to address any counterarguments. *Example*: "TV is beneficial because it offers PBS, The History Channel, and the news."[22] (There is no mention of sex, violence, or the Kardashians.)

---

[18]From http://www.iep.utm.edu/fallacy/#NonSequitur

[19]From http://www.iep.utm.edu/fallacy/#Equivocation

[20]From http://www.iep.utm.edu/fallacy/#BeggingtheQuestion

[21]From http://ksuweb.kennesaw.edu/~shagin/logfal-analysis-falseanalogy.htm

[22]From http://www.uta.edu/english/SH/Fallacies.htm

You will discover that fallacies of all three kinds are common in arguments. As a rational and critical thinker, you must think about and analyze every bit of data that comes your way.

ACTIVITY: FINDING FALLACIES

Write a brief analysis of a text of your choice in which you critique the rhetorical appeals and fallacies employed by the author. Use the text above as your guide to some of the most common of the rhetorical fallacies.

"Remember, Remember the Fifth of November" by Judith Kim

ARGUMENT MODELS

The Classical Model

Of all the argument models, you are no doubt most familiar with the Classical Model. The five-paragraph themes you wrote in grade school were modeled on the classical form of argument. Most of the arguments produced by ancient Greek and Roman orators were in the forum of law courts and legislative assemblies, with orators interested primarily in proving truth from the facts at hand in the case. Thus, the Classical Model privileges logos-based appeals. The Classical structure consists of the following elements:

Exordium/Introduction. In this section, the author announces the subject and purpose of the argument. In the *exordium*, the author answers the "so what?" question (i.e., the argument's significance) and establishes *ethos* with the audience.

Narratio. In the *narratio* or background section, the author provides a background story for the issue at hand, in other words, what is known as fact about the issue. The author provides an overview of the issue's history and the various perspectives surrounding the controversy, outlining the *context* of the issue. Usually, at the end of the *narratio*, the author provides the *propositio*, a summary of the issues or a statement of the claim. We typically call this statement the *thesis*.

Partitio. This portion of the model's structure outlines what will follow, in accordance with the nature of the stated issue. In other words, the rhetor provides an overview of the sections of the text: that is, the reasons that the claim is valid. Sometimes, an author combines the *propositio* and *partitio* in the *narratio*.

Confirmatio. Forming the heart of the argument, the *confirmatio* provides the evidence for each of the reasons supporting the claim. Thus, the claim, given in the *narratio*, and the reasons, given in the *partitio*, are expounded upon in the *confirmatio*, with ample, credible, relevant evidence.

Refutatio. In the *refutatio*, the author addresses the counterarguments to his or her claim and refutes them one by one. Both the *confirmatio* and the *refutatio* use the *logos* appeal as the predominant method for making the argument.

Peroratio. In the *peroratio*, or summation, the author concludes the argument through reiterating the claim and making a strong call to action. Pathos appeals constitute the privileged appeal in the *peroratio*. Here, the author returns to the "so what?" question and hammers home the most important points, demonstrating beyond a doubt both the significance and the feasibility of the claims he or she has made, as well as what the audience should "take away" from the argument.

If you remember these simple facets of the Classical Model, you will be well on your way to making effective use of this structure:

- Explain why your argument is important, establishing your ethos.
- Give the context through telling the back story. Make a claim.
- Give the reasons your claim is valid. Use logos.
- Provide the evidence for each reason. Use logos.
- Address the possible counterarguments. Use logos.
- Summarize the main points and reiterate the call to action. Use pathos.

The Rogerian Model

The Rogerian Model emerged from the conflict resolution work of American psychologist Carl Rogers. Dr. Rogers developed his model in order to help the author build "common ground" in addressing audiences that are not receptive to the message, or even openly hostile to it. If you are dealing with a controversial issue, and you think you may be arguing an unpopular position, you may find the Rogerian Model useful and effective. In simplest terms, the Rogerian argument reverses the main sections of the Classical model, foregrounding the counterarguments in order to build consensus between the author and the audience. This model privileges pathos and ethos over logos, but logos still provides important support to the argument. Remember that in Rogerian argument, the goal is to get the audience to consider a viewpoint that does not align with their own, so knowing the audience's characteristics becomes especially crucial. Rogers emphasized "empathic listening," which involves a deep knowledge of the audience's needs, desires, and prejudices, as well as their baseline knowledge regarding the issue. The following sections outline the elements of the Rogerian structure.

Introduction. State the problem you hope to resolve. By presenting the issue as a problem that can be solved, you increase the chance that the audience will see the problem as well.

Summary of Opposing Views. As neutrally and diplomatically as possible, state the views of people with whom you disagree. Make sure that you provide an accurate assessment of those views. By showing that you can listen without judging and can give a fair hearing to the other sides of the issue, you demonstrate that your own views are worth attention. You create ethos with your audience in this way.

Statement of Understanding. Also known as the "statement of validity," this section demonstrates an understanding of the validity of other views. Here, you explain the circumstances in which the opposing views are valid. Which parts of the argument would you concede to be legitimate? Under what conditions are these parts legitimate? This statement allows you to qualify your argument by not making sweeping, insupportable statements.

Statement of Your Position. Now that the audience understands that you are willing to listen to and concede their views, they will now receive your argument. Here, you make your claim by stating your position on the issue.

Statement of Contexts. Describe situations and contexts in which you hope your views will be respected. By outlining specific contexts, you imply your understanding that not everyone will agree with you at all times. Opponents, however, are invited to agree with parts of your argument in the effort toward building common ground.

Statement of Benefits. End your argument on a positive note by expressing to the audience how they will benefit from considering your argument and acting accordingly. Not only does this technique appeal to their self-interest, but it also allows you to move forward into future goals and actions.

Remember these essential points about Rogerian argumentation:

- Use this model when the audience does not agree with you.
- Build common ground/consensus predominantly with ethos and pathos.
- Foreground counterarguments.
- Work up to your thesis.
- End on a positive note with explaining benefits to audience.

The Toulmin Model

Stephen Toulmin, a British philosopher, developed this model to handle arguments based on probability rather than absolute truth. The ancients who developed the Classical Model operated on the notion that philosophy must deal with absolute truth. As Aristotle developed the field of rhetoric, however, the emphasis shifted to probability and likelihood, so the rhetor argues the case that best fits the truth.

The Toulmin Model provides not only a structure for you to use to organize your argument, but also a checklist for revision. Using this list of elements, you can analyze the aspects of your argument in order to identify weak parts as well as to improve the stronger parts of your work.

The following represents the six elements of the Toulmin Model, adapted from the GSU English website for Rhetoric and Composition:[23]

- **Claims:** There are several different types of claims: claims of fact, claims of definition, claims of cause, claims of value, and claims of policy. An author may use any one or more of these claims to introduce the issue and to establish the case.
- **Data:** Information an author uses to support claims.
- **Warrant:** The assumption made by a writer in order for the claim to be true. The warrant connects the claim to the data.
- **Backing:** What the author uses to support the warrant.
- **Rebuttal:** The portion of the argument in which the author considers the opposing viewpoint and refutes it.
- **Qualifier:** Language that qualifies the claims of the author; qualifiers allow for probability rather than absolute truth, giving the argument a stronger chance of being accepted by and acted upon by the audience.

The Toulmin Model enables you to analyze your argument to find its weaknesses and strengthen them. Remember that the three basic parts consist of the claim, the grounds, and the warrant. The grounds support the claim, and the backing supports the warrant. In order to acknowledge the contingent and contextual nature of the argument, the rebuttal acknowledges the counterarguments. The qualifier shapes the claim in order to allow for the counterarguments. The ideal argument has all six components.

Toulmin Argument Example:
"Single-use Plastic Bags Should Be Banned"

Single-use plastic shopping bags should be banned in the U.S. (*claim*) because they contribute to the pollution of our environment (*data*). They cannot be reused according to law or store policy. If they are reused for other purposes, they become soiled and wind up in landfills. Only one percent of the bags placed in recycling bins are ever recycled by processing plants (*data*).

Whether the bags end up in the landfill or are burned in incinerators, they emit toxins into our environment (*data*). These toxins are harmful to soil, water, and air (*warrant*). Burning the bags emits toxic gases and increases the level of VOCs

---

[23]Handout for 1101 on Models of Argument: http://www.rhetcomp.gsu.edu/~bgu/1101/models.html

(volatile organic compounds) into the air, while landfills take up precious soil resources by holding the plastic in the earth, where it emits toxins as it decomposes (*backing*). The "trash vortex," a soup of plastic goo floating in the Pacific, covers a water area the size of Texas and kills marine life at every level of the food chain (*backing*).

Most metropolitan areas could institute the ban and enforce it, but smaller cities and towns might not have as many resources (*qualifier*). A ban would take some getting used to on the part of retailers and consumers (*rebuttal*), but the effort would pay off by decreasing the number of bags polluting the environment. A number of U.S. cities (Los Angeles, Seattle) and one state (Hawaii) have instituted the ban with positive results.

CLAIM
single-use plastic bags
should be banned

REASON
because they contribute
to the pollution of the
environment

QUALIFIER
most metropolitan
areas could institute
the ban effectively

DATA
almost all bags
wind up in landfills,
incinerators, or littering
the landscape; they
emit toxins

WARRANT
toxins are harmful to soil, air,
and water

BACKING
burning bags emits VOCs into air;
bags in landfills poison soil; the
trash vortex in the Pacific kills
marine life

REBUTTAL
the ban will take some
adjustment for retailers and
consumers

ACTIVITY: OUTLINING THE ARGUMENT

Choose an argument model and use it to outline your argument. You can do this exercise before you write the draft, and you can make another outline after you write the draft to check your argument. Make sure that you did not stray from the topics, and that you covered all of the elements. If you are a visual learner, you might want to make a diagram like the one above for your argument. Your instructor may ask you to write your argument in one of these structures, so this activity will provide you with excellent practice for using the skeleton of the model and "fleshing it out."

"The Heights" by Judith Kim

THE FIVE CANONS OF RHETORIC AND THE WRITING PROCESS

Cicero, a Roman politician and theorist of rhetoric, divided rhetoric into five *canons*, or categories. He put these categories into a particular order: *invention*, *arrangement*, *style*, *memory*, and *delivery*. While Cicero designed his system after legal and political oratory, that is, he had in mind men (yes, the spaces were reserved only for men) practicing public speaking in political forums, they remain useful for us today as we craft various types of arguments. Imagine the writing process: prewriting, drafting, revising, editing, proofreading, and publishing. The five rhetorical canons are set up to mirror the process of creating texts. When I craft an argument, I have to figure out what I am going to say; decide which order of topics is best; create the most engaging, convincing style for my audience and purpose; get it all down properly in my brain, in my notebook, or in my computer; and dazzle my audience with my ethos and my effective presentation. As you read the explanation of each of the five canons, think of the ways in which each one connects to a part of your own process as a writer.

Invention

Your instructor may call invention strategies *heuristics*. In Greek, the word "heuristic" refers to a method of finding or discovering ideas or solutions to problems. Heuristics are techniques to help you figure out what you want to include in your argument. Here are brief descriptions of several basic strategies.

Commonplaces

Commonplaces are topics that we use to make arguments. The word *topic* comes from the Greek *topoi*, which means "a place." The term "commonplace" echoes this notion of location, in its connotation of being a place from which to craft an argument. In order to know the best commonplaces, we must understand our audience's needs, desires, and background knowledge. If we know our audience values the notion of family and home, we can use the language of family and home to make our arguments. Other commonplaces help us divide and organize our topics, enabling us to move into the canon of arrangement. For example, the technique of comparing and contrasting proves to be a familiar way to talk about an issue; analyzing similarities and differences, therefore, forms one commonplace. Others include defining a term, dividing something into parts or qualities, analyzing causes and effects, or using expert testimony or quotations to make our points.

Stasis Theory

"Stasis" means to make a stand or determine a mode of proceeding. Using *stasis theory* entails asking questions and figuring out the nature of the issue from the questions and answers. For instance, a lawyer is building a case against a defendant. The lawyer might ask, "Did he do it?" This question concerns the fact of the defendant's actions. This type of stasis question is called a "conjectural stasis." There are four stasis questions that will enable you to situate your arguments around an issue.

- What are the facts? (conjecture)
- What is the meaning or nature of the issue? (definition)
- What is the seriousness of the issue? (quality)
- What is the best plan of action or procedure? (policy)

In the section on the Toulmin Model of argument, five types of claims were listed: fact, definition, value, cause, and policy. These types of claims are derived from stasis theory. In addition, the process chapter in this text discusses a strategy called "cubing," which is a modern variation of stasis theory. Asking these stasis questions will help you figure out which claim to make and will give you some direction in finding additional information to substantiate your points.

Artistic Proofs

Artistic proofs develop from the rhetor's own mind. An individual develops thoughts from prior knowledge and ethical conviction, then fashions these thoughts into a logical structure of argument. In this way, the author can explore and narrow the topic, create a thesis, and determine which ideas must be conveyed to the audience. These proofs form the only purely invented ones, and Aristotle considered them vitally important. The artistic proofs can be further categorized as deductive and inductive reasoning. A scientist uses deductive reasoning when she has a hypothesis and tests it in an experiment. She works from the general principle to the specific case. A literary critic uses inductive reasoning when he collects details of a poet's life through her poetry, and derives a theory about the poet based on these various examples. He works from the specific examples to a general principle. No one method proves better than the other, but in making an argument, we find it useful to think about how best to proceed with our reasoning, and use that model to guide us. See the chapter on analysis in this text for more on deductive and inductive reasoning.

Inartistic Proofs

While artistic proofs originate, like art itself, from the author, inartistic proofs originate outside the rhetor's mind. Anything that is not invented through careful thought and reasoning, including any material from primary or secondary sources, is considered an inartistic proof. Using statistics, expert testimony, surveys, primary documents, or other types of research can also help us make effective arguments. In order to know what to say about an issue, we need to know what has already been said. What are the various viewpoints on this issue? How and by whom have these ideas been presented?

Performing research must support our invention process rather than leading it. Consider research a discovery process. Ask questions, and let the research help you arrive at possible answers for those questions. The questions themselves, and even the topic itself, may transform in the research and writing process, which is a natural and desirable development. Often, when people do research, they seek out sources that support their own, already set-in-stone viewpoint, rather than carefully considering other viewpoints and synthesizing the arguments with their original thoughts. The best arguments form sophisticated syntheses of both artistic and inartistic proofs.

Arrangement

Once a rhetor has invented material for an argument, he or she must arrange that material into the most logical, effective order. This part of the writing process, and the second canon of rhetoric, is known as *arrangement*. The arrangement canon applies not only to ordering the parts of an argument in a model such as the classical structure, but also to ordering ideas in sentences and the construction of sentences and paragraphs that flow well and that make sense to the audience. Therefore, when you arrange your material from your own mind as well as from sources, you can refer to the argument models to give you a sense of the big picture. For example, as mentioned in the section on Rogerian argument, you might prefer to state counterarguments first if you know the audience might be initially unwilling to accept your claim. You can arrange your points using the Rogerian model.

In the next sections, two of the most common and useful arrangement strategies are presented: amplification and parallelism. The first one applies to the overall structure of the argument, and the second applies more commonly to the words, phrases, and sentences within the structure.

Amplification

In rhetoric, *amplification* refers to addressing the parts of an argument structure in the most effective fashion. Generally, the term refers to the layering of data to create overwhelming evidence for the claim of the argument. Therefore, the use of multiple facts, statistics, examples, and expert testimonials *amplifies* (or makes *louder*) the points made in the argument. For instance, the author might amplify an argument against the use of plastic shopping bags by using the following strategy:

"*Not only* does the use of plastic shopping bags contribute to the tonnage of solid waste in landfills, *but* it *also* adds to the plastic waste that gets carried into rivers and oceans, poisoning wildlife." This particular use is also known as the "But wait, there's more" pitch.[24]

The *digression* also amplifies the text if it helps to prove the argument. A digression is a kind of rhetorical tangent that serves both to divert attention away from the possible objections as well as to subtly emphasize the point. In one of his most famous orations, Cicero defended a poet named Archias, whose Roman citizenship was in dispute. Cicero delivered a long speech in praise of literature, which distracted the audience from the issue of citizenship and highlighted the importance of Archias's profession: poetry. Cicero cleverly won the argument.

Finally, *ordinatio* means ordering or numbering the divisions of an argument so that the audience can follow the author's points. Example: "When choosing whether to go to war with Iran, we must consider three crucial issues. First, we must consider the financial cost to our national budget, as well as money devoted by all parties to rebuilding the country. Second, we must think of the diplomatic cost, the cost in goodwill to our country in its relationship with other nations. Third and most important, we must privilege the human cost—the physical and mental injuries to both soldiers and civilians in all nations affected by the conflict."

Amplification consists of taking each part of the argument structure and expanding it with ample, accurate, and relevant data so that the argument proves compellingly persuasive.

Parallelism

Parallelism, or parallel structure, concerns either the entire argument structure or a smaller unit within it, such as a sentence. Parallelism is a figure not only of arrangement, but also one of style. Parallelism can be used with other strategies for heightened effect. The following are several examples of parallel structure. In the example about the possibility of war with Iran given above, the three considerations are given in the form of *costs*. They all match in terms of the way that they are framed. Therefore, the points of the *confirmatio*, or body of the argument, are parallel. The following examples provide ways to structure sentences for maximum effect.

---

[24]From Jay Heinrichs, *Thank You for Arguing: What Aristotle, Lincoln, and Homer Simpson Can Teach Us about Persuasion.*

Homoioptoton

This mouthful of a Greek word simply means the repetition of similar word endings in adjacent words, or of words or phrases in a series. Example: "I am situated, educated, and opinionated." All of the terms are adjectives in the past participle form. That is, they all end in "-ed."

Zeugma

Zeugma includes several specific techniques, but all of them involve a single verb or noun referring or connecting to more than one part of the sentence. Here are some examples:

- "The farmers in the valley grew potatoes, peanuts, and bored."[25] (the verb "grew" applies to "potatoes," "peanuts," and "bored")
- "Histories make [wo]men wise; poets, witty; the mathematics, subtle; natural philosophy, deep; moral, grave; logic and rhetoric, able to contend."—Sir Francis Bacon (the noun "histories" and the verb "make" are implied throughout the sentence)
- From *Star Trek: The Next Generation*: "You are free to execute your laws, and your citizens, as you see fit." (the verb "execute" applies both to "laws" and to "citizens")
- From *Rape of the Lock*, written by Alexander Pope: "Whether the nymph shall break Diana's law,/ Or some frail China-jar receive a flaw, Or stain her honour, or her new brocade." (The noun "nymph" is the subject of the verb "break," the one who might give a "flaw" to the "jar," the one who might "stain" her "honor" or her "brocade.")

Isocolon

An *isocolon* is simply a series of elements of the same length that have the same structure. Julius Caesar said, "Veni vidi vici," which means, "I came. I saw. I conquered." President John F. Kennedy, in his inaugural address, said, "Let every nation know, whether it wishes us well or ill, that we shall *pay any price, bear any burden, meet any hardship, support any friend, oppose any foe* to assure the survival and the success of liberty."[26] Notice the way that the structure of each phrase follows the same pattern: action verb + adjective ("any") + object (noun).

Climax

Parallel structure not only makes the text sound more musical, and therefore more memorable, but it also serves to build ideas effectively for the argument. *Climax*

---

[25]From http://fos.iloveindia.com/zeugma-examples.html

[26]From http://americanrhetoric.com/figures/parallelism.htm

makes use of parallel structure in order to arrange words, phrases, or clauses in ascending order, placing the most important idea last for more weight or emphasis. For instance, Albert, Lord Tennyson, in his poem "Ulysses," wrote, "One equal temper of heroic hearts,/ Made weak by time and fate, but strong in will/To strive, to seek, to find, and not to yield." Notice the parallel structure of the verbs, building up to the climax of heroic hearts not yielding to time or fate.

In addition to arranging sentences of groups of ideas in climactic order, the parts of the argument should also be arranged in ascending order. As pointed out previously, hide the weakest point in the middle, and begin with a moderately strong point, working your way up to the most important point.

Syncrisis

Syncrisis compares or contrasts two ideas in parallel clauses. For example, "We support the victory; they decry the cost."

Using these and other arrangement strategies will help you place your points in the most logical order for maximum impact on your audience. For information on other arrangement strategies, refer to websites such as *Sylvia Rhetoricae* or great books on rhetoric such as Sam Leith's *You Talkin' to Me? Rhetoric from Aristotle to Obama.*

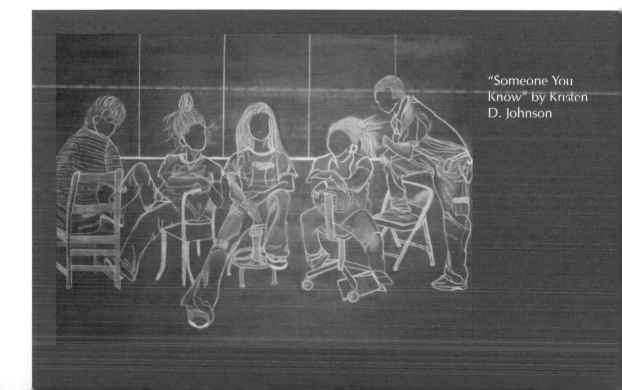

"Someone You Know" by Kristen D. Johnson

Style

Invention concerns what will be said. Arrangement has to do with the order of the ideas. And style refers to how the ideas will be expressed. Drafting and revision are the parts of the writing process in which style emerges as a dominant consideration. The style canon contains so many strategies that it would be impossible to describe them in detail in this short guide. However, a few of the most important aspects of style include the following: diction (word choice), figurative language, correctness, clarity, and level of formality.

The virtues of style described by Aristotle include *correctness* of usage and grammar; *clarity* (no ambiguity or obscurity of language); vivid *sensory detail*; *decorum* (propriety); and *ornateness* (beautiful language). Aristotle goes on to describe the quality of ornateness in detail, focusing primarily on the technique of *metaphor*. He discusses many other figures of speech, such as *simile*, *personification*, and *analogy*, but he devotes the most attention to metaphor.

Aristotle believed that metaphors teach the audience through a *visual* connection between the metaphor and what it refers to. The metaphor creates a figurative or abstract connection that *carries* meaning. In this metaphor, determine which two things are being compared and think about what they have in common: "With this faith we will be able to transform the jangling discords of our nation into a beautiful symphony of brotherhood."—Dr. Martin Luther King, Jr., "I Have a Dream." What is Dr. King trying to teach his audience about humankind through using this metaphor?

The ancient Greeks developed three levels of style: the high or grand style, the middle style, and the low or plain style. The academic arguments you write in your First-Year English classes use predominantly the middle style. You may remember someone—a peer, family member, or teacher—telling you that you must write in a more formal than the way you speak on an everyday basis. The accepted form of our language among academic and professional audiences is called *Standard American English*, and it is a kind of currency for us to use, just like money is a currency. When we use this middle level of language—not slang, but not technical jargon, either—we have the greatest chance of being respected and understood by our audiences.

A careful consideration of style will enable you to write skillful, engaging, and persuasive arguments. Refer to a writing handbook for more detail on achieving an excellent writing style. However, practicing your writing "voice" helps more than any other strategy. Once you find your authentic, original voice, you can enhance its effectiveness with techniques such as sensory details and figurative language.

Pay attention to places in your argument that seem flat and uninteresting. These are the points at which you need to create a more engaging style.

Memory

Unlike the ancient orators, we no longer have to memorize speeches. Our forms of rhetoric have expanded tremendously, and our technology ensures that whatever we create is both endlessly revisable and permanent. We can change and we can save whatever we write, draw, or say. However, some of the strategies of the memory canon can still help us today.

Students and practitioners of rhetoric have traditionally kept *commonplace books* to help them generate and remember arguments. They would write down topics, quotations, ideas, and other notes in a notebook so that they could refer back to them when creating arguments, much like many writers today. In this way, the canon of memory ties to the canon of invention. The commonplace book helps the rhetor collect and categorize ideas for arguments in a memorable form. We use databases and bookmark websites, but the ancients created commonplace books. No matter which strategy works for you, find a way to record your artistic proofs as well as inartistic proofs you discover in your reading.

Perhaps you have used *mnemonic aids* when you have studied for a test or had to memorize a speech. A mnemonic device works through association, usually of a visual nature. In the ancient Greek and Roman societies, the orator memorized his speech by imagining walking through a building and creating mental associations with objects in the building. Each object would remind him of a portion of his speech. He created a mental path from object to object, and since each object had been associated with a topic, he could remember what he needed to say. For example, if the hall contains a statue of a famous philosopher, he might use an aphorism, or wise saying, from that philosopher. Try leaving mental bread crumbs through a virtual space the next time you need to memorize talking points in a presentation.

While commonplace books and mnemonic devices help the memory of the rhetor, the *conclusion* of an argument helps the memory of the audience. Many writers neglect the conclusion, usually because they are tired of writing. However, the power of the conclusion should not be underestimated. This part of your argument helps your audience remember your points. People tend to remember the last thing they see or hear, so the ending of any argument proves vitally important for its impact. Be sure to end with a bang—give your audience a "takeaway"—a colorful and relevant fact or quote.

Delivery

Like the canon of style, *delivery* concerns *how* something is said rather than the content of the text. Even though you may not be delivering an oration, you still deliver a paper or a multimedia project to your instructor and your peers. Often, this canon is omitted from texts on rhetoric, but if we think of delivery as *publication*, or submitting written, oral, or visual work, we can still use it as a vital aspect of argumentation.

Delivery varies by the form or *genre* of the text. For example, if you write a traditional MLA-style paper, you might hand in a hard copy to your instructor, or you might email it or submit it in an online portal. In each of these forms, you are *delivering* the text. You might read it to your peers, or they might read it in a peer review session. That also constitutes a form of delivery. If you create a PowerPoint, Prezi, website, blog, video, or podcast, you might present these texts to the class in a multimedia presentation. The oral, written, and visual techniques that you use during the delivery of the text contribute to your ethos. In your final draft, consider the importance of proper grammar, usage, mechanics, documentation, and formatting. In order to deliver the text properly, you must revise for content and organization, edit for style and sentence structure, and proofread for mechanics and formatting. Every step is important, and you may loop back through the steps a few times on your way to delivery. Think of the text as your résumé, your elevator speech, and your video interview all rolled into one. You want it to shine because it reflects your brilliance.

ACTIVITY: FIRING THE CANONS!

In your next assignment, try at least one of the techniques suggested in the sections on the five canons of rhetoric. Write about whether and how it was helpful in your writing process. Answer these questions:

- Which technique did you select and why?
- How helpful was it and why?

Finally, select another strategy to use in your next assignment and explain how you will go about employing it.

Peroratio

This chapter argues that argument and rhetoric are valuable fields of study for the personal, academic, and professional life of every person. Rhetoric surrounds us every day, and by studying it, we can be better critics of the multitudinous arguments around us, and we have the power to convince other people through creating our own arguments. We analyze and synthesize far more arguments than the ones we write in English class. Arguably, argument is the most useful, most enjoyable, most challenging field of study and practice at Georgia State University.

In this chapter, you have read about the rhetorical situation, the three appeals in arguments, various fallacies of argument, the models of argument, and the five canons of rhetoric. By using this short but awesome guide to rhetorical concepts and strategies, you can impress your audiences with your knowledge and develop skills through practicing the suggested techniques. Just as in yoga or basketball, practice brings results. So, start arguing and feel the power! What's stopping you?

Research

INTRODUCTION TO RESEARCH

In college writing, you will be expected to think critically; to offer strong, compelling, and appropriate research to advance your arguments; to discern between scholarly and non-scholarly sources in your research; and to write directly and clearly.

Academic writing has conventional practices, like any other endeavor. For example, it is accepted practice that scholars writing in their fields include a "Literature Review" in their academic papers, showing that they are familiar with the works of scholars who've gone before. With effort, the conventions of academic research can be learned, and your research skills will expand and improve with practice.

You do research every day. If you're in the market for a car, you may research online or talk to a knowledgeable family member about which car fits your needs. If your car requires repair, you may consult online reviews to find a trustworthy mechanic near you. Perhaps you've read the nutritional information on the can to find the sugar content of your favorite energy drink or an online medical article about artificial sweeteners. The information-gathering you will do for college research simply builds on these informal research skills.

By the end of ENGL 1101, and throughout ENGL 1102, you will be expected to write a *researched argument paper*. In this type of paper, you will make an argument—a *claim*. Your claim may be an opinion, an interpretation, a policy proposal, or a cause-and-effect statement, among other things. In your paper, you will be expected to:

1. Make a concise, compelling claim (your argument), and
2. Support your argument with evidence gathered from your research.

MLA DOCUMENTATION STYLE

In college writing, you will be expected to *document* all of the research sources you use. Each discipline uses a particular style according to the priorities and nature of their written discourse. The American Psychological Association (APA) style, for example, is used in business, social sciences, and education, and the Chicago Style is used in journalism. In the humanities, such as English Studies, scholars use the documentation style of the Modern Language Association (MLA).

The MLA Handbook for Writers of Research Papers, Seventh Edition provides guidelines for the MLA style of documentation, which has two parts.

Part I: Part 1 entails "parenthetical citation," which means that wherever you summarize, paraphrase, or quote an author, name that author (and page, if available) in parentheses at the end of the sentence (Smith 2). If there is no author, use a shortened version of the first element of the Works Cited entry (see Part II), which would be the article name for an Internet page. For example, this would be the entry for an Internet site with no author and no pagination: ("Stetson Kennedy Dies at 94").

Part II: Part II entails the end documentation known as a Works Cited page (elsewhere, this is called the References page or Bibliography); in order to complete this part, list author and work on a Works Cited page at the end of your paper. (See the sample Works Cited page later in this chapter).

It will be helpful to review the "MLA Documentation" section of your First-Year textbook. But the best way—by far—to get the hang of documentation is to read the model research essays in this and other textbooks. Note how they 1) smoothly incorporate and synthesize research sources into their texts; 2) make the end-of-sentence parenthetical citations; and 3) format their Works Cited pages.

If you are like many First-Year students, you may be intimidated by the prospect of thorough scholarly documentation, not only because there are multiple documentation styles that each have their own minute rules to be cognizant of, but also because of the looming spectre of plagiarism. First-Year students frequently, and rightfully, worry about using the words or ideas of others; unfortunately, though, if students don't know how to document these uses, the tendency for most is to try and hide the fact from the instructor.

This is foolish, not for the fact that the deception will always be discovered, but because all scholars stand on the shoulders of those that came before, so to speak. For example, if you are studying biology, you are not expected to discover the structure of DNA molecules on your own; rather, we build on the work of those that have come before. Scholarly documentation is about our responsibility to acknowledge the work of others and is what maintains our individual credibility while working with others.

For help, you might try EasyBib Automatic Bibliography and Citation Maker (www.easybib.com). You can enter sources as you work, and EasyBib will format them according to MLA Works Cited style for books, journals, newspaper articles, databases (EasyBib is not error-proof; students are responsible for checking the formatting for the Works Cited page). The site will also format according to APA guidelines, if you are required to write papers in the social sciences, business, or education. EasyBib is very helpful in the research writing process; you can record and format sources for your Works Cited page as you go, creating a working bibliography. You don't want to scramble at the end of writing your paper to create a bibliography; it will already be finished.

"Stairway to Heaven"
by Judith Kim

EVALUATING SOURCES

In researching and writing rhetorically, you boost your *ethos*, or credibility as a writer, by synthesizing your own knowledge with expert knowledge in a field. The question to keep in mind from the very beginning is "How will this source strengthen my argument? Is it truly relevant and timely?" The goal is to find sources that are appropriate, compelling, complete, and expert. For any source, the key factors are *academic credibility, argument, accuracy, and currency.* Scholarly journals and books published by university presses carry the most credibility in academic writing. Some popular sources (popular = written by journalists, not by experts in the field) are credible, depending on context; a news item from *The New York Times*, for example, may be a source of accurate, up-to-the-minute data on a topic. Many popular sources that are meant for entertainment—glossy magazines like *Glamour*—are not credible as sources in academic writing. In addition, most instructors discourage citing Wikipedia as a source because its entries are written by volunteers; most readers have no way of evaluating their accuracy. Wikipedia articles on your topic, however, can provide excellent bibliographies and links as starting points for your research.

To succeed in academic writing, you must develop a practiced eye for the difference between scholarly and popular sources, and commit to using scholarly sources.

Scholarly Journals
- Are written for an audience of PhDs, professors, and students in an academic field
- Often published by a university press
- In general, if an academic journal or book, no glossy color or color photos
- Few, if any, advertisements
- Highly specialized vocabulary
- Articles, graphics, tables, charts
- Extensive bibliography at the end of each journal article or book

Examples:
JAMA: The Journal of the American Medical Association
(Written by experts in the field of medicine for others in the field.)

The Journal of Economic Theory
(Writer/audience of economics PhDs, researchers, and students.)

American Literature
(Published by Duke University Press for an academic audience.)

Popular Publications

- Are written by journalists or others
- Published by a news or popular press
- Glossy or eye-catching color, many photos
- Non-technical, basic vocabulary
- No bibliographies

Examples:

The Wall Street Journal (Despite "journal" in the title, it is a popular
source—a newspaper written by journalists for a wide audience)

The Economist (Written by journalists, full color, with many ads)

PCWorld (Full color, many ads. Written by journalists for a wide audience)

Primary and Secondary Sources

You'll also need to know the difference between primary and secondary research.

Primary research involves first-hand interaction with your subject; this includes interviewing people and analyzing/working with primary sources like diaries, novels and films (rather than working with second-hand *analyses* of these primary sources). Primary sources stand alone in that they are not interpreting anything else. An example of a primary source is *The Diary of a Young Girl* by Anne Frank.

Secondary research materials, on the other hand, interpret and analyze primary sources. Secondary sources include scholarly journal articles, analyses, and biographies, like *Anne Frank: The Biography* by Melissa Müller.

"We Want a Better World" by William Walsh

THE VALUE OF A LIBRARY SEARCH; OR, WHY YOU CAN'T "JUST GOOGLE IT"

Google searching returns a world of information—but often not a world of credibility. Say you are researching the history behind Dr. Martin Luther King's "Letter from Birmingham Jail." You Google "Martin Luther King," and you click on the link for "www.martinlutherking.org."

As a "dot-org," it's an organization, so it sounds credible. It is visually orderly, in terms of neatness of layout. At first glance, you think it might be the Martin Luther King Center, or a memorial foundation, or a reputable archive of King's speeches. You read the website heading: "Martin Luther King Jr: A True Historical Examination. A Valuable Resource for Teachers and Students Alike."

Unfortunately, this page is indeed the work of an organization—a supremacist hate group offering their take on King's life and on the accomplishments of African Americans in general. The site has a wealth of hateful statements about African Americans and other groups.

A good rule of thumb: To be used in an academic paper, a Web source 1) must list an author (the above source does not); 2) must cite its sources, and 3) should not exist to sell something.

GoogleScholar—not just Google—is an excellent search engine for online scholarly articles. What is the downside of GoogleScholar? Unlike a library database search, it doesn't always give the full text of an article; often, you must pay for the article. The good news: Scholarly articles are available free of charge through a GSU Library search.

QUICK-START: SEARCHING THE GSU PULLEN LIBRARY WEBSITE

You can search the Georgia State University Pullen Library website and its wealth of scholarly databases from your own computer. Go to http://www.library.gsu.edu/ and click "Libraries" and then "University Library." Last year, the library's website was visited 1.7 million times. If you're searching for books, the library houses 1.5 million volumes. Whether you are accessing the library from home or from a library computer, use the following steps to complete a simple and quick search.

http://www.library.gsu.edu/

For Academic Search Complete, click on "A" in Discover's "Databases A to Z" field. Then, click "Academic Search Complete."

Finding Articles in Scholarly Journals

To establish credibility in your academic writing, be sure to find and use peer-reviewed scholarly journal articles in your research. "Peer-reviewed" means that articles have been reviewed by experts in the field for reliability and relevance before being published and used by other scholars.

Go to the library webpage http://www.library.gsu.edu/ and view the Discover field.

You can use Discover for your search, as it searches many other databases. The results, however, are often cumbersome, and many will be irrelevant.

For a more efficient search, go to the bottom of the Discover search box to click "Databases By Name A-Z." Click "A," and then choose the database "EBSCO Host/Academic Search Complete." You will be asked for your campus ID and password.

Academic Search Complete is a comprehensive, multi-disciplinary source of more than 10,000 scholarly publications. Once you're in Academic Search Complete, conduct a basic search using keywords from your topic (*water quality*), a title, or an author. Academic Search Complete also will limit the results to scholarly journals if you click "Search Options" and then "Scholarly Journals Only." You can also choose to see only articles with full-text available. You also can earmark desired articles to an electronic folder.

Use Boolean operators to tailor your search. Use quotation marks to search for *phrases*, like "bipolar disorder" or "a midsummer night's dream." Use *AND, OR and NOT*, and make them ALL CAPS, as in biomedical AND engineering NOT nuclear. Use an asterisk* for *wild card searches*; cinema* will return "cinematic" and "cinematography." Use multiple search terms to narrow the results; a search for "environment" will yield millions of hits.

Note: EBSCO Host/Academic Search Complete is one of more than 100 databases available through the library, serving a wide range of disciplines. For discipline-specific databases, seek out the Subject Librarian for your field (art, for example), or browse "Databases A-Z" in Discover. You'll find everything from NASA's database to MedLine to ARTstor to Rock'N'Roll and Counterculture. Here are some suggested databases for different disciplines:

- Humanities, including Languages and Literatures—EBSCO Host/ Academic Search Complete, JSTOR, MLA International Bibliography, Project Muse
- Social Sciences—ERIC, Government Document Catalog Services, PsychInfo
- Business—ProQuest, LexisNexis Academic
- Sciences—Academic Search Complete, Web of Science, General Science Index
- News, Legal Cases—LexisNexis Academic

Finding Library Books

Scholarly books treat academic topics with in-depth discussion and careful documentation of evidence. They are often published by university presses, like Oxford University Press and the University of California Press. Sometimes, a well-researched popular book with a thorough bibliography is a good research find; its bibliography can point you toward scholarly books/articles on your topic. Remember: In academic writing, we build on the work of scholars who have come before us.

It's easy to search for library books. Go to the Discover window and click "Catalog"; under "All Fields," search by title, subject, or author. At the bottom of the catalog entry for each book, you will find the location of the book in the library:

"Library North 3"—and the call number by which you can find the book on the shelves: "RC516 .B526." Proceed to third floor north and find the RCs on the shelves.

Using Internet Sources Wisely

The World Wide Web is an incredible resource for research. Through it, you can find full texts of pending legislation, searchable online editions of Shakespeare's plays, scholarly articles, environmental impact statements, stock quotes, and much more. Finding credible sites for research, however, is not that easy. Sites range, in terms of credibility and usefulness, from the spectacularly good (like Google Books, with millions of searchable titles) to the spectacularly bad. While the scope of this topic is beyond this book, consider the following bare essentials when evaluating a web site. Don't be part of the proliferation of misinformation.

A rule of thumb for Internet sources: Make sure that the source 1) lists an author, 2) lists its sources, and 3) isn't selling anything.

Researchers, in general, evaluate web sites for *relevance, reliability, accuracy and currency* (as in, how *recent/timely* is the source?) In addition to asking *"How does this information fit my research purpose?"* they ask questions like the following:

Who is the author of the site? Is he or she a legitimate expert? What organization or entity does the writer represent? Think of the credibility gap—and the gap between the writer's rhetorical stance and tone—between the American Medical Association website (ama-assn.org) and "The Anti-Liberal Page" (a .com site). Researchers view .com sites, short for "commercial," with a healthy dose of skepticism. The .edu suffix, indicating a college or university, indicates credibility, as does .gov, which indicates a government agency or search engine like www.searchusa.gov.

What is the purpose of the site? What is its agenda? Compare the purpose of a recognized informational website (like the United Nations web site, at http://www.un.org/en/), to the purpose of the www.MartinLutherKing.org. site cited earlier. One seeks to provide accurate information; one is a supremacist-group smear campaign that seeks to destroy reputations.

To help you in your Internet research, two specialized search engines yield only results that have been vetted by university librarians for accuracy and credibility. They are:

Information You Can Trust, http://www.ipl.org, and Infomine: Scholarly Internet Resource Collections @ http://infomine.ucr.edu.

"So Much Needs to Change" by Oana Povian

THE THESIS STATEMENT AND RESEARCH PROPOSAL

To review, an *argumentative* paper makes an *argument*—a claim—which is supported with specific evidence gleaned from your research.

Early in your research process, your argument—the main claim of your research paper—will begin to take shape, and you will have an idea of how you will use your preliminary sources. In the research proposal, you specify the argument and sources for your research project. The proposal is not a contract, and you are not locked into the topic at this point. In fact, your proposal most likely will be refined, narrowed, or changed based on continual conversation with your instructor and peers. As your research proposal develops, think of it as a guide to keep writing and research laser-focused on your thesis.

The art of crafting a research statement (or question) requires study and practice; consult your writing textbook for techniques and examples. As for the research proposal, requirements vary from instructor to instructor; they range from a bare-bones outline (see example below) to a multiple-page written document. Here is an outline-form proposal with some typical required elements, as assigned by one instructor:

SAMPLE RESEARCH PROPOSAL

My Classical Argument Proposal: Why Writing Teachers Should Study Depression and Bipolar Disorder in Student Writers

My Audience: Writing teachers, including my writing instructor, and my 1102 class members

My Thesis/Argument: Composition teachers should study how depression and bipolar disorder affect student writing.

Three Reasons Why:
1. Depression and bipolar illness have long been associated with writing creativity.
   I knew this, and will find more examples in research.
2. Seven percent of undergraduates nationwide currently take antidepressants; a full one in four say depression has hurt their academic performance.
   I knew this generally, but didn't know the numbers until I researched. Wow!
3. Depression can cause writer's block; perhaps not all late papers are due to laziness.
   I didn't know this; I found more data to illustrate it.

Possible Counter-Arguments
THEY SAY: Writing teachers don't need to study this. They're not therapists.
I SAY: True, but this affects the writing of many, many students. It's relevant for the study of composition.

Preliminary Research Sources:

At this point, I have found three main source candidates:

1. A website (The National College Health Association's major mental health study of 200 colleges nationwide). *I will use data from this study to illustrate the breadth of depression and bipolar illness in the student population.*
2. An article (from the academic journal *Comprehensive Psychiatry*) *I will use this article for Reason No. 3, that depression can cause writer's block, which may affect students' academic performance.*

3.) A library book (published by Columbia University Press) *I will use this book for background on depression and mania in writers in English.*

"Art Appreciation" by Kaitlyn Winey

PLAGIARISM

Before we discuss how to quote, paraphrase, and otherwise work with sources, you should become familiar with the basics of plagiarism.

Intentional plagiarism ranks high in the pantheon of really bad ideas. Its stigma follows students throughout their academic careers. Plagiarism means handing in something you didn't write, and it can be long or short—from an entire paper from an online paper mill to an unattributed catchy phrase. The basic concepts of plagiarism are relatively easy to grasp with a little effort.

At Georgia State, *"The student is responsible for understanding the legitimate use of sources . . . and the consequences of violating this responsibility."* In other words, the burden rests upon you as the writer to give credit where credit is due.

It is in your best interest not to put your instructor in the position of discerning accidental from deliberate plagiarism.

Some very common types of plagiarism

1. Turning in a paper that was written by someone else as your own. This includes papers obtained from online paper mills.
2. Copying from a source without acknowledging that source in the proper format (in English courses, this would be MLA documentation, which includes a parenthetical citation at the end of the sentence and a source entry on the Works Cited page).
3. Paraphrasing materials from a source without attributing them to the source.
4. Copying materials from a text but treating them as your own, leaving out quotation marks and acknowledgement.

The penalty for plagiarism is, at the very least, an "F" on the paper; at the instructor's discretion, it can mean an "F" in the course. GSU students have too many resources to even consider plagiarizing. To learn how to avoid plagiarism and how to properly cite sources, students have not only classroom instruction but also one-on-one conferences with their instructors, tutoring appointments at the GSU Writing Studio, and the availability of comprehensive web sites like The Purdue Online Writing Lab (owl.english.purdue.edu/).

Internet searches, anti-plagiarism software like turnitin.com, and instructors' in-depth knowledge of students' writing make it easy to catch plagiarism among composition students. The "easy way," paradoxically, is simply to do the work.

From the GSU Policy on Academic Honesty (Section 409 of *GSU Faculty Handbook*)

"The University expects students and faculty to be academically honest, and it expects faculty members to communicate expectations to students in their syllabi. That said, it is the student's final responsibility to understand plagiarism and avoid it. See the definitions below.

GSU's Definitions of Academic Honesty

The examples and definitions given below are intended to clarify the standards by which academic honesty and academically honorable conduct are to be judged. The list is merely illustrative of the kinds of infractions that may occur, and it is not intended to be exhaustive. Moreover, the definitions and examples suggest conditions under which unacceptable behavior of the indicated types normally occurs; however, there may be unusual cases that fall outside these conditions which also will be judged unacceptable by the academic community.

A. **Plagiarism:** Plagiarism is presenting another person's work as one's own. Plagiarism includes any paraphrasing or summarizing of the works of another person without acknowledgment, including the submitting of another student's work as one's own. Plagiarism frequently involves a failure to acknowledge in the text, notes, or footnotes the quotation of the paragraphs, sentences, or even a few phrases written or spoken by someone else. The submission of research or completed papers or projects by someone else is plagiarism, as is the unacknowledged use of research sources gathered by someone else when that use is specifically forbidden by the faculty member. Failure to indicate the extent and nature of one's reliance on other sources is also a form of plagiarism. Any work, in whole or in part, taken from the Internet or other computer-based resource without properly referencing the source (for example, the URL) is considered plagiarism. A complete reference is required in order that all parties may locate and view the original source. Finally, there may be forms of plagiarism that are unique to an individual discipline or course, examples of which should be provided in advance by the faculty member. The student is responsible for understanding the legitimate use of sources, the appropriate ways of acknowledging academic, scholarly or creative indebtedness, and the consequences of violating this responsibility.

B. **Cheating on Examinations:** Cheating on examinations involves giving or receiving unauthorized help before, during, or after an examination. Examples of unauthorized help include the use of notes, computer based resources, texts, or "crib sheets" during an examination (unless specifically approved by the faculty member), or sharing information with another student during an examination (unless specifically approved by the faculty member). Other examples include intentionally allowing another student to view one's own examination and collaboration before or after an examination if such collaboration is specifically forbidden by the faculty member.

C. **Unauthorized Collaboration:** Submission for academic credit of a work product, or a part thereof, represented as its being one's own effort, which has been developed in substantial collaboration with another person or source, or computer-based resource, is a violation of academic honesty. It is also a violation of academic honesty knowingly to provide such assistance. Collaborative work specifically authorized by a faculty member is allowed.

D. **Falsification:** It is a violation of academic honesty to misrepresent material or fabricate information in an academic exercise, assignment or proceeding (e.g., false or misleading citation of sources, the falsification of the results of experiments or of computer data, false or misleading information in an academic context in order to gain an unfair advantage).

E. **Multiple Submissions:** It is a violation of academic honesty to submit substantial portions of the same work for credit more than once without the explicit consent of the faculty member(s) to whom the material is submitted for additional credit. In cases in which there is a natural development of research or knowledge in a sequence of courses, use of prior work may be desirable, even required; however the student is responsible for indicating in writing, as a part of such use, that the current work submitted for credit is cumulative in nature."

Two Examples of Plagiarism

Plagiarism takes many forms; two definitive examples follow. Examine the following original passages and student use of them. Determine which one is which:

1.) Word-for-Word Plagiarism
2.) Too-Close Paraphrasing/Lack of Acknowledgement of Sources

Original Passage:

"As you read the book, you really do feel for Ender. He's used like a tool, honed and shaped against his will, with no one to turn to, which is pretty much the point. If he's in the midst of battle, there won't be a grownup there to turn to. His childhood is ripped from him, bit by bit, and perhaps that's why you feel sorry for him. By the time the book comes to its climax, he's only eleven years old. He's very smart, and very talented, but he's still only eleven." (From www10brinkster.com/MShades/books/e/ender.html)

A Student's Use:

As you read the book, you really do feel for Ender. The idea of a child being used like a tool, having their childhood bypassed and eliminated, is a harsh thing, and perhaps that's the lesson of this book.

Ender is used like a tool, honed and shaped against his will, with no one to turn to. If he's in the midst of battle, there won't be a grownup there to turn to. Ender's childhood is ripped from him, bit by bit, and perhaps that's why you feel sorry for him. By the time the book comes to its climax, he's only eleven years old. He's very smart, but he's still only eleven.

Original Passage:

"At about 1:01 p.m. on March 18, 1925, trees began to snap north-northwest of Ellington, Missouri, and for the next three and a half hours more people would die, more schools would be destroyed, more students and farmers would be killed, and more deaths would occur in a single city than from any other tornado in U.S. history. Records would be set for speed, path length, and probably for other categories that can't be measured so far in the past. The tornado maintained an exact heading, N 69 degrees E, for 183 of the 219 miles, at an average of 62 mph, following a slight topographic ridge on which a series of mining towns were built. These towns were the main targets of the devastating winds. No distinct funnel was visible through much of its path, yet for over 100 miles, the path width held uniformly at about three-quarters of a mile." (http://www.carolyar.com/Illinois/Misc/Tornado.htm)

A Student's Use:

A terrible tornado passed through north-northwest of Ellington, Missouri at about 1:01 p.m. on March 18, 1925. The trees began to snap, and for the next approximately three hours, many people died, many schools were destroyed, and the U.S. record was set for deaths occurring in a single city. Records also would be set for path length and speed. The tornado maintained the heading of N 69 degrees E, and traveled at an average of 62 mph for the length of its path. You couldn't see a funnel, but for more than 100 miles, the monster left a destruction path three-quarters of a mile wide. Big tornadoes like this are the reason that towns and cities should install more tornado warning sirens.

Determine which is word-for-word plagiarism and which is too-close-paraphrase/didn't cite sources plagiarism. Then, let's revisit the idea of common and uncommon knowledge:

> **Common Knowledge:** Every year, tornadoes kill people in an area of the central U.S. known as Tornado Alley. (You do not have to name a source for this).

> **NOT Common Knowledge:** "The 1925 Missouri tornado maintained an exact heading, N 69 degrees E, at an average of 62 mph." You did not know this as you came into your research. In MLA format, you must name the source of this data, both in 1) parentheses at the end of the sentence, and 2) in the Works Cited page.

In the second example, the student did not *credit a source* when he/she directly quoted and paraphrased facts that are *NOT common knowledge.*

Remember the important rule of thumb: *If a fact wasn't in your head when you began your research, assume it is NOT common knowledge. By the same token, if a fact is new to you but common knowledge to your audience, you may not need to cite it.*

Citation strategies you would use for the Ender example:

Review and practice what it means to summarize and/or paraphrase the piece.

Review how to quote the author. Use a page number if available. Here is how: According to Smith, Ender "is used like a tool, honed and shaped against his will" (1).

Use parenthetical citation at the end of sentences both quoted AND paraphrased.

Citation strategies you would use for the tornado example:

Put quotation marks around all direct quotes (whole sentences AND phrases).

Use a looser, more contextual paraphrase (combine it with text above and below).

Use parenthetical citation at the end of fact-laden sentences, both quoted AND paraphrased (Smith 1).

For more on researching and note-taking, understanding plagiarism, and plagiarism examples, consult the "Is It Plagiarism?" and "Safe Practices" sections of the Purdue OWL at http://owl.english.purdue.edu/owl/resource/589/03/. The OWL is an excellent source across the board for research paper writing. These two sections cover reading, note-taking, summarizing, paraphrasing, quoting, and safely writing about the ideas of others.

PLAGIARISM:
EASY TO COMMIT, HARD TO LIVE DOWN

In 2006, Harvard undergraduate Kaavya Viswanathan wrote the best-selling novel *How Opal Mehta Got Kissed, Got Wild, and Got A Life*. The novel was subsequently recalled by the publisher—who took the unprecedented step of destroying all copies—because Viswanathan plagiarized throughout.

This is one of many examples of how the writer followed sources much too closely:

From Salman Rushdie's 1990 novel *Haroun and the Sea of Stories*: "If from speed you get your thrill, take precaution, make your will."

From Viswanathan's novel: "If from drink you get your thrill, take precaution—write your will."

"Out in Full Force" by Graham Robson

TAKING NOTES FROM SOURCES

To "plagiarism-proof" a research paper: As you take notes, ALWAYS indicate which words are YOURS and which are quotes from sources. Find a way that works for you—large quotation marks, highlighting for "mine," etc.

Careful note-taking is the best defense against plagiarism. Note-taking strategies differ among researchers. The purpose of note-taking is to allow you to keep source material organized; it also helps you internalize source material, and makes research writing easier. Whether you're taking notes on paper, on your computer (using a different page or file for each topic), or on a program like Zotero (a Firefox plugin available through the library), be sure to keep neat and organized notes. Here is the basic note card format, for paper or computer:

Write a subject heading at the top—a category that makes sense to you. Then, carefully enter either 1) *a direct quote of the source, with quote marks* 2) your *summary* of the source, or 3) your *paraphrase* of the source. Write which of the three you have created at the bottom of the card or file.

Google's Data-Gathering Practices (subject heading)

Stallworth," Googling for Principles in Online Advertising," p. 470

" Google's enormous data-crunching machine is able to make calculated assumptions about consumers based on their searches, or on information consumers reveal when registering for Google's free services."

Direct quote.

Common and Uncommon Knowledge

Once again, to avoid plagiarism, *you must credit a source* when you quote, paraphrase, or summarize *any facts that are not common knowledge* (see below for instructions on how to quote, paraphrase and summarize). For example: "In March of 2012, the population of the United States was estimated at 313,232,882." Or, "The *RMS Titanic* sank on April 15, 1912." Or, "The University of Texas has seven museums and 17 libraries." These facts are not common knowledge, so its source must be cited at the end of the sentence.

You don't have to credit a source for facts that *are* common knowledge: "The United States government is divided into three branches: executive, legislative and judicial." "The University of Texas is in Austin." Depending on context and audience, however, writing "The population of the United States is around 300 million" may be considered common knowledge.

IMPORTANT: Two rules of thumb: *If a fact wasn't in your head when you began your research, assume it is NOT common knowledge.* By the same token, if a fact is new to you but *common knowledge to your audience*, you may not need to cite it.

Preparing Sources for Your Paper

If you've copied words directly from a source without changing them, these copied words must be enclosed in quotation marks. Failure to put quotation marks around copied material is plagiarism, since the reader will believe they are your own words.

Always introduce the quotation with a signal phrase of your own (see below, "For William Styron"), and insert an ellipsis if you take words out of the quote (Use "insert, symbol," in Word, then click on Ellipsis). End the sentence by crediting the source of the quote. Here are the original sentences from William Styron's memoir *Darkness Visible*:

> (Original) "The madness of depression is, generally speaking, the antithesis of violence. It is a storm indeed, but a storm of murk. Soon evident are the slowed-down responses, near paralysis, psychic energy throttled back close to zero."

Here is an example, using an ellipsis (…) to mark excised words:

> (Student Example) For William Styron, the experience of severe depression is "a storm of murk … of slowed-down responses, near paralysis, psychic energy throttled back to zero" (47).

Even when you summarize and paraphrase, you still must credit the original author. The preceding example did this in the signal phrase "For William Styron" and by listing the page number in parenthesis at the end of the sentence (47).

IMPORTANT: Never copy words verbatim to your paper unless you use *direct, essentially unchanged quotes in quotation marks*. Changing only a word or two here or there is plagiarism, and is easy for instructors to catch. To guard against plagiarism, use the following read-think-write strategies.

Direct Quoting of a Source

When using a direct quote, use the source's exact language, and always set off the quote in quotation marks. If you take words out of the source's exact language, always replace them with an ellipsis (…) Always end a quote with a parenthetical citation (often, a page number).

IMPORTANT: Never just drop quotes into your paper. The effect on your audience is jarring, and meaning is often lost. Always use an introductory "signal" verb or phrase.

Examples:

> According to Smith, "Quote" (21).
>
> Smith argues, "Quote" (21).

Refer to your writing handbook or a rhetoric text for a list of these "signal" verbs that add smoothness and sophistication to your writing.

Indirect Quoting of a Source (Paraphrasing)

Sometimes, you'll want to paraphrase a quote—to put it simply, in your own words, rather than use it verbatim. This is fine as long as you 1) get the source's meaning exactly right and 2) cite the source at the end of the sentence.

Example:

> At a July 15 press conference, President Obama said he would launch a new job creation program (20).

The Rhetorical Précis

The rhetorical précis (pronounced "pray-see") is a highly specialized, brief and useful summary you may be asked to write; it is an excellent way to summarize sources (as opposed to the simple summary outlined below). It places emphasis on the rhetorical aspects of the work, like author, purpose, and audience. The précis is based on four very specific sentences, which are highlighted in the example below:

1. The first sentence provides the author's name, the genre (article, book), the title, and the date of the work in parentheses. Then, it uses a concise verb (like "claims" or "argues") followed by a "that" phrase stating the thesis of the work. The thesis can be either quoted or paraphrased.

2. The next sentence explains how the author supports his/her thesis. Stay general here; avoid details.

3. The third sentence uses an "in order to" phrase to state the purpose of the piece. Why is the author writing this piece?

4. The last sentence names the author's intended audience.

Durland, Stephen. "Witness: The Guerrilla Theater of Greenpeace." *High Performance* 40 (Winter 1987). *Community Arts Network Reading Room Archives.* Community Arts Network. 1999. 15 February 2009. Web.

> In his article "Witness: The Guerrilla Theater of Greenpeace" (1987), writer Stephen Durland argues that the performative environmental rhetoric of Greenpeace should be considered art and should not be overlooked by the world of performance art. In order to make his argument, Durland traces the beginnings of Greenpeace's brand of theater to the "guerrilla theater" of the Yippie movement of Abbie Hoffman and Jerry Rubin in the 1960s, narrates the major symbolic acts of the organization, and interviews Action Director Steve Loper about the group's philosophy and purpose. The purpose of Durland's article is to call attention to the need for an expansion of the sort of activism through art that Greenpeace practices. The audience for Durland's article includes primarily the readers of *High Performance*, a (now-defunct) magazine for the subgenre of performance art.

Taking Notes: Summarizing a Source

A *summary*, as opposed to a précis, simply condenses the original material, presenting its core ideas *in your own words.* Use it to condense long passages that emphasize your point, and when details are not critical. Don't use "I," or evaluate the piece. Just condense.

1. In the first sentence, state the article's main claim, or thesis; begin with the author's full name, the title of the article (in quotation marks), and page numbers.

2. State the major supporting points in their original order. Omit details and examples.

3. End with the author's conclusions or recommendations.

Taking Notes: Paraphrasing a Source

A *paraphrase*, on the other hand, reflects *your* understanding of the source. It is a by-product of your learning process, and as such communicates the ideas in your own words without condensing the material. Use your own language and structure.

Paraphrasing with The Look-Away Method—Read one or two sentences over several times. Then set the article aside and paraphrase the meaning of the sentences without looking back at the article. When you are finished, review the article and make sure your paraphrase is accurate and that you didn't actually quote it.

Consider this original text from page 141 of Nicholas Carr's *The Shallows: What the Internet is Doing To Our Brains* (2010):

> **Original:** "Given our brain's plasticity, we know that our online habits continue to reverberate in the workings of our synapses when we're not online. We can assume that the neural circuits devoted to scanning, skimming, and multitasking are expanding and strengthening, while those used for reading and thinking deeply, with sustained concentration, are weakening or eroding. In 2009, researchers from Stanford University found signs that this shift may already be well underway. They gave a battery of cognitive tests to a group of heavy media multitaskers as well as a group of relatively light multitaskers. They found that the heavy multitaskers were much more easily distracted by "irrelevant environmental stimuli," had less control

over the contents of their working memory, and were in general much less able to maintain their concentration on a particular task."

Student Paraphrase: Carr makes the assumption that heavy use of brain pathways involved in scanning and skimming information online has a strengthening effect on those circuits, while pathways used for deep reading and concentration atrophy. He cites a 2009 Stanford study suggesting that multitaskers were more distractable and less in control of memory and concentration. (141)

Note: For each summary or paraphrase, always record the relevant page numbers for the article in parentheses. This will save you a great deal of hunting and work toward the end of your paper, when you prepare the Works Cited list.

Taking Notes: The Annotated Bibliography

At some point in the research project, you may be asked to create an Annotated Bibliography. For each entry, you annotate the source (write a brief summary or paraphrase), and include a few sentences on how the source is relevant to your research project. An annotated bibliography, written as you research, is an ideal reference for you to use as your prepare your final paper. Here is a sample annotation:

Ehrenreich, Barbara. "Nickel and Dimed." *Mothering.* 2001. Academic Search Complete. Web. 10 May 2011.

> In this article, Ehrenreich discusses welfare assistance in America as it applies to single parents, as well as how minimum wage affects these households. She argues against the idea that putting single mothers on welfare increases the likelihood that they will keep having children they cannot take care of. She uses statistics to prove that most people who go on welfare are hardworking individuals who just do not make enough on their own to support themselves, much less their children. This article will help me to show that while the government does offer assistance to single parents, it does not offer enough, and it offers assistance in a way that makes the general public scoff at and belittle those who accept it. This also will help me highlight what individuals who received welfare really do with the money, to build the credibility of hardworking single parents who do not abuse the system.

"Networking" by Divya Sawhney

THE WORKS CITED PAGE

You must follow the exact page format for the MLA Works Cited page. The Works Cited title is centered—no quotation marks, underlining, bold font, or italics. The entries are alphabetized by the author's name or the article name. All are double-spaced. Use hanging indentation. In MS Word, go to Paragraph, Special, Hanging, and OK, and Word will automatically indent the all lines but the first in every entry.

To help you format the entries, use www.easybib.com. Alternatively, click "cite this" on library pages where applicable. But remember—these tools are not foolproof. It is your responsibility to check the order and punctuation of all entries against the MLA Documentation section of your textbook.

The following provides a model Works Cited page in MLA style:

Works Cited

Bell, Bernard W. "Percival Everett. *Erasure*—Book Review." *African-American Review*. Summer-Fall 2003. Look Smart—Find Articles. 12 November 2006. http://www.findarticles.com/p/articles/mi_m2838/is_23_37/ai_110531707/print Web.

Booth, Wayne. *The Company We Keep: An Ethics of Fiction*. Berkeley: U. of CΛ P., 1988. Print.

Everett, Percival. *Erasure*. Hanover, NH: U. P. of New England, 2001. Print.

Gates, Henry Louis Jr. *The Signifying Monkey: A Theory of African-American Literary Criticism*. New York: Oxford UP, 1988. Print.

Hardin, Michael. "Postmodern's Desire for Simulated Death: Andy Warhol's *Car Crashes*, J. G. Ballard's *Crash*, and Don DeLillo's *White Noise*." *Literature Interpretation Theory*. (2002) 13: 21-50. Web.

"Nightmare! The Birth of Victorian Horror." Vol. 1. *A and E Home Video*. 1996. Video.

Stevenson, Robert Louis. *The Strange Case of Dr. Jekyll and Mr. Hyde*. 1886. New York: Glencoe McGraw-Hill, 2000. Print.

By now, you've been introduced to the "whys" of research writing. You've gained an understanding of plagiarism, and perhaps conducted a quick library search on your own. You've learned some important standard formats your instructor may require (like the Works Cited format), and you've learned some basics of working with sources.

Your textbook will contain many details not covered in this quick guide. Review it and all materials your instructor may assign on research strategies. Your research writing will benefit.

What Are You Looking At?
Analyzing Images

THE IMAGE/TEXT DILEMMA:
SEEING IS NOT SAYING, SAYING IS NOT SEEING, BUT…

Critical response or analysis is almost always constructed with language, and so is description of an event or object. Have you ever tried to describe something that happened and found yourself saying "you had to be there"? If so, you probably know already that language just isn't the same thing as seeing something. So, descriptive or analytical language tries to represent an image or object, but it can never completely produce the visual. There are things specific to the experience of the visual that language just cannot get at; however, if we want to discuss

"Slammed"
by William Walsh

or communicate with others about what we have seen or experienced visually, language is our most likely tool for doing so. For this reason, developing an understanding and vocabulary for what it is that you see is so important for effective analysis and communication about images and objects.

IDENTIFYING AND DESCRIBING VISUAL IMAGES: TELL ME WHAT YOU SEE...

One of the first steps in a critical analysis of images involves identifying what the image is for—is it meant to be an illustration of an event or concept? Is it an example of something?—for instance, a single, general image or object to help us understand or visualize a bigger category or circumstance? Is it perhaps a visual image or object meant to be seen for itself, like paintings or art photography in galleries and museums? Sometimes, we can rely on the image's context to help us determine the image's purpose; where we find or see the image can communicate a great deal, immediately, about what the image is intended to do. If it appears on a billboard, we can probably safely assume that it is meant to persuade and inform, or advertise, for something. If it is in a museum, or hanging on the wall of a friend's home, it is probably meant as an art object, something for us to look at and think about, or enjoy. But because we live in a visually dense culture, and because of the availability of digital technology, we often see images that are removed from their original context. In this circumstance, knowing how to ask questions about what the visual elements of the image are can help us determine what the image is meant to do. Criteria that can be useful in identifying and describing what we see include ethos, pathos and logos.

VISUALIZING ETHOS, PATHOS, LOGOS SHOW AND TELL

You should be familiar with ethos, pathos and logos from the chapter on argument in this text. (If you need to, check out the definitions in that chapter.) In visual images, ethos, pathos and logos are represented visually, rather than (only) as text or narrative elements. Two important visual elements are *form* and *content.*

Most likely, you are already familiar with form and content in written texts. For instance, you could take a glance at a printed text and determine if it is a poem, a play or prose by the way the text is arranged on the page. In this case, *form* is the *structure* that the document follows in order to reproduce a play or poem format. *Content* in written text refers to the *ideas, concepts, and objects* that make up the narrative or argument. Characters, places, times, and actions are also elements determining content. Form and content in visual images are similar to the concepts of form and content in written texts, but they are different in some important ways.

Form in visual images refers to *how the image was produced*. Is it a painting? A photograph? A digital game or film? Form is important because it specifies what an image is capable of doing.

To expect a portrait painted in the 18th century to look like and convey the same information as a photographed portrait does not make sense because of the different capabilities of photography and painting. But this does not necessarily mean that one form is superior to the other, or has more accuracy and more truth or meaning; it simply means that these are different *media* (types of production tools) and that each should be considered in its own terms.

"Welcome, Citizens of the Lofts!" by Judith Kim

MEDIA SPECIFICITY: LOCATION, LOCATION, LOCATION

As we saw with form and content, knowing what kind of media is used to produce an image is very important for getting a sense of the meaning, cultural value, and production possibilities or limitations an image has. Considering this factor means knowing and understanding different production options; in visual studies or analysis, this is called *media specificity*. Another way to consider media specificity is through location or place. Certain kinds of images, with specific kinds of production design, are found in specific and intentional places. We expect billboards to communicate by and through a limited range of content and form, for example. But when we see an image or object out of expected or routine contexts, that disruption or surprise communicates to us as well. Think of the three-dimensional cows attached to some advertising billboards. When that advertising campaign first began, the disruption of expectations, and the surprise experienced by viewers, helped make those advertisements more effective not only because they stood out visually, but also because they communicated a sense of humorous and whimsical visual cleverness. So, the company created two kinds of positive response and generated more business for itself.

FOR DISCUSSION:

Examine the image below. In small groups or as a whole class, discuss the following questions:

1. What medium was used to produce this image? What capabilities does it have?

2. What can you tell about the form and content of this image?

3. How does the image disrupt the audience's expectations?

4. How is the location of the image an important part of this disruption?

"Occupied" by Nnerika Adibe

Ethos: "Just the facts ma'am…"

In a written argument, ethos constructs the credibility of both the writer and the text, and visual ethos works to accomplish the same thing. Good examples of visual ethos include photojournalism and documentary filmmaking—news media photography and film or television documentaries have the cultural value they do only when and if we trust that the photographer is showing us an accurate representation and not (only) the photographer's own opinions or viewpoints. The visual form and content of the image provide the visual criteria for assessing the ethos of both the photograph and the photographer.

An author creates visual ethos by emphasizing the objectivity of both photographer and the image. By minimizing or eliminating artistic or interpretive form and content, and presenting content that is factual or verifiable, the photographer or filmmaker establishes her professional objectivity. In other words, these genres try to present images in a style that reproduces what we would see for ourselves if we could see the person, place, object or event ourselves and through that autheticity, the genres argue for the trustworthiness of the photographer or filmmaker.

THINK ABOUT IT…

Can you think of other instances in which a visual image is seen as an extension of, or equal to, the credibility of the person(s) who created it?

What might be useful and/or problematic with this kind of expectation?

Is it possible for a photograph to be objective? Why or why not?

Pathos: Feeling is Believing (sometimes…)

Pathos is the visual quality, (form and content), that causes us to respond or react emotionally rather than logically or objectively.

In the instance of documentary film or photography, even though emotional reaction is not typically the main purpose, (as we saw in the previous section, ethos, or objectivity, is far more critical), it is not unusual for these films to intentionally use some elements of pathos. For instance, nature and science documentaries can generate an emotional response from us by showing us baby animals—ducks, or dolphins or even dinosaurs—or by using special filming techniques that can capture sweeping aerial views of the grandeur of the Rocky Mountains or vast and incomprehensible stretches of our own galaxy, all of which can generate feelings of awe and wonder.

Documentary films that focus on human experience or crisis, like *Born into Brothels* or *An Inconvenient Truth,* have an emotional appeal as part of their argument as well. Even though this type of documentary is intended to inspire action, increase awareness or educate us about important environmental issues, pathos makes it more likely that we will experience the filmmakers' commitment to the represented issues, making it possible that we will become involved as well.

THINK ABOUT IT...

If ethos (reliability and objectivity) proves vitally important for some kinds of images, why would pathos be intentionally included and used to support the argument or statement?

Usually, it is fictional, or narrative, film that relies most overtly on pathos. However, some narrative films also seek to inspire, inform or educate. I think of an example or two and identify what strategies (form and content) the film uses to inspire, inform or educate the viewer. How would you define or describe that form and content? (Is it scientific evidence, historical record, sociological data, etc.?)

Logos: Numbers don't lie (right?)

Logos in a documentary film concerns the information that motivates or inspires the filmmakers, as well as the information the film seeks to communicate to the viewer. An awareness of climate change and a desire to inform the audience about ecological concerns come from data or scientific texts; the filmmakers use that information and the visual elements that will communicate the information to viewers in order to construct and organize the film's content.

These two concerns, the information/data and the visualization of the information/data, work together to generate the viewer's understanding of the film's focus and argument. Logos is crucial for producing and supporting the film's claims. Including visuals of scientific data and sources that can be vetted, or verified; having experts in the field as consultants for the film; supplying visual images as evidence or phenomena are all examples of visual logos. In terms of content, then, logos might be supplied by interviews, a narrator describing data or information while related images are shown (this is called a *voice-over*), or by including footage of people, places or events from other sources (news media, historical archives, or witness/bystander recordings of events).

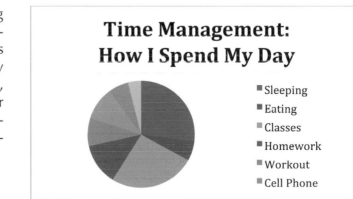

Time Management: How I Spend My Day

- Sleeping
- Eating
- Classes
- Homework
- Workout
- Cell Phone

THINK ABOUT IT...

How might form, in the instance of information media, influence content? Think about documentary and/or news media interviews you have seen and describe what the interview looks like; what is in the shot (what you see on the screen)? How is it set up? Where is the camera? Where is the interviewer?

What other kinds of visual communication emphasize logos?

The public and commercial spaces that we frequent also make use of visual argument through ethos, pathos and logos.

Analyze the image above and identify/discuss:

- What are the visual objects and elements that you see?
- What colors, shapes, sizes and contrasts are there?
- How are these things arranged?
- How does the space encourage or restrict movement?
- How do form or content support the visual and physical space?
- What might these elements indicate about the uses of ethos, pathos, and logos?

ANALYZING A VISUAL IMAGE: BREAKING DOWN THE CONTENT

The purpose of this assignment is to practice isolating, describing and assessing the visual elements that help construct an image.

1. Select a color image from a magazine, a book, or a website.

2. Scanning the image, write down what you think the image is about or what it is saying.

3. Make a list of the content (the objects that you see) and note the location in the picture plane of the objects (i.e. bottom left, left of center, etc.).

4. Make notes as well of the composition: which images are larger, smaller, which are in the foreground, background, etc.

5. Describe how the images are rendered—which ones are in sharp focus, which are in softer focus, etc.

6. Describe and list these elements in the image (refer to the Glossary of Art Terms at the end of this chapter):
    a. Color
    b. Contrast
    c. Value
    d. Style or Genre

7. Note any other significant elements (is the context important? Is it an image of an historical event or person(s)?).

8. What is the most important or the most dominant visual element in the image?

9. Looking at your first assessment of what the image says or does, identify and explain how the visual elements you have identified and described helped you "read" the image. Has your opinion of what the image says or does changed after looking more closely at the elements? If so, how?

10. Revise your original response so that it includes the visual elements that create the image's message or meaning. Use visual terms and concepts to describe how the image is constructed to your reader.

"Showdown" by Judith Kim

VISUALIZING ETHOS, PATHOS AND LOGOS: EYE SPY

In addition, and just as in the rhetorical strategies of written argument, an image or object almost never depends only on one of these elements. As the examples of documentary film and photojournalism show us, usually a complex system of supports for the argument exists, and those supports are usually an intentional production of all three. However, the presence or influence on one may be minimized, hidden or accidental. Typically, one component will be more visible, or more easily identified. But sometimes, one or more components become apparent only when we use critical readings and tools to analyze how the form and content work together to produce visual claims or arguments.

FOR DISCUSSION:

How does the photograph of the police officers and protestors above use these elements to create a dynamic image?

VISUAL CONDITIONING AND CONDITIONAL VISUALIZING:

What You Get is What You See

When we consider visual images from a critical perspective, we can begin to see how arguments are constructed using visual elements and components. However, we may not recognize as easily the ways in which we favor certain ways of seeing over others, or how we may miss visual meanings because they don't show, or show in an expected way, the things that we are taught or encouraged to see. For this reason, we need to be aware of the expectations, exclusions, and biases reflected and revealed when visual images are thought to be acceptable, correct, or "true," and when they are felt to be inappropriate, problematic or "bad." How we think or feel about visual images and objects can tell us a great deal about ourselves and our communities, belief systems, and cultures. For instance, the information you are reading reflects a very particular, and therefore limited, perspective on how the visual functions and how it can be analyzed. Just as media specificity restricts or enables some kind of elements but not others in an image, *cultural specificity* restricts and enables, or privileges, some kinds of analyses over others. Keeping this in mind will not only allow you to create more effective critical responses, but will make you more aware of the rich variety and multiple meanings of images. It will also give you a sense of how communities, cultures and contexts tend to produce some kinds of images, but not others.

This photograph is a good example of cultural specificity. What do you need to know about local culture to understand the content in the image? What might someone from another place or time not understand?

"Bleed Blue" by William Walsh

For instance, photographs are widely accepted if not required as evidence in legal and judicial situations (bystander videos of natural disasters, criminal behavior or social/political conflicts), as crucial elements in scientific or historical understanding (ultra-sound imaging of fetuses or fossil records embedded in rock formations, space probes that take and send photographs of other planets or solar systems, archives of historical photographs), and as objects that capture and preserve our own change over time (school pictures, driver's licenses, and the family photo album). All of these uses of the photograph indicate a cultural bias towards one kind of image over others. Photographs are not the first, or only, or even necessarily best, record of an historical or natural record. They *are* the most recent technology for recording people, events, and places.

Before photography, other images such as engravings, paintings, sculptures and sketches served the purpose of recording and preserving events and people, and they were, in their time and context, felt to be sufficient and accurate for those purposes.

Today, we are much more likely to see these kinds of artists' drawings and renderings as too subjective, too dependent on the individual artist's interpretation, to actually support demands for truth or evidence or data. (One exception to this is the courtroom artists' drawings that are still accepted as objective representations of court proceedings in which cameras are not allowed).

The notion that the camera acts without prejudice, that it records objects mechanically and without human interference (it does not respond to or act in consideration of what we think or want or feel when it captures an image), is in large part the reason that we believe photographs have a special ability to show us reality or the truth. However, if you have ever used photo imaging software, or are aware that this technology is widely available and routinely used in all kinds of situations, you know how easy it is to change photographic content and thus change its "meaning" or truth claims. Before the advent of digital imaging software, changing the content of photographs, especially to the degree that it could fool forensic or investigative photographic experts, was very difficult and something that only very skilled professionals could do. It is pretty easy now for even the most casual user to manipulate the content, delete objects or features, or add to the content, of digitized photographs. This new technological ability causes issues for us about what photographs do and mean, now and in the past. One of these issues concerns the photograph's *indexical* quality or nature.

Indexicality, the Indexical, and Photography: Where there's smoke…

Indexical qualities, or *indexicality*, describes a kind of cause and effect circumstance. Smoke rising from a chimney indicates a fire in the fireplace, the movement of a weather vane or wind chimes indicates the presence of a breeze, and the tracks of an animal in snow indicate that the animal was there at some point. In this way, indexical images or objects are both *visual objects* that we apprehend through our senses (we see and smell the smoke, we see and hear the chimes, we see and follow the tracks) and *active recordings* of a process or occurrence (the fire burns, the wind blows, the animal has moved over a space). They are thus imprints or records of events or moments. The technical aspects of photography—light reflected from an object is directed through the camera lens onto a surface covered in light sensitive chemicals (camera film)—can be understood as a similar kind of cause and effect. In order for the reflected light to act on the film, the object and camera had to be present at the same time, on a specific and definite day and place. It is this quality that has allowed us to accept photographs as evidence or data.

DIGITAL IMAGING AND DIGITAL IMAGES
PICTURES DON'T LIE... (BUT PEOPLE SOMETIMES DO)

With digital imaging technology, which does not rely on a chemical reaction to reflected light or that the camera and object be present together, the indexical relationship between camera and objects, or photographs and events, is not a given. We can no longer assume that the photograph shows us what was, captured at a unique and definite moment by an objective mechanical apparatus. Just as we have doubts about artists' renderings of historic events or people, newer imaging technology is causing doubts about the objectivity of older but still-in-use technology. Much of our individual and cultural histories are preserved and represented to us by photographic records and archives. When we place the photograph in

the context and history of other images, and consider the cultural, political and historical privileging of some visual products over others, we can begin to see how our interpretations and beliefs about how and what visual images produce may *mean* truth or objective fact, but cannot be held to *be* truth or objective fact. Because of this difference between meaning and being, having a critical awareness of visual images can let us see how we interpret our past, present and our future from images. Developing a critical capacity about understanding and analyzing the form, content, function, rhetorical claims and strategies that images produce and are produced by gives us greater capacities for thoughtful, active, and productive engagement with visual and textual communication options and needs.

Methods for Analyzing Visual Texts/Images: Just Being Critical

Visual analysis can be organized into three broad areas of research and critical study: focus and use, meaning and purpose, and history and networks.

Focus and Use

Focus and use tell us about the function of the image. For instance, a pie chart, graph, wordle or prezi are visualizations of data; the focus and use (understanding of complex or large amounts of information) determine to some degree the visual qualities or form of the visual image. Images that are used to communicate complex or large amounts of information are typically very precise and simple in terms of lines, shading and colors.

The purpose of this kind of visual representation is to make the information more easily understood, not more complex or dense. The form (simple lines, shapes, colors, etc.) reflects this intention and the content (complex or large amounts of information) creates the need for the form. The analysis of focus and use helps us understand why and for what purpose an image was created, and allows us to assess whether the image and the production choices communicate the information in such a way that something abstract (percentages or averages of something) or too large or small to see (populations of people or animals, or microscopic organisms in water) is not only made visual but visualized by the viewer.

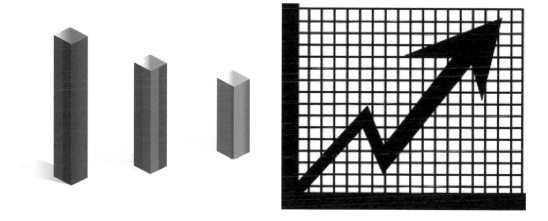

Meaning and Purpose

These two criteria may sound very similar or even the same as focus and use, but keep in mind that focus and use identify and describe the formal aspects of the image—what does it do and how does it do what it does? *Meaning and purpose* are questions about what effect or response the image creates and how that effect or response is created. Another word for this concept is the affect of the image.

INDIVIDUAL AND CULTURAL AFFECT AND IMAGES

Sometimes *affect* is immediately apparent to us; for example, there are visual images that immediately make us laugh or cry or feel afraid. Advertising provides an excellent visual space for seeing how affect works on both an individual and cultural level. When advertisers employ baskets of puppies in soda commercials, charismatic and energetic spokespersons in infomercials, everyday "Janes" and "Joes" in exercise before-and-after ads, or, conversely, celebrities in weight loss programs, affect is working to create an emotional or psychological response in the viewer. While the surface message might be an attempt to appeal to our identity or sense of who we are (or want to be), the emotional and psychological appeal is aimed at our desires for belonging or connection, or the feelings we associate with cuddly animal babies, and these appeals rely on some level of generalized, uniform cultural attitudes or sentiments. As you can see already, this general and uniform response is possible because of cultural specificity—our culture has dominant, widespread, and shared belief systems and values that, even if you don't personally share in the affect of images associated with those belief systems and values, you can recognize because you are part of this culture. This means too that advertising images in other cultures may not use the same kinds of affective images as we do. Looking at what kinds of images provide successful advertising images can give us some insight and understanding about a culture's or historical moment's value systems and belief structures.

The purpose of a visual image is reflected in the visual elements and compositions used to create its affect. Cuddly kittens selling fabric softener are meant to create both a tactile association (kittens are fluffy, warm and soft, just like your towels will be if you use this fabric softener) and an emotional association: (kittens="aawwww, cute…"=fabric softener).

"Luke" by Marissa Graziano

Meaning is not about a moral or lesson that might be part of a visual image or narrative (although the kinds of images used to instruct or direct behavior can be analyzed for their meaning and purpose). Rather, meaning, as a critical approach, tries to understand and identify how the visual image creates and reflects the way we make sense of our world, our experiences and ourselves.

Sometimes, an image that has been pretty limited in its distribution suddenly becomes really popular and effective. Have you ever wondered why there are so many zombie films, television shows, and games recently, or why so many teen and young adult romantic dramas involve vampire/human couples? Many more examples of visual images and visual elements fit with this kind of questioning: Why is one kind of jeans, or hairstyle, or interior color scheme in restaurants or

hospitals or kitchen appliances popular? In addition, these visual elements change over time and can come to stand in for, or reference, specific cultural moments. In the case of kitchen appliances, you might suspect that manufacturers manipulate our emotions and psychologies to sell more appliances—if your toaster is not the "in" color, what does that say about you? (and you would be right, to some degree)—but just a few years ago the idea of "cute" or "comic" zombies would have seemed pretty unlikely. What's more, it is not unusual for cultural objects to come from non-commercial spaces of production.

Youth subculture greatly influences the kinds of images and objects we recognize and respond to—the flower-power, psychedelic motifs of the 60s; the punk influenced ripped and safety-pinned garb of the 70s and 80s; and the flannel-shirted grunge look of the '90s all came from youth subcultures. So, important images are generated from many different areas of any culture.

Analyzing political, economic, social, and cultural *exigencies* (the needs and demands of specific situations, communities and moments) is useful for connecting and understanding the visual images and objects that are associated with those times, spaces and places. Meaning is the critical understanding that we can derive from looking at both the visual image and its moment of production and consumption.

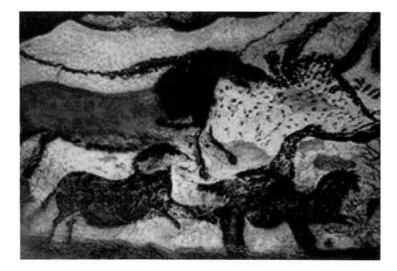

Looking at the Past to Understand the Present:
Hindsight is 50/50

You may noticed that the subheading above differs from the saying commonly used about seeing past events more clearly from a present perspective. (The original malapropism[1] comes from Yogi Berra, an American baseball figure). The traditional saying is that "hindsight is 20/20," meaning we see with accurate and unimpaired vision when we look back on past events from our current vantage point. But that is not necessarily the case, and for critical analysis, it is definitely not an accurate assumption to make. Saying instead that our ability to "see" historical events, circumstances and people is "50/50" acknowledges that we have just as much chance of getting it wrong as we do right, and that it is the historical and cultural distance that creates this possibility. The reasons that we need to be aware of the limitations of our hindsight are several: we cannot occupy the past, be part of the moment that generated it or be free of the influence those images have on our present cultural moment. And even as a person who lived in the cultural moment of an image, that person is a single individual, and therefore not representative of every other member of a time and place. We are all also part of a larger culture and influenced by the larger culture in terms of how we see and think and feel about these images. While this influence does indicate the subjective quality of meaning, it does not reduce meaning to individual opinion, bias, tastes, inclinations, or prejudice.

If we keep in mind the limitations around our objectivity, and develop the critical viewing and research skills that can help inform our understanding, we can add our own perspectives to the analyses and understanding of cultural images.

As writers and researchers, we contribute to the conversation about images through careful observation, by informing ourselves of what others have written about our research interests, by critically analyzing both our own ideas and

---

[1]Absurd or humorous misuse of a word, especially by confusion with one of similar sound. Adjective: *malapropian* or *malapropistic*. http://grammar.about.com/od/mo/g/malapterm.htm

those of others, and by offering our response and perspective. We cannot exhaust everything there is to see and say about an image, nor can we generate one, universal and definitive explanation or critique of an image. Your job as a critically engaged writer is to get a sense of where your reading and critique fits with the critical history and reception of an image. Not that your response needs to agree or reflect others' opinions, but you should be able to account for other responses, and explain why you respond as you do. In this way, you are offering a thread of communication and discussion to an ongoing dialogue. Think of it as a more formal construction of the kinds of discussions you probably have with friends or family after watching a movie or playing a game together. In the best of situations, everyone gets a chance to speak and respond, everyone's opinion is considered (and perhaps agreement or rejection of these opinions happens, but with considerate and open-minded engagement), and this kind of conversation extends the enjoyment of watching the movie or playing the game.

History and Networks of Images

You have most likely read a poem, play or novel from other cultures and times. You might have had some trouble interpreting the way sentences were constructed, or words were used, or how themes or concepts were developed. You may have spent time with classmates or instructors or friends figuring out the meaning or import of these phrasings and usages in order to understand more fully the meaning that you were constructing as you read and discussed the work. Even if you did not read multiple texts from any given era or culture, you have a sense that the ones you did read are part of, and reflect to some degree, a way of using words and ideas that were part of writing practices or even ideals at the time the work was produced. Visual images have the same kind of *contexts*, not only to other visual objects of that particular place and time, but to the cultural, political, and technological capacities of that locale.

There is a huge existing store of visual images, and we add new images constantly. Because of the effectiveness of visual images in communication and due to the speed and ease of (digital) production and distribution, older visual images are often embedded in newer ones. This use of culturally and historically recognizable or important images is called *appropriation*. Being able to recognize how a current image appropriates an image from the past can help you identify its connection with the history of images and also analyze how its meaning is supported or enhanced by using the earlier image. An example of this kind of appropriation shows up in several James Bond films.

Ursula Andress, Halle Berry and Craig Daniels have all struck poses that recreate or reference the central image in Botticelli's *The Birth of Venus.* Botticelli's Venus is a very blonde, blue-eyed and fair-skinned, western idealization of beauty. Ursula Andress would seem to continue in that tradition, but replacing Venus with Halle Berry and Craig Daniels gives us new or different ways to think about concepts like "ideal" and "beauty." As viewers, when we make the connection between the Botticelli painting and the film characters, we get a more complex and interesting way to see the painting, the characters, and the films. The practice of generating or creating meaning or more complex meaning through the relationship images (and texts) have to each other is called *intertextuality*.

Appropriation is not the only instance of intertextuality. Distinguishing how other images or image elements are used to make new images is also important for making effective critical analyses of visual objects.

Leonardo Da Vinci's *Mona Lisa* and Grant Wood's *American Gothic* are images that have been frequently reused or reinterpreted. Some of these appropriations provide examples of *parody, pastiche,* and *allusion* or *homage.*

Parody repeats or copies enough specific, recognizable elements of the original in the new work that the original is obvious in an image. Parody creates ironic or humorous effect by distorting or adding content or form that changes or plays off the original meaning.

Pastiche uses a well-known image's formal elements or content in order to produce new readings of the work. By isolating and focusing on those elements, a new image can create richer meaning within its own content and add to understanding of the older image.

An *allusion* does not necessarily reproduce form or content, although it might, but instead references another work. *Homage* is similar to allusion, and found more often in film or music rather than paintings or photography; homages are a way of honoring and recognizing an influential or accomplished work or individual within the content of a visual text. In *The Untouchables* (1987), the sequence in which a woman struggles with a baby carriage as she tries to climb a long staircase is an homage to a sequence called "the Odessa Steps" in *The Battle Ship Potemkin,* a film made in 1924 by Sergie Eisenstein, an important and foundational film director.

Understanding the differences between these kinds of reinterpretations or reproductions and the Botticelli example concerns *genre* and *media specificity.*

Genres are categories of texts, images or objects that share similar, specific, and identifiable characteristics and qualities. If you have ever walked in on a movie after it has started, or paused on a channel without knowing what was on, but could still tell category of movie or program you were seeing, you are aware of how genre works. Visual elements like lighting, narrative, characters, camera and editing techniques, and music provide clues for figuring out the film's type. Those identifiable elements are characteristics of genre.

Media specificity is the idea that there are certain capacities and limitations for any of the production means, or media, that you might use to create texts or images. For instance, what you can see visually in a reproduction or digital version of an image is limited to the reproduction's media, and some information and qualities that are in the original image are lost. Photographs of sculptures are good examples of this concept—sculptures are three-dimensional objects but photographs or digital images are two-dimensional. The size of the sculpture, its location, and its physical features are all changed by the medium in which it is reproduced.

In parody, pastiche, allusion and homage, the connections between the original image and the new image are often made by using the same or similar media. With Botticelli's *Venus* and the Bond examples, the painting's content and meaning are reconfigured as *filmic images*. Another way to think of this concept is in terms of form and use, and meaning and purpose: in the case of parody, pastiche, etc., form and use are emphasized in order for the interpretation or reproductions to work successfully. In the *Venus* images, meaning and purpose are more important for the reference to work.

CREATING CRITICAL ANALYSIS: USING CRITICAL CRITERIA TO DISCUSS VISUAL IMAGES

The following assignment will help you apply the critical criteria in this chapter to images.

For this assignment, choose an advertisement image, either in print media or on-line.

Write an analysis of how ethos, pathos and logos are used in the ad; be sure to use visual terms and criteria for identifying how these elements work in the ad.

Describe how focus/use, meaning/purpose and image history and/or networks support the ad's message. Describe how and where these criteria intersect and reinforce each other. Again, remember to identify and describe the visual elements in the image rather than only describing the narrative or action.

To give you an idea of how this analysis is done, see the Analysis Chapter for excerpts of Jocelyn Lopez's analysis of a Frappuccino ad.

Rewind

You may have noticed that there are some similarities in the critical methods and concepts discussed thus far. Logos and focus/use address the information that visual images convey—data, numbers, scientific or mathematical theories, are often expressed visually in a way that emphasize focus and use. Pathos and meaning/purpose are found in the emotional content and viewer response to the images (baby animals in documentaries and fabric softener commercials are an area of similar visual affect). Histories and contexts of images are similar concerns in both ethos and locating the image's relationship to other images. Knowing where and how a documentary or photojournalistic image was created proves important in a similar way to knowing the production history of a current or past image. Seeing how these methods and concepts work together or reinforce one another can be very helpful for increasing your understanding about how to develop and use critical criteria.

However, keep in mind that these are starting places for you to begin your own thinking and research. You should develop the skills to use these methods interchangeably, and to do that you need to become familiar with how and where they work best. But critical analysis is not like math or science, and these methods are not like equations or formulas. Critical analysis is a skill that can be developed and strengthened, and it can become an intentional, reliable way to engage with information. Most of all, it is a creative act—you are *producing*, through skill, dedication and practice, a response to the visual images and objects that interest you. You may be asked to produce your own visual statement or argument by your instructor. Knowing how to analyze other images, understanding how they are constructed and why (or why not) they are effective will help you make decisions about how to do that as well.

Writing about the Visual: Show Time!

When your assignment is to analyze or produce a visual argument, your instructor does not want a plot summary of a film or list of content in a photograph. Instead, you need to identify and explain how visual elements work together to produce our understanding of what we are seeing. At no point in a horror film, for example, does the director stop the action, step into her own film, look at the audience and say "Right now, see, she's really scared and she doesn't know the monster is right behind her in the closet!" And yet, the director communicates to us exactly that emotion. But she does it visually (and in the case of film, with sound as well) not by talking us through what her intentions are or what is going on in the film, but by visually constructing the information we need to see and understand so that we follow the action and meaning of the film. You need to analyze visual objects on these terms as well. Tell your audience what it is that *visually* makes the argument.

The best way to learn to develop this skill is to *practice*. You might try watching a movie or television show with the sound off. Can you figure out what is going on? How are you able to get a sense of the action or narrative? Another good way to practice is to watch one sequence of a favorite and familiar film multiple times. Watching it frame by frame can help you *see* the number of cuts or edits, the kinds of shots used and how the editing moves (fast or slow for instance). These film techniques communicate information to you visually.

SLOWING DOWN MOVING IMAGES: ANALYZING FILM AND TELEVISION IMAGES

The purpose of this assignment is to help you become more aware of the film techniques that communicate narrative, action, and/or character.

You will need to view the film or television program in some format that will allow you to control the speed and direction of the moving image (fast forward, reverse, image by image, etc.) so make arrangements to have access to a DVD player, a computer, or another similar viewing device.

Choose a film or show that you are familiar with (the better you know it, the better this will work for you). Choose one sequence, 2-3 minutes long, and after watching it once, describe what is going on in the sequence. Is it establishing a character's identity or personality? Is it setting up or resolving action or plot? Is the dynamic tense, or romantic, or suspenseful?

After writing down your description, go back to the beginning of the sequence and count the number of edits; how many times does the shot change? Does the point of view change? Does the lighting or framing change?

After making notes of these film techniques, describe the changes you saw and describe how they communicate the action or narrative. Does the editing move more quickly or slowly to increase or decrease tension? Does the lighting change to indicate a change in sentiment, or understanding? How does the sound (the music or sound effects) work to support the affect of the film?

(The questions above are for getting you started so don't limit your analysis to them—include and describe as many filmic and visual elements as needed to effectively analyze the sequence)

Review your initial description and revise it so that the visual elements you identified form the major part of your analysis criteria.

You might also spend some time looking closely at other visual objects. Try looking at advertisements from a visual criteria perspective, or the interior of a coffee shop or retail store. Books on genres or periods of art are also very useful for developing an eye for the elements of genre or art styles. A book on a single artist can make you aware of how an artist's work changed over time, or what her influences were. Visiting a museum, gallery or art show is an excellent chance to see how different media look or are used, and how different artists can use the same medium in very different ways.

Most importantly, practice, practice, practice! If you are writing about a film, or several films, you will need to take the time for multiple viewings and for taking notes while you view. If you are writing about ads or specific art genres, you should study the images with the same focus and commitment you would for studying any other text or focus in any other class.

And, last but definitely not least, remember that a visual image or object needs to be *cited* and *credited* in your writing just as any poem, play or book would be. If you are using images from a website, it is your job to track down the information needed to cite it properly. MLA provides several sections that address proper in-text citations as well as works cited lists for visual and digital sources.

The following is a short, and incomplete, list of some visual terminology to help get you started with your research and analysis. You should supplement this list with vocabulary and concepts from the area of visual study that you are analyzing.

Art Terms

Color—the hues or pigments in an image or object

Composition—the arrangement of objects in the picture plane

Contrast—the difference in light and dark areas

Medium—the materials or form used by the artist to create an image

Context—the place or moment that a work references or represents, or the place or moment in which the image was created

Genre—the categories of images or objects: impressionism, cubism, abstraction, etc.

Form—how something is made; the production and material construction of an object or image

Content—the objects depicted in an image

Perspective—the technique that creates the illusion of three-dimensional space in a two-dimensional image

Rule of thirds—an imaginary division of the picture plane by three vertical and three horizontal lines; the central, middle section is the least dynamic of the areas and the composition focuses on the outer sections.

Point of view—the implied positioning of the viewer through the composition and perspective in the image

Texture—the quality of surface in an image or object

Value—the degree of lightness or darkness of a color or pigment

Sources and Resources

http://www.bluemoonwebdesign.com/art-glossary.asp

http://reference.yourdictionary.com/word-definitions/art-terms-definitions.html

http://www.artlex.com/

Film Terms

Camera angle—the placement of the camera relative to the objects in front of it. High angle—camera is above and looking down on the object; low angle—the camera is below and looking up at the object. Used to convey information about power and point of view.

Close up—a small object (the size of a human head) that takes up the entire space of the frame

Composition—the way objects are distributed in a shot

Editing—selecting and ordering shots into sequences, and sequences into a narrative whole

Frame—the edges that contain the shot/photographic image

Framing—the choices made by the director about what is in the shot

Long Take—an unedited shot that goes on, continuously, for longer than usual

Mise en scène—everything that can be seen in a frame

Montage—a series of shots edited together in order to create a sense of change over time and/or connected action or narrative in multiple spaces

Point of view (POV)—a shot that presents a character's perspective

Script—the written narrative of a film including dialogue, scenes, timeline, setting, etc.

Sequence—a series of shots edited together that forms one part of the film's narrative

Shot—unedited section of film; this is the basic unit of all film, from which the film is constructed. There are multiple kinds of shots (close-up, medium, long, establishing, etc). The designations refer to how much of an object or objects can be seen in the shot.

Shot/Counter Shot—a sequence of shots edited together that shows reactions to dialogue and/or action

Tracking shot—a shot that follows the action along a horizontal line

The people who make film:

Director—the person in charge of all creative aspects and decisions for a film

Editor—the person who selects and arranges the shots and sequences of a film

Director of Photography (DP)/Cinematographer—the person in charge of filming and photography

Producer—the person responsible for the film in terms of everything except creative decisions

Writer (script or screen)—the person who creates the text/narrative version of the film, including dialogue, descriptions, scenes, events, etc.

Sources and Resources

http://www.filmland.com/glossary/Dictionary.html

http://www.imdb.com/glossary/

http://www.filmsite.org/filmterms.html

Architecture

Sources and Resources

http://www.nyc.gov/html/lpc/html/glossary/glossary.shtml

http://www.buffaloah.com/a/DCTNRY/vocab.html

http://www.aviewoncities.com/_architecturalterms.htm

Photography

Sources and Resources

http://www.photographytips.com/page.cfm/1587

http://www.betterphoto.com/exploring/allDefinitions.asp

http://www.betterphoto.com/exploring/allDefinitions.asp

http://www.digital-photography-tips.net/digital-photography-terminology.html

Photo Credits from Online Sources (in the Public Domain)

Frederick Douglass:
https://encrypted-tbn2.google.com/images?q=tbn:ANd9GcQm_j41aUXHIZc6OPDQyi_
d9TqNwp2LWA8jIiyrQ_LxigADlMa78g

Napoleon:
https://encrypted-tbn0.google.com/images?q=tbn:ANd9GcQoYlEATB8vyysvOrGAxiiLqz
AuzKwltPQ72MXwWnb97lPHYq-W

Korean Girl:
https://encrypted-tbn2.google.com/images?q=tbn:ANd9GcR-M4t5Oe-eaH3Ttay-
SNATRGSvhfd3JJh0tv6c0Eg6zi3hXuU8V

Baby Penguin:
https://encrypted-tbn0.google.com/images?q=tbn:ANd9GcQxx8WWCaTE6P2-B1kPx0N-
L6JsGo-a8fGpMPp3tyHxLAMHy5gKX

Gulf Coast Dead Zone:
https://encrypted-tbn3.google.com/images?q=tbn:ANd9GcR8jhH9PUlHVdLkuQRkoZpH
Z0KNz428pKK0lnNLqpfqWDDEeKDV

Pie Chart (by Diana Eidson)

Atrium:
http://www.public-domain-image.com/interiors-and-exteriors-design-public-domain-images-pictures/atrium-interior.jpg.html

The Great Chicago Fire:
http://1.bp.blogspot.com/_TZ4zYEBSw1I/TK-ZxwL0-yI/AAAAAAAANkA/0_krc1MJUXk/s1600/The_Great_Chicago_Fire_2.jpg

NASA Footprint:
http://www.helloari.com/wp-content/uploads/nasa-footprint.jpg

Snow Tracks:
http://farm6.staticflickr.com/5127/5322606521_f654c8e7ef_m_d.jpg,

Bigfoot/Sasquatch:
https://encrypted-tbn0.google.com/images?q=tbn:ANd9GcSXWK49hT0QeHIqOM6XegX
KAKAtzszMMxn-BXtuXVgj5jNkjzInSQ

Color Graph:
http://www.clker.com/clipart-chart-3d-column-dsfdf.html

Black-and-White Graph:
http://www.clker.com/clipart-stocks-arrow-up-chart.html

Kitten:
http://farm2.staticflickr.com/1155/540833164_566c0df363_q_d.jpg,

Atomic Age Vampire:
https://encrypted-tbn0.google.com/images?q=tbn:ANd9GcSkCa-epHXXnBEYOwgG713f-
5kZJBinVNPcaTQypxr3HAU2K1TM

Punk Girls:
https://encrypted-tbn0.google.com/images?q=tbn:ANd9GcQwukuFT0PhdJq0UY16WGb
CG5gQYBOhAuv--_V15g-T1MjGOu7u3A

Lascaux Cave Painting:
https://encrypted-tbn3.google.com/images?q=tbn:ANd9GcSc-ScL0354brXGNrwNQF-
NhRWRFQV_NCq4W-nJ0igrF4fKeLchH

1900s Woman:
https://encrypted-tbn2.google.com/images?q=tbn:ANd9GcQG6qlAMyCvi6yq8Yp8ELig5t
B7mmCEdLw8c5iJc5T2BJfbhjFIPg

Two Guys at Woodstock:
https://encrypted-tbn2.google.com/images?q=tbn:ANd9GcS5If12WuSjwl2IykCkf0F6r2Yo6UnKsZDfZkZgYs66PqmRinoy

Botticelli's *The Birth of Venus*:
http://www.flickr.com/photos/floraflorence/5525753489/

Ursula Andress in James Bond Film:
https://encrypted-tbn2.google.com/images?q=tbn:ANd9GcQafSr0ruAyqzW36AoA5uwISuTDc2V0VWg9PmQMqZgOUWbacH_UCg

Grant Wood's *American Gothic*:
http://farm8.staticflickr.com/7069/6931149292_a5af4ffd3e_d.jpg,

***American Gothic* Parody:**
https://encrypted-tbn0.google.com/images?q=tbn:ANd9GcQmFuZvGd_jiVzMLaa9sH-3Cew5FKdSkHixmso_fQK64jOuPtXjV

Legos Version of DaVinci's *Mona Lisa*:
https://encrypted-tbn3.google.com/images?q=tbn:ANd9GcTiJDgsxUHjDSVzaO5mbourhfZHnhx4n4SkQHx3xL0rxXq-h0gSfg

New Media Literacy

How do digital practices—mostly, the things that we do when we interact with the Internet—affect our lives? We can look to our economic activity and observe how frequently people shop, pay their bills, and manage investments online. We choose restaurants, concerts, and films based on feedback that we receive digitally from both advertisers who don't know us and friends who do. Most of the work that you did to apply to this university probably happened online. Our culture is no longer fascinated by the existence of the Internet; in fact, we often take it for granted. However, the last five years of collaborative, social activity on the Internet is a subject of intense academic study right now. As the Internet shifted from a location where one could receive information to a place where one could participate in information, a new model of activity developed. This transformation is commonly called Web 2.0, a term that describes how online users have moved from consumption to production of content. This chapter will address how that consumption and production relates to the act of composing in your ENGL 1101, 1102, and 1103 courses at Georgia State University.

Let's begin by defining terms. "New media," we can loosely assert, are the host of programs, apps, and collectives that enable and produce participatory digital culture. Television and radio do not count as new media, but as soon as we say that, we see the boundaries of these concepts dissolving. Maybe you watch a program on NBC (a TV broadcasting network that started as RCA in 1926), but you watch over an ATT connection that is also your pipeline to the Internet. You might watch it on a television that, with one click, can enable browsing on the Web. More to the point, you might watch that NBC content on Hulu, the website that streams NBC's television content on the Web. Movies are technically not "new media," but they are certainly embedded in the culture of the Internet, considering the millions of people who stream movies from Netflix or watch movie trailers on YouTube every day. New media certainly interacts with and cross-pollinates with "old media" (as silly as that sounds), but the defining quality of new media forms is engagement. Pre-Internet media produced static content; new media invite and depend on user content.

"Disregard Series #3" by Mike Black

FOR THOUGHT AND DISCUSSION:

Consider how the Internet delivers new media to users who may or may not have the digital experience to interpret those media.

This section will address how three terms in digital culture have an impact on our work as critical thinkers and composers. We will examine *attention*, *participation*, and *audience* in the context of new media and the composition classroom.

ATTENTION

Early computer users sat down to their boxy towers with specific tasks in mind—"I will write an email," for instance. Increasingly, the phrase "sitting down at a computer" seems antiquated, as many of us carry the functionality of a small computer around in our pockets. Our cellphones can quickly gain and delete new programs (apps), connect us to instantaneous live conversation (Twitter or chat programs), and sometimes serve as one of our main sources of media consumption. Whether you consider your cellphone or tablet, your laptop or the desktop computer in the library's digital commons, you are rarely removed from the constant stream of multimedia content that the Internet provides. How does this stream, sometimes a flood, affect our academic work, our theory of knowledge, or our control over our activities? In short, how does being five seconds away from the Web impact our attention?

You might not find it surprising that interest in the field of neuroscience has increased parallel to our digital activity. After all, the more we learn about the world through our computers, the more we have to think about how we manage that learning and how it impacts our future learning. For example, you may think that the Internet automatically provides you with a wider lens on world events than citizens had before the Internet. Back then, radio, television, and newspaper media held control over what most people could realistically "know" outside of their own experience. With the Internet—blogs, Twitter, online newspapers, YouTube, etc.—you might be tempted to say that that control has been transformed. Now, you can learn anything that you want. However, consider what happens when we decide to follow someone on Twitter or friend them on Facebook, when we add a blog to our RSS reader account or subscribe to a YouTube channel. We are selecting or curating our own list of regularly updated media. However, if we collect that list according to our pre-existing and unexamined tastes, we are essentially avoiding Web content that we feel is irrelevant. Our curation, if not reflective, can put a boundary around our learning.

Therefore, attention involves what media we attend to. It also involves *how* we pay attention. Studies over the last several years have attempted to understand whether we learn differently when we use digital technologies. Consider the iPad or the Kindle, even the laptop; are these items ideal for reading specific kinds of material and not for others? Given that many of us work these days with several Internet browser windows up at the same time, we toggle back and forth among several sites: email, social media (like Facebook or Twitter), research, and writing. We chat with our collaborative partner who posts a link to a *New York Times* story, which links to an academic study, which in turn includes a graph that we want to drop into our presentation. That process entails several steps, but we move through them without much effort and without thinking about the implications of all of those windows, all of those platforms.

In *Net Smart*, Howard Rheingold describes what he calls "infotention": "intention added to attention, and mixed with knowledge of information-filtering … a coordinated mind-machine process" (17). Rheingold explores how digital, networked activity strains our attention in unique ways, and we should train our brain to be more focused when we do work online. Cathy Davidson suggests, on her syllabus for "This Is Your Brain on The Internet," an interdisciplinary undergraduate course at Duke University, that if the metaphor for the brain in the 20th century was the CPU, then the brain metaphor for the 21st century is the iPhone. Think about it. The iPhone works across multiple platforms and applications, it organizes networks, and it shares data in a variety of different forms. Its strength as a piece of technology is its ability to connect pathways among a variety of different programs and applications.

One of Rheingold's goals in *Net Smart* is to get people thinking about how to exercise control and focus over their attention during online work. Many of us have had the experience of sitting down "just for a minute" to Facebook, YouTube, or Tumblr and discovering two hours and multiple browser windows later that we have no idea where the time went. Consider our compulsive reaching for cellphones and our instinctive clicking on hyperlinks in a news story, just to satisfy curiosity or, deeper, to fulfill a less explicable psychological "need." In *Alone Together: How We Expect More from Technology and Less from Each Other*, Sherry Turkle studies the psychological complexity of human/computer relationships. She worries about the effect of "always on/always on you" networked devices on our ability to attend to others, to listen, and to empathize.

FOR THOUGHT AND DISCUSSION:

Our attention is demanded in our physical and virtual lives. How does a trip across the GSU quad focus our attention in ways that online activity does not?

"The Associates" by Judith Kim

The iPhone connects different media just like the brain makes connections among different languages, senses, social groups and activities. However our brain works differently from a machine in that it can pay attention to only one process at a time when we ask it to complete a complicated task. Before we begin an investigation of reading new kinds of media, it behooves us to acknowledge the challenges of that exploration. Do digital consumption and production encourage us, as Nicholas Carr writes, "to dip in and out of a series of texts rather than devote sustained attention to any one of them," or is the abundance of information beneficial, according to Clay Shirky's response to Carr? Either way, as citizens of the virtual world, investigating the question becomes imperative. Rheingold writes that "[j]ust as the ancient arts of rhetoric taught citizens how to construct and weigh arguments, a mindful rhetoric of digital search would concentrate attention on the process of inquiry—the kinds of questions people turn into initial search queries" (64).

Is paying attention or staying focused while online difficult for you? Take a minute to examine your ability to monitor your attention online by trying some of the exercises below.

- Find a friend who will let you study an "hour" of his or her online time. Take notes on where your friend goes, how many browser windows are kept open, and where links lead. Collect the raw "data" on what your friend consumes and produces (status updates, tweets, and emails count as "production"). After you are finished, try organizing the data: Into what categories can you divide the visited sites? Where did your subject spend the most time? Did activity seem linear (progressing along a logical path) or more organic or impulsive? Ask your subject to record the same "data" for you and discuss your data. What does it teach you?

- Research the Pomodoro Technique of time management and the application Focus Booster (www.focusboosterapp.com). Divide your time online into 25-minute segments according to Pomodoro and write realistic goals for what you are going to do during the time period (whether or not for academic purposes). How successful were you at staying on task for 3 different time segments?

- Read John Tierney's article "When the Mind Wanders, Happiness Also Strays" in *The New York Times* (Nov 15, 2010) and Jocelyn K. Glie's post "10 Online Tools for Better Attention and Focus" on the productivity website *99%*. Experiment with some of the tools and compose a response to both texts that is personal to your own experiences online. Do Glie's and Tierney's pieces convince you that time spent wandering online is a problem to solve?

PARTICIPATION

Our early uses of the Web involved an excited amount of access to information—information that was always available and timely. Schools, businesses, non-profit organizations, the government, any organized group could publish current data about its work. The Internet was supremely useful for checking movie times, ordering gifts, and generally just "finding things."

As time progressed, however, the Web became more dynamic. The O'Reilly Media Web 2.0 Conference, started in 2004, introduced the use of the term "Web 2.0" into common usage. "Web 2.0" distinguishes between prior uses of the Web that were mainly consumptive and the evolving ability of digital citizens to *produce content*.

Plenty of people participated in digital culture before 2005, but after that time the Internet became more participation-friendly. Facebook, Wikipedia, and Flickr, among many others, signaled a new orientation for digital culture: they encourage user-generated content. Just think—what is Facebook without the pictures and text that its users contribute? Not much. It simply provides a very attractive and share-able frame that users are happy to populate with their own content. The shift in digital culture designated "Web 2.0" is significant, even if no one really agrees when it officially started (or if it has already ceded to some new paradigm/model). Think of the stereotypical couch potato watching television for hours; this person illustrates the once passive media consumer. While being online may not appear any more physically active, online activity is now a thoroughly more interactive way to engage with media.

We can think of all this "production" actually as a new form of publishing; comments on an *Atlanta Journal and Constitution* editorial, posts to a blog, reviews of a book on Amazon, pictures to Picasa, or posting videos to YouTube represent dissemination of your thoughts. If everyone is publishing more, then everyone must be composing more; the inherent goals of First-Year composition begin here. You may not think that a "writing" class has any relationship to how you interact with the Web, but think for a minute: is there another environment, apart from the web, where you write more?

Consider Wikipedia. Perhaps the most useful participatory experiment on the Web, Wikipedia presents an open model for knowledge production. We can all contribute to its vastness. In the early days of Wikipedia, teachers often scolded students for using Wikipedia in any scholarly way (many still do, in fact). However, Wikipedia has developed from a collection of thousands of dubious, argumentative posts to millions of entries that are constantly under revision by the citizens of the Web. Wikipedia is still not a recommended source in an academic essay, but it can be a great starting point when you begin to write something new. Wikipedia entries provide links to other, more verifiable sources, and these sources provide researchers additional places to search for credible content. If managed carefully and critically, mass-crowd participation can produce infinitely useful media on the Web. The lesson we learn from Wikipedia is this: our participation, as minor as it may seem, remains important to the digital environment.

"0100101001001" by Fenton Thompson

FOR THOUGHT AND DISCUSSION:

Wikipedia, in its ability to open construction of "stable" knowledge to a variety of digital users, suggests a new culture of comment, revision, and re-imagination. What other websites offer new cultures to their users? Describe the "cultures" of these websites.

Because participation has become an integral component of Web culture, it behooves us to understand and assimilate it with our own behavior, if and when appropriate. This strategy means moving from a place of consumption (reading a restaurant review) to production (writing a review ourselves after our visit). The Internet has become such a useful collection of media *because* millions of people have taken it upon themselves to contribute to it. These discrete and numerous contributions to the content of the Internet result in enormous cultural changes to publishing, journalism, entertainment, and education. On a deeper level, they have an influence on how our culture defines "knowledge."

When we interact with the content of the Web, we encourage more interactivity and connection. When we post pictures or comments to our friends' content on Facebook, others can reply and we can start a conversation. We learn from social media, on an unconscious level, that the more we put into it, the more we get out of it. The content of our contributions to social media networks, and to the Web in general, has a large impact on response. If we type "great pics!" to a new album that someone has uploaded to Google+, we will probably not get much response. However, if we engage the photos in some creative or narrative way, other people on the network are more prone to participate with us. We might post "this picture reminds me of that time that we all met for dinner at Eats; when was that? who was there?" and with that, the digital "ball" starts rolling. Other people within the network are encouraged to answer the questions, link to more pictures, or make their own reflections.

The important lesson for the composition class, and any academic experience for that matter, is that participation increases our engagement in learning and connects to other people. Discussion boards are a common feature of digital education portals (like Blackboard, Web CT, Desire 2 Learn, etc.), and teachers who use them are encouraging engagement and community. Rather than contributing an answer that is flat, we should approach a forum like we do a conversation validating the opinions of others, making distinctions, and encouraging more response. Consider the following exchange in a hypothetical class:

Prompt: "How are the lessons of this lab useful?"

Melora: I found this lab useful because it helped me answer questions that will be on the test.

Jack: The lab was difficult because I kept getting different results from the tests. Was I doing it wrong?

Ahmad: I had the same experience as Jack, but I think that is part of the conclusion actually. If the results of the various tests are not consistent, doesn't that mean that we should consider outside variables?

Stephanie: I agree with Ahmad: like time of day, how the testing might change after multiple uses, temperature?

In this exchange, Melora interacts like a passive consumer. She gives the instructor back the answer that she thinks he is seeking. Jack, Ahmad, and Stephanie however, approach the forum with questions, suggestions, and connections. They express an intuitive value in the scholarly members of the forum community, and they participate in ways that foreground critical thinking, citation, and community. Our active and critical participation in digital environments, whether on the open Web or on classroom projects, are valuable to others. Digital culture invests knowledge sharing and knowledge production with more democratic potential, and we should take these opportunities seriously. On the next class discussion forum, peer review assignment, or information gathering trip across the Web, consider how your participation helps others. If you have something to contribute, think critically about how to provide comments in a detailed way that encourages community and interaction.

Do you have experience in the participatory culture of the Web or does it seem foreign to you? Here are some suggestions of how you can explore the dynamic capabilities of the Web.

- Choose a recent online article in *The Atlanta Journal and Constitution* (www.ajc.com) or *Creative Loafing* (www.clatl.com) that has a number of comments on it. Read through the comment chain, and post a response that agrees or disagrees with the contributions of previous commenters, citing their user names. See if you can get a discussion going between you and the community around the article to further explore the topic. Remember: engage in dissent civilly and carefully. Your goal is to encourage courteous, intelligent discussion.
- Use an online discussion forum provided by your instructor to identify classmates that share your interest in a genre of music, film, or literature. Use the open-endedness of the prompt to practice community engagement: ask others to clarify statements that interest you and try to make overt connections between your interests and theirs. Analyze the thread in order to determine who makes the most engaging comments that move others toward participation.
- Conduct a scavenger hunt related to material for your class via one social media network. Post the list of the items across the platform in a way that allows team members to share information (pictures of items acquired, interesting interactions, etc.) dynamically. Analyze which team's platform or use of the platform best supported the experience.

AUDIENCE

Audience has always been one of the trickiest issues for a writer to consider. Once, the audience for any text was limited to those who had economic access to the work, geographic proximity, and interest in the text. Whether it was the newspaper or a physics textbook, all three of those variables had to line up for us to begin to think about audience. Does someone have the money to buy the text or the ability to borrow it? Can someone physically get to where the text is located? Who is interested in this text? These questions acted as controlling factors, limiting and shaping an audience.

"Caricature" by Judith Kim

FOR THOUGHT OR DISCUSSION:

An artist often has to work hard to "find" her audience, even to the point of relocation. How does the Internet affect how a composition can find an audience?

The digital landscape has blurred or erased all of those variables. Certainly people still purchase texts, but the fact that texts *can* be obtained for free has resulted in millions of people writing content without asking for payment (consider the

realistically read dozens of tweets during a five-minute period. This kind of reading is not thorough, but it does not need to be. Twitter users quickly develop an understanding of the usefulness of the network and can discard large amounts of what they read in order to get to information that is personally or professionally valuable. Because tweets can include links to more developed content, Twitter can become a suggestion board for longer texts.

"Update" by Judith Kim

FOR THOUGHT OR DISCUSSION:

Twitter messages can reach a ready audience in seconds with updated information about a local gathering, news-worthy event, or protest. Police have used Twitter in order to keep informed of mounting protests or safety issues. What are some other professions that use social media like Twitter extensively? Why is audience an important consideration when using social media, especially in the professional realm?

The new media available to digital composers require a revised understanding of audience. When we compose for online spaces, whether a long-form blog post or a short tweet, we should do so with an appreciation for the texts' potential interactivity and reach. Active digital readers want to participate in the texts that interest them, and the best Web compositions court that kind of participation. If you are assigned to compose a digital text for your class, pose questions that invite the replies of your readers. Open questions will suffice, but your post should steer readers toward a particular understanding and ask pointed questions about it. For example, your professor may ask you to respond to a reading from the textbook in a discussion forum open to the class or compose a text that explores the trickier questions of the reading. Do not be afraid to "think out loud" about what seems contradictory in the reading or about what terminology is unclear. Discussion forums, blog posts, and tweets are never intended to be closed circuit communication. They engage in constructing knowledge through participation and engagement.

Consider how these exercises prompt you to rethink the idea of "audience" across the Web.

- Choose a regular blogger in a topic you enjoy (fashion, film, religion, politics, travel) who also maintains a Twitter presence. Spend some time researching who follows the author's Twitter account and who follows the blog. Are they the same people or are there some clear differences? Is one group significantly larger than another? What contrast exists between the topics of the blog posts and the content of the blogger's tweets? Often you will find that bloggers use Twitter to inform readers of new posts, but often the tweets will wander into different topics. Contrast the author's interaction with audience members between the blog and Twitter account.
- Read Clive Thompson's *Wired* article "How Twitter Creates a Social Sixth Sense," published only a year after Twitter's launch. Then read Katrina Gulliver's "10 Commandments of Twitter for Academics," published this year in *The Chronicle of Higher Education.* Thompson's article displays no comments (this feature has been closed by *Wired*), but Gulliver's article includes long responses. How do each of these authors attend to the idea of audience within the Twitter platform?
- Choose a YouTube video that you find hilarious—you know, one of those memes that goes viral over a two-week period— and a blog post from any regularly posting author. How do the comments attached to one relate to the comments attached to the other? Analyze the difference between the two groups. While the video may have thousands of comments, evaluate the amount of engagement each audience has with the content. How does the composer's relationship with the audience affect its engagement?

While the use of new media in your composition classroom may be new to you, many professors are beginning to use new media sites or practices. College students have always had to embrace their identities as writers to be successful. New media spheres encourage us to think of ourselves as composers, too: of conversations, of visual images, of research projects. Digital learning, whether in a physical class that uses an online portal or a hybrid or fully online course, asks us to employ skills that we have already learned and to evaluate them critically. Exploring the definitions of *attention*, *participation*, and *audience* within a new media context helps us make sense of an increasingly digital world. Gaining new media fluency is an essential part of our development as critical thinkers, writers, and composers.

FOR FURTHER READING

For more on digital media and on the production of digital texts in the Web 2.0 environment, take a look at these sources:

The Agenda with Steve Paikin: *The Myth of Digital Literacy* (video)

John Brockman: *Is the Internet Changing the Way You Think?* (book)

Collin Brooke: *Lingua Fracta* (book)
Nicholas Carr: *The Shallows* (book)
Tyler Cowan: "Three Tweets for the Web" (article)

Cathy Davidson: *Now You See It* (book)
David Eagleman: *Six Easy Steps to Avert the Collapse of Civilization* (video lecture)

Howard Rheingold: *Net Smart* (book)
Clay Shirky: *Here Comes Everybody* (book)

Sherry Turkle: *Alone Together* (book)

STUDENT WORK

To find out more about producing digital texts, please visit lds.gsu.edu. Click on "Resources," then "Student Resources," then "Technology." Here, you will find student examples of digital composition. Produce your own digital creations and share the links with the webmaster. She will add your work to our website to expand your audience.

English 1101/English Composition I

English 1101 introduces you to college writing, increasing your ability to construct written prose. It focuses on methods of organization, analysis, research skills, and the production of short expository essays. The course will introduce you to readings on issues of contemporary social and cultural concern.

At GSU, English 1101 instructors use a writing workshop format centered on the theory and practice of writing as a process. Early in the course, we introduce you to the writing workshop format, in which your small group works to revise drafts from first thoughts to final essays. Plan to hand in all drafts for every major assignment. Early drafts of an essay are often messy, which is acceptable and expected. Rest assured that your instructor and workshop group will place heavy emphasis on the revision process. Only the final draft must be clean, neat, and proofread, following MLA page format exactly (see your course handbook for examples).

Like other writing courses, English 1101 emphasizes forms of expository writing, a type of discourse that informs, explains, describes and/or defines; however, assignments will cover a range of genres, including personal narrative, descriptive essay, and researched argument paper. Most instructors take a rhetorical approach to this course, encouraging you to write with rhetorical strategies in mind. These strategies include, among other things, identifying your purpose for writing; developing a deep sense of audience awareness; learning strategies for invention, arrangement and style; and enriching your writing through awareness of ethos, logos, and pathos.

In GSU's Freshmen Learning Communities program, students progress through First-Year courses with the same group of peers, based on an area of academic interest. Most 1101 instructors relate FLC themes to the writing work of the class. However, the primary goal of all 1101 courses is to teach logical, clear writing within a specified context or situation and with a specific audience in mind.

In English 1101, we want you to think about writing as a motivated, purposeful activity, and we try to develop assignments to meet that goal. We also introduce you not only to the conventions of academic writing but to research, including

"Guitar" by Marissa Graziano

use of the library, the Internet, computer-based writing, and other means of communication. This review will include what some of us call grammar and Standard American English, and you also will learn how to develop paragraphs and effective topic sentences, use transitions for reader-friendly prose, summarize sources, draw conclusions from sources, and synthesize sources effectively.

The best 1101 survival tip we can give you, second only to the foundational importance of attendance: *Read the assignment in order to fully understand its complexities.* Many less-than-optimal grades on assignments are attributable to students ignoring or rushing this basic step. Finally, you can easily see the importance of regular attendance as part of any grade strategy. This fact barely needs reiterating. Miss class, and you will miss essential, grade-influencing activities and information. In 1101, a passing grade is C.

OUR GOALS FOR YOU: THE OFFICIAL LEARNING OUTCOMES FOR ENGLISH 1101

By the end of this course, you will be able to engage in writing as a process using various invention heuristics (brainstorming, for example). You will learn the basics of considering your audience, gathering evidence, drafting an essay, revising, and proofreading.

You will engage in the collaborative, social aspects of writing and use writing as a tool for learning by critiquing your own and others' work in written and oral formats. You will use language to explore and analyze contemporary multicultural, global, and international questions.

You will demonstrate how to use writing aids, such as handbooks, dictionaries, online aids, and tutors. You will learn how to gather, summarize, synthesize, and explain information from various sources, using grammatical, stylistic, and mechanical formats and conventions appropriate for a variety of audiences.

You will learn how to produce coherent, organized, readable prose for a variety of rhetorical situations. You will learn to reflect on what contributes to your writing process, and you will learn how to evaluate your own work.

"America" by Michelle Ha and Erin Fielding

"Aesthetically Pleasing" by Kaitlyn Winey

THE PERSONAL NARRATIVE ESSAY

In English 1101, you may be assigned a personal narrative essay. This is not a research paper, but an essay drawn from your own experiences. As a narrative, your story must progress through time and contain characters, a plot, and a setting.

In line with the rhetorical focus of the course, you will be required to articulate your purpose as a writer and an understanding of your audience. Questions like *"Should I write about this? Is it appropriate to say that?"* depend on your knowledge of your audience (example: readers) in any given rhetorical situation. In the beginning, your audience may be your 1101 class members and instructor (again, you must read your assignment sheet to determine fundamental requirements like target audience and length). You will craft a thesis for your essay, whether explicit (see the last sentence of "It Happened to Me: On How I Worked at Hooters") or implicit (unstated, but easily summarized by readers).

Most narratives use a first person narrator, with the story unfolding from introduction to conclusion. Alternatively, you may begin *in medias res*—in the middle of the action—and tell the story through flashback.

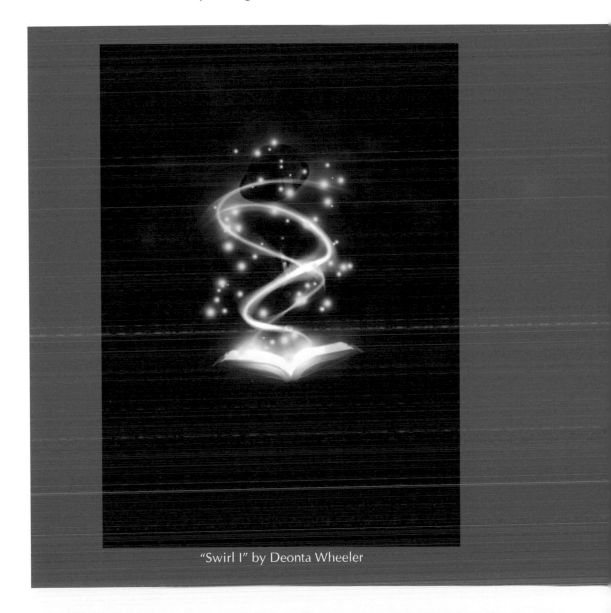

"Swirl I" by Deonta Wheeler

Just as when you tell a story orally, you must enliven the narrative to engage your audience. Description, detail, and dialogue provide the color your story needs to "pop" amid the stacks of essays your instructor will grade. It takes nerve to write an effective personal essay, which by nature exposes something about yourself. Writing workshop groups must operate on the principle of mutual respect, creating a safe intellectual environment for writers to give and receive structured feedback.

Find below a Personal Narrative Essay assignment sheet for your familiarization, followed by an essay from a student in English 1101. Here is the assignment:

ENGL 1101—Mrs. Sara Hughes

Essay #1 Assignment (Personal Narrative)

Final Typed Draft Due: Friday, September 19

<u>Requirements</u>: 3 to 5 pages in length

<u>Format</u>: All final drafts must be typed, double-spaced, in Times New Roman, 12 pt. font. Papers should have 1 inch margins. Make sure to include a "Name Block" in the top left or right corner which includes your name, my name, the class, and the date.

<u>Assignment:</u> In a **well-organized**, **focused** essay, tell a story about something that has happened in your life. Do not try to tell your entire life story; instead, narrow down your topic to one single incident (consisting of mainly **a single narrative**), and completely describe it with some underlying **purpose** (thesis), which may be a lesson you learned or taught someone else. In other words, don't let this essay merely become an accounting of a personal story. An effective or engaging approach may be to start with the action of your story and put the thesis in your conclusion. Think about the specific moments in your life where something happened that at the time may have seemed insignificant, but which turned out to be a turning point in your life. Remember to keep in mind your audience for this piece, and choose a topic about which you are comfortable discussing. Some possible topics to consider:

- A memorable experience from your early life

- A lesson you learned the hard way

- A trip into unfamiliar territory

- A time you were really jealous of someone else

- An embarrassing moment that taught you something

- A monumental misunderstanding

- An accident (vehicular or otherwise)

- An unexpected encounter

- A conflict or contest

- A time when you were really scared

Objectives: This assignment is meant to support the following Learning Outcomes outlined by the GSU Department of English for 1101:

- Engage in writing as a process, including drafting, revising, editing, and proofreading

- Use grammatical, stylistic, and mechanical formats and conventions appropriate for a variety of audiences

- Critique your own and others' work in written and oral formats

- Produce coherent, organized, readable prose for a variety of rhetorical situations

Assessment: Your paper will be evaluated on the following four criteria:

1. *Purpose*—Your purpose should be clearly stated as a direct thesis statement or at least strongly implied throughout the essay as an implicit thesis statement.

2. *Support*—You should vividly and accurately describe all of the events surrounding your experience, focusing on concrete details and strong images.

3. *Organization* –You should include narrative transitions, such as time transitions, etc. between paragraphs so that your reader can easily follow the narrative. Chronological order is usually an effective way to organize the events in a personal narrative.

4. *Language/ Mechanics*—You should always avoid major grammar errors in an essay, but in particular, pay attention to your verb tense and point of view. Try to use vivid language to evoke a strong image in your reader's head.

The following student example on the next page illustrates this assignment. Note how the page is formatted, and note that you will be expected to follow this page format when you turn in major (graded) essays:

Mollie Mason

ENGL 1101: Personal Narrative Essay

Dr. Laurah Norton Raines

1 November 2011

"It Happened to Me: On How I Worked at Hooters

and Learned Not to Judge by Appearances"

I applied as a joke. On a whim, I stopped into the restaurant to pick up an application, as I had nothing to lose by filling out some paperwork. I made the rounds to other restaurants in the area, and my need for a job reached levels of desperation. There I was, broke and unemployed, living in Atlanta. Granted, I could have made an appeal to my parents explaining I was too busy studying to hold a job and consistently attend classes, but I was too independent and prideful to ask for extra help. Grasping the forms detailing the past two years of my employment history, I braced myself for the punch line.

I remember walking into the wood-paneled entrance, the eyes of countless owls staring into my soul. *I shouldn't be here*, I was thinking to myself, a walking masterpiece of self-doubt. I was greeted by a statuesque woman who had the most beautiful hair I had ever seen. "Wait here," she said as she took my application and ran it back to the Manager on Duty, Rob. Rob emerged from the managerial closet and gave me the initial onceover. "Well, we usually won't hire anyone over eighteen for a host position. The money

Mason 2

blows and you are old enough to serve beer," he began. "You would do better as a Hooters Girl!" At this point I almost stopped breathing. ME? A Hooters girl? Impossible. I was convinced I was lacking in the two most important qualifications: the confidence to skip around in tights and my underwear, and the desire to sell my body. Waitressing? I had that down, but this seemed like a whole different ball park. I was not accustomed to showing off my pear-shaped figure; nor was I a fan of spandex, in any form. Even aside from the uniform doubts, I did not consider myself to be the dumb, tanning bed-loving picture of valley girl perfection. Rob looked over my application, occasionally asking questions until he saw my work history. "Canyons Burger Company? Do you know Sonny?" Of course I knew Sonny. He was one of the owners of the small restaurant I worked at over the past two years. "He and I opened Moe's together!" Rob exclaimed! I had officially signed my death certificate. After a few minutes of name dropping and general small talk, Rob handed me a business card and sent me on my way.

Talking to my roommate and laughing about the whole incident later, I felt a tingling sensation from my pocket. I checked my phone and saw the call was from an unfamiliar number. "Hi! This is Jess from Hooters," I was surprised to hear. "Would you mind stopping in tomorrow at two for an interview?" I immediately went into customer-service mode and made an appointment for the following day. "Great! Be sure to wear your hair down, but look *glamorous*. Wear *glamorous* makeup -- not too much, not too little --

and dress in something form-fitting and business casual." Never before in my life had my attire been assigned to me by a stranger. I was slightly offended. Nevertheless, the next day was a complete frenzy. I spent an hour abusing my hair into what resembled a chic 1940s-style curl, applying more makeup than I knew my face could carry, and digging out the Sunday best I never wake up early enough to sport. I arrived early. Too early, so I walked around the city block once or twice to work out some pre-interview jitters. I was approached by a young man selling gym memberships who gave me a name of the modeling agency he was represented by because I had "serious potential." Needless to say, it was just the boost I needed to walk into that interview as if I owned the planet.

"The blue has got to go," Jess said flatly, assessing my hair. "At Hooters, we go for a wholesome, All-American, Dallas Cowboys Cheerleader look. Unfortunately, extreme hair colors will not be tolerated. Is that going to be a problem?" I assured her that it was semi-permanent and would be taken care of as soon as possible. "Great!" she said brightly, moving on to the same speech Rob gave me about the benefit of becoming a Hooters Girl (as opposed to just hosting). She looked over my application and asked me to describe myself. Figuring I had nothing to lose (the whole situation was still surreal to me) I was blatantly honest. "Well, I go to school down the street and I think it would be really cool to not starve this semester" inspired a laugh from the woman who would decide the fate of my employment. After my brief self-description, she

Mason 4

began to inform me about the practices and the history of Hooters in Atlanta. "You will be photographed. You will be filmed. You will be in the public eye." I was not fazed. Between social networking and the perks of hailing from a small town, local celebrity was no new concept to me (at home, I'm known as the Canyons Beer Girl because of my past employment). She then moved onto the biggest topic of dread: the uniform. "This is standard; all girls must wear it and wear it appropriately." I noted the skin-tight orange shorts and the cleavage-baring tank top. *No more bread. No more bread ever again,* I thought, trying to figure out how I was to squeeze myself into the ensemble. Before I knew what I had gotten myself into, Jess concluded our time together with "We'd love to have you as part of the team! You seem smart and friendly and you would fit in really well!" My eyes glazed over with shock. I walked home in a daze clutching the paperwork she presented me with as a parting gift. I was not expecting that outcome.

The whole next week I spent time researching: reading blogs by Hooters Girls and excerpts from the employee manual, even learning how to cover tattoos with makeup (as they are not supported by the Hooters image policy). I was a mess of self-doubt. I kept thinking that I would never be like the other girls. It was mentioned in the interview that a lot of girls use Hooters as a starting point for modeling and acting careers. I did not want that. I wanted to pay my phone bill. I had a different build (pear, not hourglass), personality (snarky and smart, not shallow and dumb) and overall way of life (student, not escort) than the other women employed by Hooters. Even so, I paid for an online alcohol awareness course and ordered the required chunky white tennis shoes in hopes that I would not be fired within the foreseeable future. I received emails over the next few days with details about the upcoming orientation I was to attend. I was one of six new hires, and I was to bring my social security card along with a state-issued ID. Again, I was told to look *glamorous* and dress in a "Dressy Casual" style. I spent the two hour break between my classes that day and the orientation to perfect my look. I never felt more like a sell-out in my entire life.

Orientation was not what I expected it to be. I was surrounded by average people. Every girl sitting around me was as nervous as I was sitting a little more straight in their chairs than usual. They all had questions and concerns about the job. No one was any different than I was. We were given folders of paperwork to fill out and sign. After forty-five minutes and what seemed to be a thousand signatures later, we finally began the orientation process. We were shown a short video about the history and ideals of Hooters. We learned about the basics of uniform wear and maintenance, sexual harassment (it *is* Hooters), and the terms of payroll. After a brief restaurant tour, we received classroom and training schedules, were thanked, and left with smiles and the beginnings of an exciting new opportunity.

A week later, I began my training. I rushed to the restaurant, pantyhose under my jeans, a face full of makeup, and my hair expertly curled. Once

Mason 6

inside, I was directed to the back where the other Hooters Girls were beginning to select sections and making final adjustments to their "All-American Cheerleader/Girl Next Door" facades. I was horrified. All of these women were perfect; no cellulite or tummy pooches, immaculate hair, and there I was looking like I just walked out of a drag show. The surprising thing is, they were all so nice. Every girl was willing to help me out with my uniform, covering my tattoo, and letting me know which tables in their section were available while I was playing hostess for the night. After the longest shift of my life (nine hours, standing at the door telling people to wait to be seated), we all changed into street clothes (it's against policy to have any part of your uniform visible outside of the restaurant) and the girls were talking about their troubles. My trainer, Lauren, was worried about low merchandise sales which could lead to the end of her employment. Angie, another coworker, was dealing with a jealous ex-boyfriend. Morgan was trying to pay off some student debt before her baby is born in February. Taylor was trying to decide on a major (after seven changes). That's when it began to hit me. They have problems just like me. They all feel anxiety before they come to work, and we all deal with that in similar ways. I did not know that those women had real feelings and real problems. I did not know they were just like me.

Once my training was over, the similarities between myself and the other girls on staff became increasingly apparent. I was refilling drinks at the wait station one night when Liz asked Lauren if she wanted to share an order of

Tater Tots. "NO!" Lauren exclaims, "Potatoes are the enemy." In the dressing rooms, the girls always complained about their thighs or their (imaginary) love-handles. Marta was upset because one of her tables did not leave a tip (working for $2.13 an hour means you rely on the generosity and basic math skills of others). These women had the same insecurities I carried. The difference was that I was too afraid to point out my perceived flaws to them. Because they recognized their "imperfections," the others would help them recognize the invalidity of the claim or would help them fix the problem. Every time I walked into the dressing room, someone was helping another curl her hair or apply makeup. Hooters was not about "perfect" women serving food and flirting with the clientele; it was about teamwork. It was about owning up to your problems and letting others help. Hooters was a test of pride.

I started my employment at Hooters with as many preconceived judgments as I felt they had towards me. Even though I haven't spent much time working for the company, I can tell that it is too quickly judged. The girls serving wings and beer are not always attention seekers with "daddy issues." Often they are just trying to make ends meet. It happened to me: I work at Hooters. Next time you visit a location, remember to tip your Hooters Girl and treat her well. You do not know the life she leads outside of the orange shorts.

FOR DISCUSSION

In whole class discussion or in small groups, answer the following:

1. How did the writer meet the specifications of the assignment?

2. How does the writer establish an *ethos* (writerly credibility)? How does the writer use descriptive detail to support her thesis, which is stated in the last paragraph? What emotions does the writer convey—both hers and those of the other women? Does emotion (*pathos*) make her thesis more effective?

3. A deep understanding of the "rhetorical situation"—audience, purpose, message—is the foundation of effective and persuasive writing. In whole class or group discussion, imagine you are the writer of the Hooters piece; how would you adapt or rewrite it for the following genres? Discuss audience, purpose and message for each:

   - A speech before a national convention of conservative churches
   - A company blog for other Hooters women
   - A thoughtful email message to a teenage girl you know, a girl with Hooters aspirations
   - A motion picture script for a romantic comedy? A drama?
   - A documentary?

THE DESCRIPTIVE ESSAY

In English 1101, you may be assigned an essay designed to strengthen your creative abilities through the use of description. Creative flexibility and an eye for detail serve students well in their academic writing careers.

In a common descriptive assignment, the student 1) picks a place that intrigues her; and 2) observes it for a period of time, taking detailed notes describing the place, its people, and its sensory details (vision, sound, smells, touch, taste). Students may choose from innumerable places to observe, within the bounds of safety; students have described truck stops, domestic violence centers, VFW halls, tattoo parlors, day care centers, cemeteries, concerts, etc. The following GSU 1101 course assignment requires students to visit and describe Atlanta's Sweet Auburn Market:

Food Essay No. 2
Professor: Marta Hess
Description and Analysis
Draft Due in Class Next Week for Peer Review

As we discussed in class, a significant element in becoming a dynamic writer is learning to be an excellent observer. In this essay, you have the opportunity to demonstrate your observation, analysis, and writing skills.

Using the notes you made during your visit(s) to the Sweet Auburn Market, write a well-developed, 3-5 page essay. The first part of your essay should include the detailed observations and responses that you made at the market. While you will use your notes as a guide, I don't want only a list of your observations, but instead, I expect a narrative consisting of smoothly-written, well-developed paragraphs. Tell me in vivid detail what you saw, heard, smelled, touched, and tasted, and your responses to those things. The more details you include, the better your essay will be. If you talked with a vendor, include information about your conversation with him/her.

Next, analyze your responses by answering the following questions:
What surprised me about what I observed? Why?
What intrigued me about what I observed? Why?
What disturbed me about what I observed? Why?

Last, conclude your essay by summarizing your experience in three or four sentences.

The superior essay will be free of grammar errors, use vivid details, and demonstrate that you have made thoughtful connections between your observations and your responses. Make sure that you submit your observation notes along with your essay.

The following student example illustrates this assignment:

"Mercado" by
Judith Kim

Lauren Taronji

ENGL 1101: Descriptive Mini-Paper

Ms. Marta Hess

10 September 2011

Sweet Auburn Curb Market, Atlanta, Georgia

Sweet Auburn Market does not boast extravagance. In fact, its exposed ventilation, blinding white lights, and concrete floors give it a cold and industrial feel. The scent of fish overpowers every other smell in the building, and raw meat fills display cases for as far as the eye can see. A constant humming fills the air: a loud combination of voices, meat saws, coffee grinders, cash registers, squeaky shoes, and other various sounds; it is not exactly the place to spend a cold and rainy Monday morning.

Take a seat on an overstuffed gold couch in the market's only coffee shop, Café Campesino. This tiny café, situated in a corner of the market, offers only four tables and the couch. A heavenly aroma of roasting coffee beans lazily floats throughout the small room. The vibrantly red-haired barista, the only employee at this time of day, wears a forest green apron around her waist and quietly rings up the few customers in the shop. She takes her time preparing their drinks. Unknowingly, she creates the music of the café: grinding coffee beans, clinking metal cups, frothing milk, opening and closing cabinets, and her own voice as she calls out the drinks to waiting customers. The coffee tastes delightfully sweet, with just a hint of a bitter aftertaste. The coffee beans are organic, mixed with creamy milk and white chocolate shavings, with a dollop of whipped cream on top. The cup radiates heat from the warm liquid inside, perfect for a cold and wet Monday morning. The couch in the coffee shop offers a view of the bakery next door. Here, a smiling baker displays cupcakes, pies, brownies, flavored cheesecakes, whoopie pies, and more delicacies in glass display cases. A small girl presses her face against this glass and points to a chocolate chip cookie as big as her head, while her mother opens her purse to purchase it for her. The sweet smells of the bakery make their way into the coffee shop and weave themselves with the aroma of roasting coffee.

Over at small gathering of white tables situated in the middle of several food stands, almost every table has either a nurse on break or a college kid with a textbook. An Afro Dish restaurant serves Jamaican staples, including jerk chicken, fried plantains, oxtails, stewed goats, and other island favorites. An old woman walks up to the counter to order her food, and while she waits for a man to make her plate, one of the women behind the counter pulls out a picture of her newborn baby and hands it to the old woman. She smiles and her eyes crinkle at the edges as she warmly congratulates the waitress. She happily kisses the picture of the baby several times, then takes her food and goes on her way. At the Gyro restaurant across the way, they serve everything from sandwich wraps and gyros to pizza and ice cream. Men and women sit at the counter and converse, laughing and talking with mouthfuls of food, and these cheerful sounds mix with the noises of sizzling chicken, clinking silverware, chairs sliding across the floor,

Taronji 3

and the turning pages of books and newspapers. The smells are so numerous that they cannot be distinguished from one another.

I step out of the doors of Sweet Auburn Market to find that it is no longer raining. The sun peeks out from behind the clouds and the wind has died down to a gentle breeze. A friend and I happily chat about nothing in particular as we make our way back into the frenzied bustle of downtown Atlanta.

FOR DISCUSSION

In whole class discussion or in small groups, respond to the following:

1. What adjectives does the writer use to describe Café Campesino? The food stands? The employees and the customers? Make a list. See how many you can find.

2. How does the writer use *pathos* (an appeal to emotions or to the imagination) to paint a picture of the Sweet Auburn Market?

3. Is the writer foregrounded or backgrounded? In the second paragraph, the writer invites the reader into the Sweet Auburn Market by subtly shifting to second person ("Take a seat on an overstuffed gold couch in the market's only coffee shop, Café Campesino."), allowing the reader to vicariously experience the sensory details. In the final paragraph, the writer shifts from this "invitation" or "tour guide" mode to first person in the last paragraph ("I step out of the doors of Sweet Auburn Market to find that it is no longer raining."). Describe whether this strategy is effective (or not) as an ending for this piece.

English 1102/English Composition II

English 1102 focuses on argumentative writing and is designed to increase your ability to construct persuasive appeals based on the highest academic standards of logic and evidence. Like English 1101, this course focuses on methods of organization, analysis, and research skills, but all with the goal of increasing your ability to build scholarly arguments that synthesize your ideas with the work of other academics.

Your 1102 experience will expose you to topics that range from civic issues and political arguments to readings of literary texts or other cultural artifacts. Your instructor will also introduce you to the study of argument and rhetoric through the use of texts (including this handbook) that focus on rhetorical theory and various argumentative models. You may also work with supplemental readings from a variety of genres, including nonfiction essays/articles, documentary films, advertisements, or other texts. Additionally, in English 1102 you will practice active reading strategies, scholarly note-taking techniques, and research methods that are vital to success in any degree program.

In this course, you will try out a variety of arguments that draw on different types of sources as evidence. Although you began to research and complete other library related work in English 1101, English 1102 will introduce you to additional research instruction and guidance for particular assignments. English 1102 requires that you practice writing from sources, including basic scholarly skills like summary and paraphrase; quoting and citing sources; evaluating and drawing conclusions from sources; synthesizing sources; and other techniques for researched writing. Additionally, you will learn more sophisticated argumentative strategies, including how to develop appeals to fact or logic, values, character, and emotion; building credibility; developing effective reasoning; using appropriate evidence; and analyzing various arguments composed by other writers.

English 1102 continues 1101's emphasis on college-level and professional standards for formal prose, mechanics, and formatting. However, English 1102 focuses attention on style and usage more as rhetorical strategies; the awareness of audience, purpose, and other aspects of the rhetorical situation such as constraints and exigency that you were introduced to in 1102 are brought to the forefront in 1102.

"Fandom" by Graham Robson

OUR GOALS FOR YOU: THE OFFICIAL LEARNING OUTCOMES FOR ENGLISH 1102

In addition to the skills acquired in English 1101, by the end of the course, you will be able to analyze, evaluate, document, and draw inferences from various sources, both primary and secondary. You will also identify, select, and analyze appropriate research methods, research questions, and evidence for specific rhetorical situations. Using the rhetorical situation of text, audience, and purpose as a guide, you will learn how to perform research driven by your research questions.

You will use argumentative strategies and genres in order to engage various audiences. Of all the components of the rhetorical situation, audience is arguably the most important.

In order to be an ethical researcher and practice academic honesty, you will learn to integrate others' ideas with your own and properly document all sources.

You will learn grammatical, stylistic, and mechanical formats and conventions appropriate to rhetorical situations and audience constraints. Writing with these in mind enables you to review and practice grammar and mechanics, applying what you know about language conventions to what you write.

You will produce well reasoned argumentative essays demonstrating rhetorical engagement. This engagement means that you are *engaging* your audience in a rhetorical act: an exchange of ideas and evidence that encourages their interest in and attention to your ideas, whether you want them to consider another perspective, change their minds, or go forth in action.

Finally, and importantly, as an emerging writer, you will reflect on your writing process and evaluate your own work.

"The Girl from Ipanema" by Timothy Short

The Argumentative Essay

In English 1102, you will typically spend the majority of the semester composing assignments that entail pre-writing, a topic proposal, and/or initial research tools (like an annotated bibliography) that culminate in a longer researched paper. However your instructor chooses to structure the class, though, you can be certain that you will compose at least one major argumentative paper that employs primary and secondary sources.

What follows are two provocative examples of the type of research project and argumentative essay you will complete in English 1102. For both, you will see the assignment sheet the student received, then the complete essay, followed by questions for discussion.

Assignment Description: Final Written Argument
Instructor: Juliette Kitchens

The argument is the final element within the major research project that you have developed over the course of the semester (the exploratory paper and the proposal with an annotated bibliography are the other two major components).

The first step is to choose a topic that interests you (as you will be working with it for the duration of the class) and begin to narrow this topic to focus on a specific issue within it. The topic proposal needs to be a short paragraph describing the topic you are interested in exploring and how you plan to focus your topic (i.e. make it specific). Keep in mind that your original focus might change as you develop your exploratory paper. The topic proposal is merely to get you started on your research path and is, therefore, given full credit upon completion (if handed in on time).

For example: If you are interested in solar energy, you can narrow the topic like this:
1. First, narrow by type--Residential, rather than commercial.
2. Narrow again by type: "passive solar" (orienting buildings for maximum energy efficiency), as opposed to "active solar" or "photovoltaics."
3. Then, narrow by place: Phoenix, AZ, which has 300 sunny days per year, yet (you've noticed) very little residential solar energy.
4. Possible proposal: "New neighborhoods in Phoenix should be built with passive solar energy in mind, but very few are. Why not?"

Topic proposals must be typed and formatted according to MLA guidelines (proper heading, header, title, 12 pt. typeface, 1" margins, etc.).

The **written paper** must present a logical, well developed, and researched argument. For this paper, you will synthesize your source materials into your own argument, taking a clear stand on the issue you have chosen (note, however, that you can take a stand that strikes a balance between opposing positions). Your thesis statement should clearly state your position on the issue, and the body of the paper should support that position. Remember to use your sources as support for your argument rather than using your argument as a way to weave sources together.

Your final paper must be 4-6 pages in length and in MLA format. It must contain a correctly prepared works cited page (which does not count in your final page requirement), and it must contain **4-6** sources, **3** of which need to be scholarly (unless you can demonstrate a reason why they should not); a minimum of **3** should have been in your annotated bibliography. Remember, you can't put a source on your works cited page unless it is cited in the paper, and I will be checking for the accuracy of your citations. MLA formatting weighs heavily in the assessment of this paper, so if you have questions about it, now is the time to ask for help....

Here is a submission in response to the assignment sheet excerpted above. Note how the pages are formatted, and know that you will be expected to follow this page format when you turn in your argumentative essay:

Chelsea Johnson

Juliette Kitchens

English 1102

3 July 2010

The Case for Decriminalizing Polygamy

The criminalization of polygamy in the United States is an affront to the American concept of individual liberty, an example of a continued trend toward erosion of personal freedoms. According to *A Corrected Ethnographic Analysis* by George Murdock (1999), polygamy is practiced in more than 1,045 ethnic groups and subcultures worldwide, although in many of these, only a small number of families (often those with means and resources) practice it (89-90).

Americans should be allowed to practice polygamy in the United States freely and without fear of persecution or prosecution. State laws criminalizing polygamy are drafted not to preserve the social order but to allow the majority to dictate morals to a minority. The laws should not dictate morality, and should consider social practicality. Despite the general cultural acceptance of multiple-partner sexual relationships, undocumented polygamy in the form of multiple common law relationships, and time-lapse polygamy in the form of serial monogamy, society at large is still morally opposed to polygamy and denies polygamists' rights based solely on moral abhorrence. Any attempt to retool existing laws prohibiting polygamy must begin with an examination of the beliefs supporting these laws.

The current federally-backed state laws make polygamy illegal and a felony offense punishable by up to life imprisonment, depending on the extent to which the law is broken. Because of this law, polygamists live in constant fear of government reprisal. Those who openly live as polygamists can have their children taken away, their employment compromised, their financial viability damaged, and their freedom taken away through incarceration if they are fully prosecuted. Immigrants coming to the U.S. with a plural marriage structure can be denied citizenship and are subject to expulsion (Ling). In 2008, the state of Texas forcibly removed 486 children from polygamous homes only to have them returned after lawyers for the defendants cited the unjustified and illegal nature by which they were seized. This persecution breeds distrust of the government as well as an insular behavior that negatively affects everyone. One woman remembers her life growing up in a polygamous family as being ruled by fear of a shadowy tyrannical authority: "We were always taught to hide. We couldn't play in the front yard. When we drove somewhere, it was always 'Duck!' when you passed a police car" (Egan).

Supreme Court Justice Antonin Scalia, in his *Lawrence v. Texas* dissenting opinion, stated that he believed removing a state's ability to enact morals-based legislation would culminate in mass legalization of immoral activities, which would in turn undermine state efficacy (Greenhouse). However, the criminalization of polygamy inhibits polygamists' right to

free association, and it infringes upon their right to privacy. Justice Anthony
Kennedy assesses this issue in *Lawrence:*

> [T]he issue is whether the majority may use the power of the
> State to enforce [its moral] views on the whole society through
> operation of the criminal law. Our obligation is to define the
> liberty of all, not to mandate our own moral code. (*Lawrence*).

Polygamy is a lifestyle choice, which is protected by both the ninth and tenth
amendments (*Lawrence* 589-2). Because the federal government has no
constitutional authority over freedoms that are not specifically enumerated,
polygamy is not only guaranteed to the individual, but also is not subject to
the jurisdiction of the federal government. For polygamists, the government's
interference is analogous to the past criminalization of homosexuality (Bauer).
The hypocrisy is palpable: if a man maintains a mistress and sires illegitimate
offspring, society generally turns a blind eye in unstated acceptance, but if he
were to cohabitate with another woman besides his spouse, call her "wife" and
support her children, then he has committed a third-degree felony carrying a
penalty of zero to five years imprisonment (Ling).

Non-morals-based arguments in favor of the current laws cite the First
Amendment's appointment of the legislature to regulate "actions which [are]
in violation of social duties or subversive of good order" (*Reynolds* 164).
A commonly held belief, verbalized by Senator Harry Reid during a Senate
judiciary hearing, is that polygamists engage in abusive behavior and various

Johnson 4

types of fraud (US Senate). Some people believe that decriminalizing polygamy leads to the acceptance, by absentia, of various illegal acts (Greenhouse). When abuses are referenced in tandem with polygamy, the focus is almost always specifically on the Fundamentalist Church of Jesus Christ of Latter Day Saints, a small Mormon sect. The FLDS has received negative press in recent years, with compound raids and the prosecution of various leaders for crimes like incest. Though widely publicized, the splinter Mormon group is not the only group of polygamists in the U.S. They are, in fact, a very small, insular group of religious polygamists. According to an FBI polygamous sect investigator, "[a]t least 99 percent of all polygamists are peaceful, law-abiding people, no threat to anybody. It's unfortunate that they're stigmatized by a band of renegades" (Stumbo). There is no greater propensity for abuse within polygamous families than within monogamous families (Ulve 166).

Polygamy is not *de facto* child abuse, child marriage, forced marriage, subjugation and marginalization of women, or unique to any one religious doctrine, but it has become synonymous with those issues in the minds of many Americans. These negative, stereotypical assumptions about polygamists allow people to justify criminalizing polygamy without legitimate grounds.

With *Lawrence's* affirmation that due process liberties extend beyond morality, the primary reasons for prohibiting plural marriage are no longer enough to justify the proscription. Non-morals-based rationales for polygamy prohibition have yet to pass the rational basis test, a measure that determines whether a legislature passed a law based on a reasonable rather than arbitrary basis. Proponents of the current laws give child welfare protection and women's rights as secondary and tertiary non-morals-based rationales for continuing the criminalization of polygamy (Rowen). These issues, however, are extrapolated to the whole of all polygamous practice when the groups providing this type of data are a small percent of polygamists. Assuming that the problems arguably prevalent in a small and regionally insular religious fundamentalist Mormon sect are indicative of problems found in all polygamist families is a fallacy of hasty generalization, one that strips the rights of many based solely on the crimes of a few. The logic is analogous to denying the right to all monogamous marriage based on a possible proclivity for spousal abuse.

The illegal actions perpetrated by those few FLDS members are not a feature of polygamy but a byproduct of a specious interpretation of the Mormon worldview. The error in prohibiting polygamy, based on those supposedly consequent activities, is that there are already laws and social systems in place to handle those illegal behaviors. A sexual relationship with a minor is a crime regardless of relationship nomenclature. Statutory rape and pedophilia laws are enforceable in polygamous unions just as they are in monogamous unions. Child neglect and endangerment is unacceptable for single parents, married parents, plural-married parents, and everyone else. The laws pertaining to child welfare and women's rights are not exclusively enforced among monogamous couples; they are germane to all citizens, including polygamists. It is irrational to prohibit polygamy due to an assumed predilection for negative corollary effects that are already criminal.

Women in polygamous families are not without rights. As some polygamist practitioners put it, polygamy is their choice –they chose it, and should they ever become unhappy with the decision, they would simply leave (Ling). Throughout the world, there are cultures that emphasize sharing and communal commitments rather than disjointed nuclear family structures. This concept of community growth extends to the single-family unit as well. Sharing resources, love, child rearing duties, etc., allows a freedom of movement in an otherwise rigid familial structure. Sharing a marriage bond with someone going through similar trials and triumphs can foster a meaningful familial bond, and the adage "It takes a village to raise a child" takes on profound meaning (Kilbride).

Many people believe that polygamy is an expression of religious beliefs that, as long as those who practice it do not injure a third party or cause a public danger, are protected by the First Amendment (Turley). Polygamy is an accepted practice among groups in many of the world's religions, including Hinduism, Buddhism, Islam, Jainism, various Christian sects, various Pagan sects, and others (Zeitzen). This fact, however, is inconsequential according to the Supreme Court's *Reynolds* decision (*Reynolds v. United States*, 1878) that held that the government could impede religious behavior, but not religious beliefs (Ulve 166). This ruling, in and of itself, seems counter-intuitive to theological truisms like "faith without works is dead." By the very nature of religious devotion, it is almost impossible to disassociate religious devotion and adherence to actionable religious law. Asking a religious polygamy practitioner to believe in the divine instruction but not to adhere to the mandate is tantamount to asking them, under the guise of patriotism, to willingly blaspheme.

The *Reynolds* ruling's continued support for the Morrill Anti-Bigamy Act, signed into law by President Lincoln in 1862, which turned the issue from a sacred right to a social vice, resulted from the radicalized thinking of the 1800s, during which polygamy was cited as a feature of "Asiatic and African people" that is "odious" to the northern and western nations of Europe (*Reynolds* 164). The ruling was one of few to cite the modified statues of England and Wales as precedent for U.S. Supreme Court rulings (*Reynolds* 165). According to the Court, because polygamy is "contrary to social normalcy," it is therefore a crime (Bronson). The government's prosecution of people practicing their faith is an egregious offense to American religious sensibilities. The *Lawrence* case, which clarified that citizens do have the right to engage in certain intimate-sphere behaviors without government intervention, essentially challenged the court's *Reynolds* decision.

With *Lawrence's* negation of all solely morals-based legislation, and the illogical nature of prohibiting relationships based on undesirable secondary effects that are already illegal, the anti-polygamy laws currently in effect

Johnson 8

are inappropriate. They are unconstitutional and should be revised. The best revision would be a compromise in which polygamy is decriminalized, because legalizing polygamy is presently a logistic impossibility. Leaving the current laws unaltered is unacceptable. Legalizing polygamy would mean rewriting all existing marriage law, possibly destabilizing the institution of marriage. With the bulk of the population opposed to redefining what marriage is, enacting new plural marriage laws and social systems, akin to laws already in place in Canada and India, is unlikely to occur in the near future. Deciphering child custody, pensions, alimony, health benefits, power of attorney, etc., among multiple parties is a legal quagmire the government is not apt to pursue. Therefore, the most reasonable balance between ensuring constitutional freedoms and maintaining integral societal structures is to keep the illegal designation but decriminalize polygamy. Polygamous families would be penalized, but incarceration would not be an option, in a vein similar to traffic or drug law enforcement. For example, there may be a small fine for speeding because it is illegal, but there is no possibility of jail time because it is not criminal; similarly, possession of drugs is illegal, but below a discrete amount possession is no longer criminal. Courts rarely hand down imprisonment for *personal use* drug quantities. If polygamy were decriminalized, then polygamists could live openly and with dignity, confident in their constitutional rights.

Works Cited

Bauer, Robin. "Non-Monogamy in Queer BDSM Communities: Putting the Sex Back into Alternative Relationship Practices and Discourse." *Understanding Non-Monogamies*. Eds. Meg Barker and Darren Langdridge. New York: Routledge, 2010. 142-53. Print. Routledge Research in Gender and Society Series. 23. Print.

Bronson v. Swenson, No. 2:04-CV-0021 TS, U.S. District Court, District of Utah, 15 Feb. 2005.

Duncan, Emily J. "The Positive Effects of Legalizing Polygamy: 'Love is a Many Splendored Thing'." *Duke Journal of Gender Law & Policy* (2008): 321. J-STOR.

Egan, Timothy. "Polygamous Community Defies State Crackdown." *New York Times* 25 Oct 2002: A15. Web.

Garner, Bryan, ed. *Black's Law Dictionary*. 8th. West Group, 2004. Print.

Gray, J. Patrick. *Ethnographic Atlas Codebook. 1998 World Cultures 10(1):86-136.* Web.

Greenhouse, Linda. "Justices, 6-3, legalize gay sexual conduct in sweeping reversal of court's '86 ruling. Cite privacy right. Texas sodomy law held unconstitutional –Scathing dissent," *New York Times* 27 June 2003: A1-A19. Web.

Kilbride, Philip. *Plural Marriage for Our Times: A Reinvented Option.* Westport: Bergin & Garvey, 1994. Print.

Johnson 10

Lawrence v. Texas, No. 02-102 539 U.S. 558. Supreme Ct. of the U.S. 26 June

2003.

Ling, Lisa. "Polygamy in America." *The Oprah Winfrey Show.* 26 Oct. 2007.

Murdock, George Peter. "A Corrected Ethnographic Atlas." *World Cultures*

10.1 (1999): 86-136. Web.

Reynolds v. United States, No. 98-145. Supreme Ct. of the U.S. 5 May 1879.

Rowan. "Fundamentalist Mormon Abuse: Why Does It Happen?" *Irregular*

Times. Irregular Times, 25 July 2008. Web. 22 June 2010.

Stumbo, Bella. "No Tidy Stereotype; Polygamists: Tale of Two Families." *Los*

Angeles Times 13 May 1988: Part 1. Web.

Turley, Jonathan. "Polygamy Laws Expose Our Own Hypocrisy." *USA Today*.

Gannett Company, 3 Oct. 2004. Web.

Ulve, Sigrid. "Hernandez v. Robles and Goodridge v. Department of Public

Health: The Irrationality of the Rational Basis Test." *Journal of Gender*

Race & Justice (2008): 166. Pro-Quest.

United States Senate. Committee on the Judiciary. "Crimes Associated with

Polygamy: The Need for a Coordinated State and Federal Response" 24

July 2008. Web.

"Utah Senate Approves Bill To Fight Polygamist Crimes." *New York Times* 24

Feb. 2000, A12. Print.

Zeitzen, Miriam. *Polygamy: A Cross-Cultural Analysis*. New York: Berg,

2008. Print.

FOR DISCUSSION

In whole class discussion or in small groups, answer the following:

1. Did the writer meet the specifications of the assignment as listed in the assignment sheet? Are there any components neglected? If so, what?

2. Directly quote or highlight what you believe is the writer's thesis statement. Does this statement explicitly take a stand on the issue or defer until later in the paper? Do you think this is an effective rhetorical strategy given the topic?

3. What are the major claims the writer makes to support the thesis? Is each supported by secondary sources? Are they effectively organized?

4. Does each paragraph focus on a single topic, or more than one? Given the nature of the topic, how effective is this organizational strategy?

5. Is all material drawn from outside sources documented properly?

6. This writer is defending an unconventional position regarding an emotionally charged topic. Does the writer anticipate or account for potential counter arguments? Find examples.

7. Whether or not you are sympathetic to the writer's stated position, is the argument based on logic and supported by scholarly sources?

8. Ultimately, does the argument a) reaffirm the belief you already had, b) change your mind to adopt the writer's position, or 3) expand your understanding of the topic even if you remain unconvinced?

"Snowpocalypse" by Judith Kim

Essay #4: Persuasive, Research-Based Essay

First Draft (for peer review) Monday, April 18 (bring at least two hard copies)
Final Draft to Ms. Myatt: Wednesday, April 20 (bring one hard copy)

*Remember that I will not accept the essay late. It is due at the beginning of class.

Purpose: The purpose of writing an argumentative or persuasive research-based essay is to learn how to persuade your readers or to bridge gaps between differing viewpoints and offer closure to conflicts. You will draw on the research and writing you conducted in your earlier essays and bibliography to build a focused, sustained, and developed argument.

Objectives:
- Use argumentative strategies and genres in order to engage various audiences.
- Produce well-reasoned arguments demonstrating rhetorical engagement.
- Analyze, evaluate, document, and draw inferences from various sources.
- Identify, select, and analyze appropriate research methods, research questions, and evidence for a specific rhetorical situation.
- Integrate others' ideas with your own.
- Use grammatical, stylistic, and mechanical formats and conventions appropriate to rhetorical situations and audience constraints.

Assignment:
To get you started, you will need to:
1. Identify the argument you wish to pursue.
2. Identify the rhetorical situation.
3. Identify at least two points of view surrounding the issue.
4. Identify your own position.

In your final argument, you will develop and support a particular point of view in order to persuade an audience, further a discussion by posing new questions, or establish common ground and provide solutions. As a responsible and ethical writer of an argumentative essay, you must also present the complexity of the issue and distinguish the main arguments surrounding it. Draw on your research, and be sure to make your claims carefully and substantiate them with ample reasons, facts, statistics, analogies, expert opinions, etc. The conclusion should address the significance of your argument, thus the broader future implications in this area of study.

Requirements:
8-10 pages in length. You must include at least eight scholarly (or at least highly reputable) sources. You may include other sources such as interviews, pieces of artwork, films, etc. Include an alphabetized and properly formatted list of citations for

all sources on a separate page entitled "Works Cited." Also include an appropriate and creative title for the paper.

MLA format:
- 1" margins top, bottom, left and right; left-aligned
- Top left-aligned name block includes your name, instructor's name (Ms. Myatt), the class (ENGL 1102) and the date (Example: 20 April 2011)
- Right-aligned header should be ½" from the top right margin and include your last name and page number. Page number should not appear on the first page
- The entire document should be double-spaced and in 12-point Times New Roman or Cambria or Calibri font
- A Works Cited page including citations for all sources.

Assessment: This paper is worth <u>30 percent of your final grade</u> and will be assessed on the following criteria:
- Organization (following one of the argument models—Toulmin, Rogerian or Classical)
- Research and documentation (Scholarly? Thorough? Well-integrated into your argument? Avoided plagiarism?)
- Development (including appropriate level of detail, exploring the issue thoroughly, addressing counter arguments)
- Manuscript Form (MLA formatting, citations within text and Works Cited page)
- Grammar and Mechanics (spelling, agreement, sentence structures, punctuation, capitalization, etc.)
- Presentation—you will present your work in class, and part of your grade will consist of the quality of that presentation

---

The following student example is a submission in response to the second assignment sheet excerpted above. Note again how the pages are formatted, and know that you will be expected to follow this page format when you turn in your argumentative essay:

Chris Vaughn

ENGL 1102

Alice Myatt

1 November 2010

The Prison Crisis: A War on Ourselves

Most of us do not spend a lot of time thinking about what happens to those who break the law, and we just try to avoid breaking the law ourselves out of a general fear of punishment or a sense of morality. It may come as a shock to many, as it did for me, to learn that the good ol' freedom-loving U.S.A. is in fact the world's leader in imprisonment. What is our country, whose constitution has so much to say about prisoner's rights and protection from government, doing in such an infamous position? Our prisons are incredibly overcrowded, abusive to both mind and body, and shameful to us internationally. How did our criminal justice system come to such a state, and what, if anything, can we do about it?

Since 1980, the rate of incarceration in the United States has skyrocketed. According to the US Department of Justice, as of 2007 1 out of every 133 adult US citizens were incarcerated in prison or jail, and approximately 1 out of every 31 were either incarcerated or on parole/probation (Glaze and Bonczar 1). As previously indicated, while the U.S. may not lead the world in economic power or education, we have the dubious distinction—that of being first in imprisoning our citizens. As Adam Liptak, the Supreme Court correspondent for *The New York Times* reported, "The United States has

Vaughn 2

less than 5 percent of the world's population. But it has almost a quarter of

the world's prisoners. Indeed, the United States leads the world in producing

prisoners…" (1). Only Russia comes close to us by imprisoning 1 out of

approximately 160 of their people, and 59 percent of countries have rates below

1 out of 667 (Walmsley 1). On a purely holistic level, the US incarceration

rate is frightening, but it becomes more so when you take a deeper look at the

specifics.

Graphs are public domain, found at http://en.wikipedia.org/wiki/United_States_incarceration_rate*

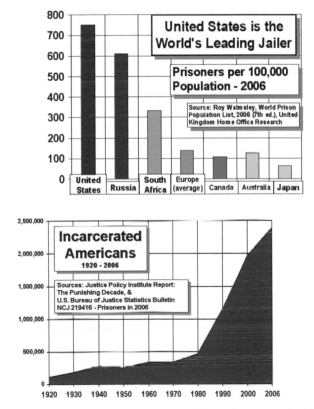

*NOTE: Most instructors do not encourage or allow the use of Wikipedia text or images. Use caution when using sites such as Wikipedia because the veracity and neutrality of some of the posts is in dispute or doubt.

These numbers would indicate that the U.S. has decided that punishing criminals is more important than stamping out the major causes of crime. During the entire decade of the 1990s, for instance, total spending on education rose only 165 percent; compare this to a growth of 521 percent in federal spending on correctional facilities during the same period, and a nearly 50 percent reduction on employment and training programs (Golembeski and Fullilove 186). Considering that approximately 40 percent of those incarcerated in the same period did not have a high school diploma or GED, and that an additional 20 percent had only a GED, it is not hard to find a correlation between a lack of education and incarceration (Harlow 1). However, it seems the poorly educated are not the only "undesirables" America enjoys punishing.

Perhaps an even more startling side of this crisis is found in the blatant incongruities between the racial and social demographics of prisoners and the nation at large. While African Americans made up only 12 percent of the general population in 2000, they represented 47 percent of prisoners (Golembeski and Fullilove 186). As there is little to no evidence of a genetic basis for such a discrepancy based on skin color, this is clearly either a failure of US cultural mores or blatant racism. Furthermore, 80 percent of those incarcerated in 2002 could not afford an attorney, and a 1991 survey of prisoners showed over half had incomes lower than $10,000 the year before their admission (186). With such a misrepresentation of black people and the

Vaughn 4

poor in prison, it is difficult to believe that the philosophy of equal protection under the law is being maintained in light of such atrocious figures.

Since discrimination against the lower classes is certainly nothing new, those unfamiliar with the American political culture in the 1980s may wonder why such an incredible increase in the rate of incarcerations began during the latter half of that decade. Thanks to the "War on Drugs," more than half of the increase in state prisoners during the 1980s were because of drug law violations, mostly simple possession charges. Furthermore, from 1980 to 1997, the rate of prison sentences for violent crime "went up by only 82 percent; for a nonviolent crime, up 207 percent; for a drug offense, up 1,040 percent" (Shelden 6). Largely as a response to the drug counterculture of the 1960s and 1970s, conservative white Americans felt a need to demonize drugs and those who use them. It seems that America has not learned from her own history and has once again created a criminal class supported by the fear that other people may not live up to the moral standards of the religious conservative. Sadly, such fear and lack of understanding has led to many problems.

Many, if not most, Americans may feel that those put in prison for crimes are worthless criminals who are completely unlike other citizens and must have some sort of fundamental character flaw that makes them irredeemable. People who hold such views should understand that, if nothing else, their attitude towards the punishment of others may in fact be very detrimental to themselves. One of the more easily understood facets of this correlation is the fact that our overcrowded prisons are a breeding ground for diseases. For example, a horribly drug resistant strain of tuberculosis was being spread at the end of the 1980s and the early 1990s largely due to overcrowding in prison populations. As stated in the *American Journal of Public Health*, "In 1989, New York City jails and prisons were the source of 80 percent of all cases of a multidrug-resistant form of tuberculosis reported in the United States" (Golembeski and Fullilove 185). Factor in the rate of AIDS infection in prisons (3.5 times that of the general populace in 2002), and it is quite possible that we are creating plague factories, just waiting to breed new strains of life-destroying diseases that will spread over the world (Golembeski and Fullilove 185). This situation proves medically unacceptable, but, more important, morally unconscionable.

For those more willing to believe that many criminals may just be normal people with problems, a closer look at the rate of mental illness in prison populations may be enlightening. During the 1960s and 1970s, psychiatrists and other scientists began to understand the neurochemical makeup of behavior, and they developed drugs to assist with serious mental illnesses. The majority of mentally ill patients, who had previously been forced to exist in mental institutions (which were quite cruel in their own way), could now live productive lives through these new treatments and drugs. Unfortunately, while mental institutions were falling into disuse, there was a failure to ensure that these new treatments were being adequately provided to the poor. The result is that the penal institutions and the larger criminal justice system began processing the disenfranchised mentally ill. These people could have been productive citizens given psychiatric help, but because of the failures of the system, the majority will not only be unable to receive the help they need, but they will also be further traumatized by the brutalities of hardened criminals. As for numbers, "The incidence of serious mental illnesses, such as schizophrenia, major depression, bipolar disorder, and post-traumatic stress disorder, is two to four times higher among prisoners than among those in the general population" (Golembeski and Fullilove 185).

For those people who believe parole programs should help rehabilitate criminals into productive members of society, a closer look at the needless barriers faced by parolees—barriers which prevent them from ever being able to reintegrate into society—may be shocking. Because they find themselves ineligible for student loans, welfare, and public housing, parolees have a hard time bettering themselves, or even finding stable living arrangements. Most employers simply will not hire ex-convicts even if they are otherwise qualified; furthermore, even if ex-convicts get jobs that they are eligible for, they still require stable housing. Parolees cannot get housing without a job, and cannot get a job without housing. In this way, we continue to punish people long after they are freed from prison, and our society makes it very difficult for them to do anything other than return to a life of crime.

Having discussed some of the pressing reasons for change in the system, it is appropriate to consider some possible solutions. One of the first steps I would recommend is that the criminalization of drugs be replaced by taxes on their purchase. This would serve the triple duty of keeping those convicted of victimless crimes out of the jails, raising the funds to pay for more far-reaching health care and educational reforms, and putting the violent drug lords out of business. How many have died in drive-by shootings over alcohol since Prohibition was repealed? Truly, there are many potential issues related to this solution that we do not have enough data about yet, such as how low the prices would need to be to prevent black markets. Nevertheless, as it is clear that the current "solution" does not work, we should try experimenting with others.

Perhaps most importantly, education may be the biggest deterrent to crime we have available, with the bonus side effect of greatly increasing the productivity of the nation. According to reports discussed by Vacca, prisoners who worked towards college degrees returned to prison at only about half the rate of the general population (298). As he points out, prisoner education is not without its own problems, and "many prisoners are likely to have poor self confidence and negative attitudes about education because they viewed their early experiences as being negative … the inmates often face peer pressure where achievement and attendance in school are discouraged" (301-2). This situation is not insurmountable, though, as a massive focus on educational and leadership programs for underprivileged children would turn these anti-educational views around.

With an investment in the education and the social skills of all children, combined with an awareness of mental illness (and greater access to qualified doctors to treat it), and a willingness to help criminals (instead of violently punishing all who will not obey the law), America could use our current crisis as the impetus to once again be a nation worthy of praise. Instead of wasting our tax money on an ever-inflating prison system to treat the symptoms of what is really a social crisis, we need to invest in curing the disease. Investing in bettering its citizens is always a sound investment in a better future for any society. Whatever his other shortcomings, at least FBI Director J. Edgar Hoover perceived this truth. He once said, "we can prevent more crime in the high chair than in the electric chair."

Vaughn 9

Works Cited

Golembeski, Cynthia, and Robert Fullilove. "Criminal (In)Justice in the City

and Its Associated Health Consequences." *American Journal of Public

Health* 98 (2008): 185-190. ProQuest.

Glaze, Lauren E., and Thomas P. Bonczar. "Probation and Parole in the United

States, 2007 Statistical Tables." US Dept of Justice, Bureau of Justice

Statistics, NCJRS, Dec. 2008. Web. 7 Nov. 2009

Harlow, Caroline Wolf. "Probation Education and Correctional Populations"

US Dept of Justice, Bureau of Justice Statistics, NCJRS, Jan. 2003.

Web. 7 Nov. 2009.

Liptak, Adam. "Inmate Count in U.S. Dwarfs Other Nations'." *The New York

Times* 23 Apr. 2008. Web. 9 Nov. 2009.

Shelden, Randall. "The Imprisonment Crisis in America: Introduction." *Review

of Policy Research* 21.1 (2004): 5-12. EBSCO Academic Search

Complete.

Vacca, James. "Educated Prisoners Are Less Likely to Return to Prison."

Journal of Correctional Education 55.4 (2004): 297-305. ProQuest.

Walmsley, Roy. "LIBRARY: World Prison Population List. Eighth Ed."

National Institute of Corrections (NIC). King's College London.

International Centre for Prison Studies (London, England). 9 Nov. 2009

Web.

FOR DISCUSSION

In whole class discussion or in small groups, answer the following:

1. Did the writer meet the specifications of the assignment as listed in the assignment sheet? Are there any components neglected? If so, what?

2. Directly quote or highlight what you believe is the writer's thesis statement. Does it explicitly take a stand on the issue or defer until later in the paper? Do you think this is an effective rhetorical strategy given the topic?

3. What are the major claims the writer makes to support the thesis? Is each supported by secondary sources? Are they effectively organized?

4. Does each paragraph focus on a single topic, or more than one? Given the nature of the topic, how effective is this organizational strategy?

5. Is all material drawn from outside sources documented properly?

6. This writer employs in many places totalizing language, makes broad claims about the thoughts and feelings of "many" or "most Americans," and draws causal relationships between the rates of incarceration and various effects. Is each of these choices rhetorically effective or logically sound? Identify and compare moments like these in the draft.

7. Whether or not you are sympathetic to the writer's stated position, is the argument based on logic and supported by scholarly sources?

8. Ultimately, does the argument a) reaffirm the belief you already had, b) change your mind to adopt the writer's position, or 3) expand your understanding of the topic even if you remain unconvinced?

English 1103/Advanced Composition

English 1103 requires admission by permission of the English Department or the Honors College.[1] This course is designed to develop your abilities to construct written texts on a sophisticated level. The course emphasizes critical reading and writing of various sources and incorporates advanced research methods. In addition, instruction in 1103 emphasizes more advanced rhetorical issues, including invention strategies, arrangement, selecting and analyzing evidence, and developing an appropriate style.

Lower Division Studies offers English 1103 to students who have exempted English 1101 and who are placed in this course through placement testing, SAT scores, or AP scores. English 1103H is an honors course primarily for Honors College students and functions as a Freshmen Learning Community. The content of the FLC course is not different from English 1103, however, unless the Honors freshmen community has a specific theme attached to it. This advanced composition course assumes a high caliber of reading and writing skills on the part of the students.

At GSU, English 1103 instructors develop their own themes, readings, and assignments in order to design a course that provides more breadth and depth than the 1102 or 1103 entails. Because each section of the course varies in theme and assignments, this course offers more flexibility for the instructor and the students. The amount and complexity of the reading load represents a higher expectation of student ability and diligence. The assignments typically focus on close readings and analyses of fiction and non-fiction texts; creative and exploratory genres; and extensive research-based argumentative essays or projects.

Like instructors in other First-Year writing classes in Lower Division Studies, instructors for English 1103 emphasize the writing process, peer interaction and peer reviews of drafts, and reflecting upon writing and learning through writing prompts and discussions. In addition, this class, like 1101 and 1102, enables you to hone your skills through extensive practice in reading, writing, discussion, response, oral presentations, and other activities that promote critical thinking.

---

[1]More information about the GSU Honors College is available on their website: http://www.gsu.edu/honors/

OUR GOALS FOR YOU: THE OFFICIAL LEARNING OUTCOMES FOR ENGLISH 1103

By the time you successfully complete the English 1103 course, you should understand and engage in writing as a process, including generating ideas, gathering evidence, drafting, revising, editing, and proofreading. The writing process, while both individual and collective, proves to be different for each student, and you will discover the benefits of recursively going through the process, writing multiple drafts and using a variety of strategies, including having conversations with your instructor, your peers, and yourself about your writing and your thought processes as you write and revise.

You will be introduced to the collaborative, social aspects of writing, including the ability to use writing as a tool for learning. Many of the assignments and classroom activities will ask you to collaborate with your peers by responding to readings, creating documents and other projects, and providing feedback on each others' work. In addition, you will find ways to engage in academic discourse through close reading and analysis and through devising original arguments about texts and issues. You will also learn more about discourse through producing discourse. For example, you might revise a piece you have written by transforming it into another genre, which enables you to think about how form influences content and how different genres speak to audiences differently.

"Lone Tree" by Michael Stevens

You will analyze, evaluate and draw inferences from information from various sources. In addition, you will identify, select, and analyze and appropriate research methods, research questions, and evidence for a specific rhetorical situation. These research questions and methods will enable you to synthesize your original arguments with evidence from a variety of credible, relevant primary and secondary sources. In order to be an ethical researcher, you will learn how to integrate others' ideas with your own in order to produce well-reasoned, logical argumentative essays with evidence appropriate to the rhetorical situation.

Finally, you will practice various grammatical, stylistic, and mechanical formats and conventions appropriate to various rhetorical situations. Writing proves a powerful and effective way to enhance your skills in language conventions.

THE RESEARCH-BASED ARGUMENTATIVE ESSAY

Although assignments vary somewhat by instructor, one of the most common and important essays for the 1103 course is the researched argument. Some instructors will ask you to create a project or presentation to go along with your paper: a blog, website, podcast, video, Prezi, or similar multimedia or multimodal presentation. Other instructors take a more traditional approach. The sample assignment and student essay provided below represents the traditional word-processed essay in MLA format.

However, the format of the course varies distinctly from the 1101 and 1102 class formats in Lower Division Studies. The instructor of the course in which this student work was produced juxtaposed novels as primary texts with cultural studies criticism, which served as a set of secondary texts providing theoretical lenses through which to interpret and analyze the novels. Students read two novels as well as a wide variety of theorists from critical race, feminist, post-colonial, Marxist and queer theory perspectives. These theories help thinkers examine representations of identities of race, class, gender, and sexual orientation in various genres: poetry, short stories, drama, non-fiction, film, visual artwork, and websites, to name but a few. *However, this innovative course design does not constitute a literary interpretation class—the students learned principles of rhetoric, and they formed arguments about literary texts using theory to do so. The instructor focused instruction specifically on the rhetorical situation and on performing extensive, scholarly research.*

For the final paper in the course, students chose a primary text, either one of the novels they had read or another text, and they researched a variety of cultural studies theories (secondary criticism) to write about their chosen text. In addition, they were required to select a cultural artifact that revealed something about their chosen text and juxtapose the analysis of the two pieces in their arguments.

In the following pages, you will see the assignment instructions, which set up the rhetorical situation and criteria for the assignment. Following that description appear the student's essay and an interview with the writer, Michael Banks, about his research and writing process.

Argumentative Research-Based Paper/Essay 4
ENGL 1103, Ms. Diana Eidson—Spring Term

Rough draft due at beginning of class on **Thursday, April 29** for peer editing. This essay is due to me by 5 p.m. on **Tuesday, May 4**, and will not be accepted late. I must have a hard copy in my hand by 5 p.m.

Purpose: The purpose of the argumentative research paper is to encourage you to employ your knowledge of literary techniques and cultural studies criticism to perform a close reading of a fictional text. The interpretation and resulting original argument will demonstrate your understanding of the text and your ability to research source material and synthesize your findings with your original thought to make a contribution to the conversation about the text and about cultural identities broadly defined.

Objectives:
- analyze, evaluate, document, and draw inferences from various sources
- identify, select, and analyze appropriate research methods, research questions, and evidence for a specific rhetorical situation
- use argumentative strategies and genres in order to engage various audiences
- integrate others' ideas with his/her own
- use grammatical, stylistic, and mechanical formats and conventions appropriate to rhetorical situations and audience constraints
- produce well-reasoned, argumentative essays demonstrating rhetorical engagement
- reflect on what contributed to his/her writing process and evaluate his/her own work

Topic: Your topic is the portrayal of race, class, gender, sexual orientation or identity formation in a chosen text. There must be some kind of theoretical lens you are using to examine the text, which comes from your secondary sources. It could be critical race theory, postcolonial theory, feminist theory, queer theory, or Marxist theory, or some other critical lens you find. Also, the primary text must be approved by the instructor ahead of time if it is not *Rule of the Bone* or *A Confederacy of Dunces*.

Throughout the semester, we have concentrated on the various ways authors explore cultural identities in their works. We have engaged in readings, discussions, and writings concerning the ways in which authors portray truths about these identities through literary devices such as tone, characterization, point of view, setting, symbols, conflicts, resolutions, metaphors, irony, satire, patterns of imagery, motifs of image or theme such as the grotesque aesthetic, etc.

Argument: We have discussed and written about how Banks and Toole challenge notions about selfhood and stereotype in their work. Your job will be to find a truth, a message, a theme in one of the works (or in a work of your choosing) and demonstrate through primary textual evidence, research of secondary sources, logical organization, and appeals of ethos, logos, and pathos how this truth is revealed to the reader.

Artifact: You must use scholarly articles to provide the theoretical lens(es) for your argument, but you are also going to add a layer: the artifact. One of your sources must be a cultural "artifact" (human-created item) that you will juxtapose with your chosen text. You must make an argument for the relationship between the artifact and the text. You might discuss why you chose this particular artifact. For example, the artifact could be a piece of sheet music, the transcript of a speech, a letter, an essay, a piece of art or handicraft, a receipt, a postcard, a journal, a recipe, a photograph, an advertisement, a birth certificate or other government document, etc. The assignment entails not only using a cultural studies theory to analyze the paper, but also making an argument for the relevance and significance of the chosen artifact to the primary text. Think of the artifact as a springboard for your argument. You could devote a section of the paper to explaining the connection(s), or you could interweave the discussion of both primary text and artifact throughout the paper.

Requirements:
1. Your paper should be 8-10 pages in length. Longer than this length is acceptable; shorter than this length is not acceptable.
2. Include a citation for ALL primary and secondary sources on a separate page entitled "Works Cited."

3. You must have one primary text, one artifact, and at least SIX secondary, scholarly/critical sources. No sites like Wikipedia. Sources need to be scholarly texts. You may use one of the articles I have posted on the portal; the remainder of the sources need to be from your own research.

MLA Format
- 1" margins top, bottom, left, and right; left justified
- Name block includes your name, instructor's name, the class, and the date in this form (7 April 2010)
- Header should not appear on first page and should be ½" from the top right margin. Header will have your last name and the page number.
- The entire document should be double-spaced and in 12-point Times New Roman or Calibri typeface
- Refer to "How to Do the MLA Stuff" and the "MLA checklist," as well as Chapter 7 of *Writing about Literature* for more information about exact guidelines.

Assessment: This paper is worth 30 percent of your final grade, and the grade will be assessed on the following elements:
- Clear, explicit thesis that states your insight into the text as well as the literary elements you will analyze in the paper;
- Insightful, thought-provoking, and focused argument;
- Organization: sentence→sentence and paragraph→paragraph; with structure, unity, coherence, transitions;
- Development: substantial and relevant details, evidence, examples, logic, arguments/appeals;
- Audience: a clear awareness of your audience that takes into account common ground and provides sufficient background information for your assertions;
- Style: clear and graceful sentence structure, precise word choice, imagery, sentence variety, formal tone;
- Grammar and Mechanics: correct grammar, spelling, and punctuation;
- Format: manuscript form and documentation in MLA style.

Refer to grading rubric posted in the portal. I will use that to grade your final essay. Do not hesitate to contact me with any questions or concerns.

The following student example illustrates the assignment given above. Note how the page is formatted, and note that you will be expected to follow this page format when you turn in major (graded) essays:

Michael Banks

Diana Eidson

ENGL 1103

1 April 2010

Homosexuality In and Out of the Closet:

An Analysis of John Kennedy Toole's *A Confederacy of Dunces*

In 1961, author John Kennedy Toole was drafted into the U.S. Army and was stationed in Puerto Rico to teach English to Spanish-speaking recruits. During his two year stint in the military, he wrote *A Confederacy of Dunces,* a satirical look at New Orleans and the life of Ignatius J. Reilly, a sexually and culturally repressed slob savant. Analyzing *A Confederacy of Dunces* through the theoretical lens of queer theory provides a deeper understanding of John Kennedy Toole's sexuality. In fact, Ignatius's homophobia is shown to be a projection of Toole's own repressed sexuality. This analysis is focused on Ignatius's interactions with Dorian Greene, the "Save the World through Degeneracy" manifesto, and the accompanying political rally at Dorian's home. Further, the character of Dorian Greene is examined as both a literary allusion to Oscar Wilde's Dorian Gray and as being influenced from a past relationship of John Kennedy Toole. Taken outside the restrictions of heteronormativity, these elements of the novel and connections with other works provide a rich context for an examination of the interplay between the personal and the political.

The concept of queer theory originated in the 1970s as gay and lesbian studies began to take shape. When cultural theorists started looking at literature in a non-heteronormative context, they created the deconstruction and discourse of gender and sexuality as a mode of research. It would not be until the 1990s that these forms of research and theorizing from that research would be referred to as "queer theory." Stephen Valocchi, in his article "Not Yet Queer Enough: The Lessons of Queer Theory for the Sociology of Gender and Sexuality," explains that "queer theory focuses on the 'deviant' cases, or the anatomies, genders, sexual practices, and identities that do not neatly fit into either category of the binaries or that violate the normative alignment of sex, gender, and sexuality" (753). In the case of *A Confederacy of Dunces,* most critics write from the heteronormative perspective. A heteronormative context pushes Ignatius into a corner that labels him as puerile to explain his actions and leaves out any possibility of ambiguity regarding his sexual orientation and identification. As an example, William Bedford Clark, in his essay, "All Toole's Children: A Reading of *A Confederacy of Dunces,*" asserts that "Ignatius's aversion to physical contact and resistance to the demands of natural sexuality have been two of the dominant symptoms of his infantilism" (276). If Ignatius's actions are analyzed through a queer perspective, however, critics can paint a markedly different picture. To illustrate, Michael Hardin discusses the need for queer perspective in analyzing the works of John Kennedy Toole in his essay, "Between Queer Performances: John Kennedy Toole's *The Neon Bible* and *A Confederacy of Dunces*." Hardin asserts that "By abandoning heteronormative readings of these texts, and looking instead at how sexuality is performed within the novels, we will see a rather clear queer subtext" (59). Several scholars believe, this queer subtext speaks to Toole's own repressed homosexuality.

No one knows anything certain regarding Toole's sexuality. However, many of the stories told by acquaintances point to a man who was clearly struggling with his sexual identity. Toole was raised a devout Catholic; the Church even now considers homosexuality to be a sinful form of sexual promiscuity. The thought of excommunication from the church because of sexual orientation or promiscuity pushed Toole into a repressive state. Many of his friends from a young age shared the same opinion; they "agreed that sexuality in general was a distasteful subject to Ken, and it would remain so throughout this life" (Nevils and Hardy 32). As Toole moved into his late teens and early twenties, he "often expressed interest in women," even though "there is no indication that he engaged in a physical relationship with anyone of the opposite sex" (Nevils and Hardy 59). The two characters who tell the most about Toole's sexuality are Ignatius J. Reilly and Dorian Greene. Ignatius represents Toole's upbringing and his aversion to all things sexual. Dorian, on the other hand, forms a foil or antithesis to Ignatius. Toole creates Dorian

Greene as a character meant to embrace and flaunt his sexuality to the point of being the satirically stereotypical "queer of the Quarter."

At the beginning of the story, Ignatius first meets Dorian Greene at The Night of Joy bar when he and his mother stop to get a drink. The reader is not sure what to think of Dorian in that moment, but realizes almost immediately that he is a flamboyant gay man. Ignatius does not yet recognize this trait in Dorian. In the reader's introduction to Dorian, Toole describes him as "[a] n elegantly dressed young man who chainsmoked Salems and drank frozen daiquiris in gulps" (29). Interestingly, Toole describes him as "elegantly dressed," a term usually reserved for women. From this early introduction in the story onward, the character of Dorian Greene is clearly meant, by clues of dress, speech, and behavior, to be the caricature of a homosexual. Furthermore, Greene's persona is Toole's clear homage to another gay author, Oscar Wilde, and to a relationship from Toole's past that did not end well.

The name Dorian Greene is a literary allusion to Oscar Wilde's character Dorian Gray from his novel *The Picture of Dorian Gray.* Toole is signifying to the reader, not so subtly, that Dorian is a man who is concerned only with his looks and fulfilling his base desires. *The Picture of Dorian Gray,* published in 1890, was the only novel by Oscar Wilde, one of the few gay authors of the time. *Dorian Gray* is the story of a man so vain that, in order to avoid outwardly aging, he sells his soul so that his portrait will age while he remains young. Wilde's novel does deal directly with the issue of

Gray's sexuality, but there is a strong homoerotic subtext in the competition for Dorian's attention between Lord Henry Wotton and Basil Hallward. Lord Henry, a nobleman and friend of Basil Hallward, the artist who creates the portrait, tells Dorian that he is to be the symbol for a new hedonism: "You might be its visible symbol. With your personality there is nothing you could not do. The world belongs to you for a season…." (49). Afraid of the prospect of his physical beauty being shortlived, Dorian proclaims he would give his soul if the portrait would age in his place. With his wish fulfilled, the painting now begins to age and deform with every sin Dorian commits. Influenced further by Lord Henry, Dorian begins to explore a life of debauchery and basks in all forms of pleasure at the expense of those around him. In the end, Dorian realizes he cannot be absolved from his sins. Fearing the consequences for his actions, he stabs the painting. Dorian believes that if the painting is destroyed, his life will end. He is later found by his servants with the knife plunged into his heart. He is now withered and aged, and the painting has returned to its original form unscathed. *The Picture of Dorian Gray* forms but half of the influence in Toole's creation of Dorian Greene. The other half is born from a friendship that Toole once had with an openly gay man. The lost friendship provides the basis for the interactions between Ignatius and Dorian.

Joel Fletcher, author of *Ken and Thelma: the Story of A Confederacy of Dunces,* believes that not only is Dorian Greene an allusion to Wilde's fictional character Dorian Gray, but that Greene is actually a composite of

Gray and Toole's childhood friend Doonie Guibet. Doonie and Toole shared quite a friendship as young men. When they were older, Doonie moved to New York and Toole remained in Louisiana. They wrote letters to each other to stay in touch. Thelma Toole, John Kennedy Toole's mother describes their relationship: "When they were young they were inseparable. Then Doonie moved to New York. Ken went to see him in his apartment there once....Ken didn't like what Doonie was doing with his life, and eventually he broke with him" (Fletcher 135). Doonie had "come out" to Toole and was living an openly gay life in New York. Fletcher discusses the impact of Doonie's lifestyle on Toole's decisions in creating Dorian, "The unflattering portrayal of Dorian Greene is more than just tinged with homophobia, and homophobia, both externalized and internalized, is not uncommon phenomenon among gay men who have not come to terms with their sexuality" (136). No one will ever truly know whether Toole was homosexual. Nevertheless, the interactions between Dorian and Ignatius reflect to some degree his ambivalent relationship with Doonie Guibet. These interactions offer insight into Toole's repressed sexuality and the possibility of his closeted homosexuality.

The major queer elements of *A Confederacy of Dunces* emerge later in the novel while Ignatius is working for Paradise Vendors. To help him sell hotdogs in the French Quarter, an area known for its large population of gay men, Ignatius "tape[s] a sheet of Big Chief paper on which he ha[s] printed in crayon: TWELVE INCHES (12") OF PARADISE" (Toole 255). Toole gives the reader a not-so-subtle indication that Ignatius knows what message will attract gay men. Later, while Ignatius is resting, Dorian Greene spots him and approaches the wagon. Their conversation starts as a flurry of insults directed towards each other's sexuality. Ignatius targets his insults towards Dorian for being extremely promiscuous, even calling him a whore. Toole shows Ignatius's stereotyping of homosexuals by directing Ignatius's homophobia towards Dorian's openly gay sexuality. Dorian, on the other hand, makes reference to Ignatius being in drag: "You look like Charles Laughton in drag as the Queen of the Gypsies" (258). Dorian also refers to Ignatius as multiple women, referring to him as "Bette Davis with indigestion" and a "sort of Hungarian Joan of Arc" (259). Even if Ignatius doesn't realize it, Dorian's comments point to his acknowledgment of Ignatius's sexuality. He seems to know more about Ignatius's sexual persuasion than Ignatius himself.

As the insults come to a close between Ignatius and Dorian, Ignatius spots a sailor walking down the street. He suggests condescendingly that Dorian go proposition the sailor in an effort to end their exchange. Ignatius is horrified to learn from Dorian that Timmy, the sailor, is not in fact a member of the Navy but a gay imposter. Ignatius concludes, "Every soldier and sailor that we see could simply be some mad decadent in disguise. My God!" (Toole 262) Michael Hardin discusses the influences that Toole gives our protagonist, "Ignatius's adventures with the gays in the Quarter provide Toole with the opportunity to lampoon the hypermasculinity of the military and expose its queer elements" (72). As Ignatius's paranoia and homophobia continue, he wonders "How many of the military leaders of the world may simply be deranged sodomites acting out some fake fantasy role?" (Toole 262) And finally, Ignatius is has an epiphany, "This could be the key to lasting peace" (262). As the thoughts build, Ignatius makes his way home to the sanctity of his bedroom and begins his campaign for peace.

During the novel's time period, the early 1960s, the world was in political turmoil. The United States and the Soviet Union engaged in a full-scale Cold War. In addition, the United States was becoming more involved in Vietnam; as a result, the threat of nuclear war with the U.S.S.R. mounted. Toole lends his voice to these world problems through Ignatius's "Save the World through Degeneracy" campaign, a satirical look at the United States' state of affairs concerning the military, global arena. Even though it is bathed in Ignatius's disdainful brand of stereotyping and homophobia, this campaign reveals Toole's covert desire for the social acceptance of homosexuality. Ignatius begins, "I cried imploringly to my god-like mind. 'This is madness.' But still I listened to the counsel of my brain. It was offering me the opportunity to Save the World through Degeneracy" (Toole 280). For Ignatius, degeneracy, as in homosexuality and all its stereotypical nuances, is the key to bringing about world peace. He believes the best way to start his plan for peace is at the top of the governmental ladder. Replacing the president with a homosexual man would take foreign policy in a new direction. This belief, in turn, leads to the next logical step towards peace: a completely gay

military. Considering the time Toole spent in the Army, he might have seen

the military as an easy target for satire. Ignatius goes on to say, "As soldiers,

they will all be so continually busy in fraternizing with one another, tailoring

their uniforms to fit like sausage skins, inventing new and varied battle dress,

giving cocktail parties, etc., that they will never have time for battle" (280).

By following the stereotype that gay men are only concerned with fashion and

flirting, Toole implies that their gayness will not logically allow any time for

war or aggression. It seems Toole's jabs at the armed forces are not that far

removed from reality. What other occupation in the world has so many different

uniforms for various occasions? The Army alone has at least five, including

everything from a combat uniform to formal dress attire. The U.S. military

branches have been either an all-male force, or, more recently, co-ed. However,

the military culture remains a blend of uber-masculinity and a dandyish concern

for matters of dress.

Ignatius thinks he has settled the problem of the American penchant

for geo-political aggression, so he turns to the issue of the Cold War. The

satirical nature of the journal continues with its mockery of the nuclear

arms race and the spread of communism. Ignatius writes that once the

United States employs an all-gay military, the rest of the world will follow

suit. And if problems arise "[i]n those reactionary countries in which the

deviates seem to be having some trouble in gaining control, we will send aid to them as rebels to help them in toppling their governments" (Toole 280). Toole seems to be addressing the United States' involvement in trying to stop communist takeovers in Cuba and Vietnam. The irony of suggesting that this practice would represent a change is completely lost on Ignatius. In his mind, the threat of nuclear war would be all but gone since "[n]one of the pederasts in power, of course, will be practical enough to know about such devices" (281). In effect, once all governments have been overtaken by homosexuals, "the world will enjoy not war but global orgies conducted with the utmost protocol and the most truly international spirit for these people do transcend simple national differences" (281). Toole not only ridicules the folly of war, but also allows the reader to see deeper into Ignatius's psyche. He infers that sexual solidarity transcends all cultural and geographical barriers. As stereotypical as this suggestion sounds, Ignatius seems to be reaching out for the camaraderie he has never had. The conclusion of Ignatius's "Saving the World through Degeneracy" journal entry is aimed towards the leaders of nations. He closes by writing, "Quarrels of any sort could easily be straightened out in the men's room of the redecorated United Nations. Ballets and Broadway musicals and entertainment of that sort will flourish everywhere and will probably make the common folk happier than did the grim, hostile, fascistic pronouncements of their former leaders" (281). With the desire for war replaced by lust, fashion, and the love of musicals, world peace would finally be possible. Even bathed in grossly stereotypical satire, Toole creates a cultural and geo-political utopia that many people of the time would have preferred to the grim reality of the Cold War.

In concluding his plan for peace, Ignatius realizes that allowing degeneracy to flourish, "[w]ill now signal peace for a troubled world," and concludes, "We must have new solutions to new problems" (Toole 281). Ignatius's layers his support for a tolerance for homosexuality with a concluding plea for gay rights:

> Almost everyone else has had an opportunity to run the world.
> I cannot see why these people should not be given their chance.
> They have certainly been the underdog long enough. Their
> movement into power will be, in a sense, only a part of the
> global movement toward opportunity, justice, and equality for
> all. (281)

Regarding the "Saving the World through Degeneracy" campaign, Michael Hardin asks, "Is this a real plea masquerading as hyperbole, the only possible way it could in a text whose protagonist uses flamboyant performance to mask or divulge deeper sexual issues?" (73). The manifesto "Saving the World through Degeneracy" is as much a satirical view of world issues for Toole as it is a way to vent his frustrations both socially and sexually through Ignatius. Following the verbal altercation on the street, Ignatius and Dorian next interact at the political rally in Dorian's apartment building. The rally, while being one of the funniest parts of the novel, forms the focal point for Ignatius's desire

to be accepted by Dorian and the partygocrs, and highlights the effects of that

desire being unanswered.

      The campaign to rally the homosexuals of New Orleans begins with

Ignatius's arrival at Dorian's apartment building. Ignatius is shocked to learn

that Dorian is the owner of the building. Dorian explains his arrival in New

Orleans and how, with money from his family, he can afford his lifestyle:

"They send me large checks every month. I simply guarantee them that I'll stay

out of Nebraska" (Toole 322). Even with living such an openly gay lifestyle in

New Orleans, Dorian still faces the hardship of being disowned by his family

because of his sexuality. The story of Dorian's departure from Nebraska is

connected to the real life events of Doonie Guibet, who left New Orleans for

New York in order to lead an openly gay life. As the rally continues, Ignatius

sees that no one is paying him or Dorian any attention. There is a hint of jealous

anger in Ignatius when he realizes that the host of the party and his partner for

the event is being ignored by the crowd. He tells Dorian: "They haven't even

nodded to their host, whose liquor they are consuming..." (327). Dorian shrugs

off Ignatius's attempt at chivalry and continues his mingling. As the night

progresses and Ignatius's discomfort of being surrounded by so many gay men

continues to grow, he harshly interrupts the festivities by halting the music

to argue his plan for peace. When the record player stops, the partygoers are

furious at this interruption of their revelry. They demand that Dorian remove

Ignatius at once. Ignatius realizes he is not accepted by the homosexuals of the Quarter as they boo and hiss at him. Dorian gives in to his guests and turns the record player back on, all the while apologizing for Ignatius, who is then left alone and ignored by Dorian. In a fit of desperation, "as Dorian swept past in the arms of the cowboy, Ignatius tried futilely to attract his attention. He attempted even to stick the cowboy with the cutlass, but "the two were a wily and elusive dance team" (334). Ignatius has now been turned away by the only man he had believed actually understood him. The frustration that Ignatius feels mirrors Toole's feelings of having lost his relationship with Doonie Guibet. This frustration on the part of Toole manifests itself through Ignatius's attack and ridicule of homosexuals, a sort of literary homophobia.

Sociologists Eleanor A. Hubbard and Kristine De Welde broaden the definition of homophobia so that not only is it the fear of engaging in homosexual acts and hatred of homosexuals, but can also "be expressed as the fear of *desire* for members of one's own sex..." (75, emphasis added). Ignatius's homophobia is a defense mechanism against his own repressed desires. Likewise, the homophobia of Ignatius can be considered an outlet for the frustration felt by John Kennedy Toole, a man who had feared and repressed his own sexuality to an extremely unhealthy level. Finally, D. G. Kehl, in his article, "The Two Most Powerful Weapons against Doublespeak," comments that Toole has given his readers "a comic satire [that] proves to be a powerful weapon against the abuses of the modern world" (63). Toole's use of satire allows him to voice his disapproval on social and global affairs while also lending a voice of levity and reason to problems that will never be easy to remedy.

This examination of *A Confederacy of Dunces* reveals several insights regarding John Kennedy Toole's repressed sexuality and about the polyvalent aims of his artful satire. Using both critical queer theory as a theoretical lens and another novel, Wilde's *The Picture of Dorian Gray* as an "artifact" revealing Toole's allusion to another gay author, this study seeks to open up more conversations about literature using queer theory to provide advocacy for a non-heteronormative view and models for new theories of identity. As stated earlier, queer theory deals with "deviant" cases in literature and permits a more open-minded examination of authors and their works. As we progress as a society, and non-heteronormative views become more commonplace, queer theory will be there to help lend a voice to the authors who can and will not be put into any prominent societally-driven box. In the case of *A Confederacy of Dunces,* a queer theoretical lens has explicated Ignatius' actions as those of a man who has repressed his own sexual identity from fears of further rejection, rather than those of a homophobic slob savant. Further, queer theory affirms the possibility of John Kennedy Toole using his novel as a veiled autobiography, which permits Toole to address both the issues of his sexuality and the broader issues of social inequality and war. The role of queer theory in literary criticism has grown exponentially

Banks 15

in recent years. Moving forward, queer theory will help to rationalize and validate unorthodox literary texts by providing interpretations informed by alternate theories of identity.

Banks 16

Works Cited

Clark, William Bedford. "All Toole's Children: A Reading of *A Confederacy of Dunces*." *Essays in Literature* 14.2 (1987): 269–280. J-STOR.

Fletcher, Joel L. *Ken and Thelma: the Story of A Confederacy of Dunces*. Gretna, La.: Pelican, 2005. Print.

Hardin, Michael. "Between Queer Performances: John Kennedy Toole's *The Neon Bible* and *A Confederacy of Dunces*." *Southern Literary Journal* 39.2 (2007): 58-77. J-STOR.

Hubbard, Eleanor A. and Kristine De Welde. "I'm Glad I'm Not Gay!: Heterosexual Students' Emotional Experience in the College Classroom with a 'Coming out' Assignment." *Teaching Sociology.* Vol. 31, No. 1 (Jan., 2003): 73-84. J-STOR.

Kehl, D. G. "The Two Most Powerful Weapons against Doublespeak." *The English Journal* Vol. 77, No. 3 (March, 1988): 57-65. J-STOR.

Nevils, René Pol, and Deborah George. Hardy. *Ignatius Rising: the Life of John Kennedy Toole*. Baton Rouge: Louisiana State UP, 2001. Print.

Toole, John Kennedy. *A Confederacy of Dunces*. New York: Grove, 1987. Print.

Valocchi, Stephen. "Not Yet Queer Enough: The Lessons of Queer Theory for the Sociology of Gender and Sexuality." *Gender and Society.* Vol. 19, No. 6 (Dec., 2005): 750-770. J-STOR.

Wilde, Oscar. *The Picture of Dorian Gray*. Oxford: Oxford UP, 1981. Print.

"Striped Panther" by Judith Kim

Interview with Student Author Michael Banks

GSU Instructor Diana Eidson interviewed her former student Michael Banks about his writing process and his research methods.

Diana: What were some of the research questions you used to get started on your project? In other words, what interested you about this text and the connections across texts?

Michael: I have read a lot of fiction. Reading A *Confederacy of Dunces* literally was easy. On the surface, it's just a very enjoyable comedy. When I started to read into the undertones, there was so much to think about. I think my age and reading experience has quite a bit to do with what I saw in Ignatius' actions. The satire and overall subversive subject matter is some pretty deep stuff, especially for the time in which it was written.

My initial research focused on Toole. I believe you have to "know" the author to truly understand the text. His biography opened my eyes to the connections between himself and Ignatius. Dorian Greene was an instant connection to Dorian Grey for me. I had read *The Picture of Dorian Grey* many years ago, but it was sitting on my bookshelf.

Diana: How did you go about finding the artifact that you used to inform your analysis of A Confederacy of Dunces? You juxtaposed Toole's *A Confederacy of Dunces* with Wilde's *The Picture of Dorian Gray*. What led to this selection?

Michael: I began to do some critical research of Wilde and his works. He was a really interesting person, whom I believe was born 100 years too early. He was persecuted for his sexual orientation. That led me back to Toole and his relationship with his mother. I inferred that Wilde was someone Toole related to or respected. Wilde was open about his sexual orientation, thus the tribute to Wilde in the character Dorian Greene.

Diana: How did you go about finding credible sources for your project? For example, which databases did you search, and what keywords did you type? Also, how did you go about evaluating your sources?

Michael: Your English class was the first semester back to school for me. You recommended J-STOR, and I was able to find an abundance of writings on queer theory, *CoD*, Toole, and Wilde. Research will take as long as the paper, if you wish to find good, credible, and fitting sources. Keywords were focused around my main topics.

Diana: When you are performing research, how do you organize your notes? What strategies do you use to organize your research? How did you synthesize your argument with the research you conducted?

Michael: I would download and save any articles I thought might be relevant in PDF form. You can highlight and put notes on PDF files, which helps. I also kept a running page for each article with brief summaries and ideas.

Diana: How did you go about drafting this piece? Revising it? In other words, what advice do you have for other students writing researched arguments?

Michael: Once I felt I had enough material to work with, I started with an outline. Then I did a first draft of my thesis statement. The paper should just flow if you have a good outline and have read your sources. I think the hardest part is the first draft. I don't worry about how bad the first draft is, because it's all about getting the ideas down on paper. It's always easier to revise than to create. The problem most students have with papers, in my opinion, is that they start too late and do not revise. A first draft is not a paper, it is a beginning. I usually do a minimum of 2 to 3 revisions. To write well, you have to start early and plan your time accordingly.

Wrapping Up

We hope that this book serves as a proper beginning for you on the progress toward becoming a more effective writer. Writing is essential to living, and great writing can change the world. To extend that endeavor throughout and beyond First-Year writing, we offer these additional resources for further exploration.

For Students

Our Lower Division Studies website (lds.gsu.edu) has a wealth of information about our program. Information on courses we offer, our staff, our services, and our policies and procedures are located here, as well as information technology and better writing under "Resources." Georgia State University has a vast amount of resources for students: the Pullen Library and the Law Library, the Writing Studio (tutoring and conversations on writing), Writing across the Curriculum (WAC), Critical Thinking through Writing (CTW), the Digital Aquarium (a high-end digital resource center), iTunes U, *The Signal*, WRAS, and Cinefest. Links to all of these and more are on the Lower Division Website under "Resources." Please browse our site and feel free to contact us with questions and comments.

For Instructors

A comprehensive bibliography of works cited in this book, as well as other teaching resources for this book, are located on the Lower Division website under the "Pedagogy" link. In addition to pedagogical resources such as syllabi, assignments, and lesson ideas, this site has a list of the WPA Composition Outcomes under "Instructor Resources." The Outcomes, comprehensive national standards for writing classes, were compiled by the Association of Writing Program Administrators. Other resources located on the "Instructor Resources" page include an instructors' handbook, professional development readings and links, a newsletter, and information on programs for students such as the First-Year Book program and Freshmen Learning Communities. Please browse the site and contact us with your submissions, comments, and questions.

"Spectator" by Marissa Graziano